"All the World's a Stage"

Major Literary Authors
Volume 9

STUDIES IN
MAJOR LITERARY AUTHORS
OUTSTANDING DISSERTATIONS

edited by
William E. Cain
Wellesley College

A ROUTLEDGE SERIES

OTHER BOOKS IN THIS SERIES:

"ALL THE WORLD'S A STAGE"

Dramatic Sensibility in
Mary Shelley's Novels

Charlene E. Bunnell

NEW YORK & LONDON

Published in 2002 by
Routledge
29 West 35th Street
New York, NY 10001
www.Routledge-ny.com

Published in Great Britain by
Routledge
11 New Fetter Lane
London EC4P 4EE

Routledge is a member of the Taylor & Francis Group.

10 9 8 7 6 5 4 3 2 1

Library of Congress Cataloging-in-Publication Data is available from the Library of Congress

ISBN 0-415-93863-5

Printed on acid-free, 250 year-life paper
Manufactured in the United States of America

In memory—

Elizabeth James Bray
K. B. Brannon
Gershom W. Bunnell

Table of Contents

Acknowledgments

There are many people whom I wish to acknowledge, but space allows mention of only a few. First, I would like to thank Charles E. Robinson, for his wisdom, expertise, patience, humor, and friendship. I have learned much under his tutelage, not the least of which has been his example of excellence in both scholarship and the classroom. I also thank Barbara T. Gates and Jerry C. Beasley for their unselfish giving of time, knowledge, and goodwill. A special gratitude for Donald H. Reiman: he has been a veritable gold mine of information and an exemplar of an established scholar's generosity and support.

To my students at University College of Widener University — thank you. You have made walking into a classroom a stimulating, challenging, and vibrant experience. I learn much from you and our discussions, and each class reminds me why I love to teach literature.

I cannot thank enough all my family and friends for their encouragement and understanding. A special acknowledgment to my husband, Timothy Detwiler, who took on more than his share and maintained his sense of humor. To our daughters, Abbey and Emma: you have patiently tolerated my absence from many a dinner table and outing, and, more importantly, you never fail to keep me grounded in reality.

A heartfelt thank you to the editing staff at Routledge for their patience and attention to this work, especially to Damian Treffs and Erin Herlihy. Thanks as well to the series editor, William E. Cain, for his encouragement.

Finally, I would like to acknowledge three people to whose memories this work is dedicated. First, my maternal grandmother, Elizabeth James Bray, from whom I inherited my love for reading: she would have been pleased to see her first granddaughter attain the education she wanted but was denied. Second, a dear friend, K. B. Brannon: she always played her role with dignity, compassion, and humor. Her presence on life's stage was too brief; nonetheless, she made this world a more humane and gracious place in which to live. Finally, for my father, Gershom Bunnell — as a fifth-generation dairy farmer, he embraced the "drama" of life that nature brings with every sunrise and every season and instilled that love in me. We all miss him greatly.

"All the World's a Stage"

Introduction

> All the world's a stage,
> And all the men and women merely players;
> They have their exits and their entrances,
> And one man in his time plays many parts,
> His acts being seven ages.
> — Shakespeare, *As You Like It*

In many respects, Mary Shelley is a representative figure of the Romantic period. As the daughter of Mary Wollstonecraft and William Godwin and later as the wife of Percy Shelley, she generally embraced the principles that we associate with Romantic philosophy: political radicalism, social idealism, individualism, primacy of the imagination, and love of nature. Like many of this period's writers, she supported democratic revolutions, questioned institutional systems that oppressed individual rights, and condemned social conventions that favored the privileged and censured the disenfranchised.

However, we can also find in Shelley's writing a pragmatic view of life and a skepticism about ambition and the Romantic quest for knowledge and perfectibility. Like Keats' "La Belle Dame Sans Merci" and Percy Shelley's "Alastor," her works suggest that such a quest often values the unattainable ideal more than the existing reality. Shelley also criticizes the subjective sensibility that centered the self and elevated the personal quest above the needs of family or society as a collective whole. No isolationist or anarchist, she asserted that personal rights and desires must co-exist with those of a larger community, and she recognized that the individual's vision, well-intentioned and just as it might be, must often be postponed or abandoned for the welfare of others.

To illustrate the dangerous effects of an egocentric sensibility, Shelley refigured the Renaissance *theatrum mundi* metaphor, so aptly illustrated in the lines of Shakespeare's doleful philosopher Jaques in *As You Like It*: "All the world's a stage, / And all the men and women merely players."[1] In her novels, characters frequently perceive their quests, and often their lives, as dramas and themselves as actors on the world's stage. They transform the metaphor of *theatrum mundi* into a literal perception of life as theater, eliminating the metaphoric relationship between world and stage. What happens, Shelley asks, when one assumes a theatrical role in a

non-theatrical world? When life becomes a personal dramatic performance? When obsession with one role hinders recognition that "man in his
time plays many parts"? What happens, Mary Shelley asserts, is an intense
confusion of boundaries between the dichotomous spheres of illusion/real-
ity, self/other, and public/private, a confusion that often results in a skewed
vision of reality, an oppression of others, and a destruction of domestic life.

Betty T. Bennett has noted that a major Romantic theme is "the ability
of the imagination to restructure experience."[2] Mary Shelley, skeptical
about the Romantic imagination's privileging of the interpreting self, suggests that restructured experience can become a dangerous illusion leading
to an irrecoverable loss both of self and of a sense of reality, reality being
what Anthony Abbot describes as "that set of social, political, and
economic structures . . . of everyday living" (4).[3] For many of Shelley's
characters, the metaphor of life as theater and of people as actors loses its
analogic function, and they become immersed in a dramatic, egocentric
illusion that governs their perception of their lives and the physical world.
The result is often disastrous for them and those around them: Victor
Frankenstein, Mathilda, and Lionel Verney structure their narratives as
dramatic tragedies that center entirely on themselves as tragic figures; Lord
Raymond, Castruccio, and Perkin Warbeck ignore the destruction their
egocentric visions wreak on domestic life; Cornelia Lodore recognizes
nearly too late the cost of social ambition; and John Falkner discovers that
the chivalric, heroic role he plays results in the death of the woman he
loves. Giving free rein to a subjective sensibility, these characters become
so caught up in the roles of their personal drama that instead of achieving
a sense of self and of place on the world's stage, they become isolated
and disconnected. Their quest or vision has failed them — or they have
failed it.

To depict her characters' egocentric visions and dramatic sensibility,
Mary Shelley incorporated literary conventions from both drama and fiction. Chapter Two of this study examines the *theatrum mundi*'s presence in
the literary traditions with which Shelley was quite familiar and the ways
in which she refigured various devices for her purpose. From Renaissance
drama, she adapted the world-as-stage metaphor and the play-within-the-
play convention as both thematic and structuring devices. The dramatic
tendency of her characters also has a direct link to eighteenth-century
novels, especially Gothic ones. The Gothic genre, with roots in both
Richardsonian sensibility and Romantic subjectivity, encouraged exploration of the human psyche and challenged the boundaries of illusion/real-
ity and private/public. Contemporary drama, especially the melodrama,
contributed theatrical devices, such as stylized language, soliloquies,
tableaux, and elaborate settings — all of which intensify the dramatic perception of Shelley's characters. Furthermore, Shelley's own predilection for
seeing the world as a stage and life as a drama reveals her sympathetic

though critical depiction of such characters. Her journals, letters, and other writings demonstrate this tendency and explain why Shelley understood her characters' excessive sensibilities and dramatic perceptions. Although biographical material is germane at times to my thesis, this study does not rely on the biographical or psychoanalytical approaches so frequently employed for Shelley's works. I am more interested in how Shelley critiques Romantic individualism by reworking literary conventions, especially that of the world-as-stage motif.

Chapters Three, Four, and Five focus on *Frankenstein*, *Mathilda*, and *The Last Man*, respectively. As first-person narratives, these novels exhibit Shelley's most explicit use of the *theatrum mundi* metaphor. Perceiving themselves as tragic heroes and heroines, characters in these works dramatically narrate or rewrite the events of their lives to reflect their subjective illusions. Chapter Three explores the motif in Shelley's first and most famous novel, *Frankenstein* (1818), whose intricate narrative structure complicates the already subjective first-person point of view. In this work, Shelley criticizes the marginalization of domesticity and the violation of natural and social order to achieve a personal ambition. She also depicts a tension between characters who are actors on the stage of life and those who are relegated to observing the action. The dramatic metaphor is less explicit in *Frankenstein* than in *Mathilda* and *The Last Man*; however, the characters' perception of life as a literary construct demonstrates that Shelley was clearly developing the metaphor that dominates the other two first-person works. Chapter Four examines *Mathilda*, a novella written in 1819 but not published until 1959. *Mathilda* offers Shelley's most accommodating example of the *theatrum mundi* motif. Perceiving herself as a tragic actress, the eponymous heroine structures her memoirs into a dramatic narrative rich in theatrical subjectivity. The work solidly reflects Shelley's affinity for the dramatic form. As we see in Chapter Five, the approach to her fourth novel, *The Last Man* (1826), echoes *Frankenstein*'s concerns with the tension between actors and spectators. Lionel Verney's dramatic account of his life and the last days of humanity exhibits a theatricality that rivals most melodramas of Shelley's time.

Chapters Six and Seven examine Mary Shelley's two historical romances, *Valperga; or the Life and Adventures of Castruccio, Prince of Lucca* (1823) and *The Fortunes of Perkin Warbeck* (1830). *Valperga* chronicles the rise of Castruccio, a Luccan prince and Ghibelline and explores his relationship with Euthanasia, a Tuscan noblewoman and rival Guelph, and Beatrice, a prophetess. *Perkin Warbeck* features a similar triangle of characters: Perkin, who claims to be Richard IV of England; Lady Katherine Gordon, his wife; and Monina de Faro, his confidant and unofficial "general" in his attempt to regain the throne. Because of the third-person point of view, the *theatrum mundi* motif in these two novels is less explicit than in *Mathilda*, *Frankenstein*, and *The Last Man*. However, the motif pervades both texts and is employed by narrators and characters alike. These novels featuring historical public figures present Shelley's strongest argument about the dangers of casting oneself into a role of public greatness according to a self-defined perception of the heroic. The characters in *Valperga* and *Perkin Warbeck* experience a disillusionment with their self-created drama and come to regret the destruction those public roles have on the private sphere.

Chapters Eight and Nine conclude this study with an examination of Mary Shelley's last two novels, *Lodore* (1835) and *Falkner* (1837). As domestic fiction, these works echo the eighteenth-century novel of manners and sentiment, and they demonstrate how the personal quest often destroys boundaries between private and public lives. Cornelia Lodore ultimately learns that the public stage is not an adequate substitution for domestic happiness, and John Falkner watches with haunting guilt the public spectacle that results from his enacted illusion, as he tragically realizes that life is not art.

Although Mary Shelley shared William Godwin's assumption that oppressive society corrupts one's natural benevolence, she also recognized that the self is often its own worst enemy; and although she respected Godwin's and Percy Shelley's belief in the individual's quest for perfectibility, she questioned the self-centeredness that often resulted. In varying degrees of intensity, Shelley employed the *theatrum mundi* motif to caution us that egocentric individualism and ambition can become as despotic and destructive as any unjust social system and that excessive self-reflexivity can result in one's perceiving life as a theatrical production to satisfy that subjectivity. The world may indeed be a stage on which we play our parts. However, the drama of human existence features an ensemble cast, with many actors and many roles; it cannot spotlight only one player or privilege his or her personal drama over that of another.

Chapter 1 Notes

1. William Shakespeare, *As You Like It*, in *The Riverside Shakespeare* (Boston: Houghton Mifflin, 1974), II.vii.139-140.

2. Betty T. Bennett, introduction to *The Fortunes of Perkin Warbeck*, Mary Shelley (New York: Norwood, 1976), I: ix.

3. "Reality" for the characters in Shelley's fiction refers to diegesis or the fictional reality of the world depicted in the text by the narrator or persona.

Roots of Mary Shelley's Dramatic Sensibility

> All the world is a stage, thought I and few are there who do not play the part they have learned by rote. And those who do not, seem marks set up to be pelted at by fortune; or rather as signposts which point out the road to others, while forced to stand still themselves amidst the mud and the dust.
>
> — Mary Wollstonecraft, *Letters Written During a Short Residence in Sweden, Norway, and Denmark*

Mary Wollstonecraft's letter, as quoted above, reflects the *theatrum mundi* motif that pervaded Renaissance literature. Although the "All the world's a stage" passage from *As You Like It* is perhaps the best known Renaissance illustration of *theatrum mundi*, Shakespeare refers to the world as a stage in several of his other plays, including *The Merchant of Venice*, *Henry IV*, and *Macbeth*, all of which Mary Shelley had probably read in the years 1814 to 1820.[1] Nor was he the only dramatist to employ this motif; Thomas Heywood, Thomas Middleton, and Ben Jonson were others. In his introductory poem to *An Apology for Actors* (1612), Heywood writes, "The world's a theater, the earth a stage, / Which God and Nature do with actors fill."[2] Several years later, Thomas Middleton in *A Game at Chess* (1624) repeated that "The world's a stage on which all the parts are played."[3] The Host in Ben Jonson's *The New Inn* (1629) says, "I imagine all the world's a play: / The state, and all men's affairs, all passages / Of life, to spring new scenes; come in, go out, / And shift, and vanish."[4] These few examples support Thomas B. Stroup's contention that this motif was so familiar to the Elizabethans that it "had become a part of their thinking."[5]

For the Renaissance character, playwright, and audience, the *theatrum mundi* metaphor assumed God, Fate, or Fortune as the ultimate director and creator of the cosmic drama; in fact, the "actors in the play, no more than the audience, know the end. They too must trust the director and the author. If they could all see and know the end, they would not only understand divine justice but be able to observe clearly the divine plan" (Stroup, 11). In her fiction, Shelley inverts this characteristic of the Renaissance motif. Her characters not only perceive themselves as actors in the drama of life, but also, as in the case of Victor Frankenstein and Mathilda, often assume the "role" of director of that drama, usurping God's or Nature's controlling and primary position. According to Henry Lok's sonnet, which plays off the *theatrum mundi* metaphor, "All creatures of the ayre, the sea and land, / Are players at his appointment of some thing, / Which to the world a proper use may bring, / And may not breake assigned bownds or band" (qtd. in Stroup, 18). From the classical to the Renaissance period, the motif illustrates that "God the artist, stage-builder, and producer, puts on his cosmic drama and tests his creature, man. In this way [people] explain the presence of evil in the world and the suffering of the innocent" (Stroup, 22).

In depicting the disastrous effects of characters who cast themselves as directors of their lives, Mary Shelley reiterates Lok's belief that one has a proper place in the world and that deviation from it through egocentric role-playing in a self-created drama can violate a natural order that Shelley believed existed. Although she was not a practicing Anglican in a formal sense, her letters and journals indicate that she assumed a hierarchy of authority and existence beyond the human realm: "I trust in a hereafter — I have ever done so," she notes in 1822;[6] and in the 5 October 1839 entry to her journal, she writes: "The God that made this beautiful world . . . made that into which I go — As there is beauty & love here — such is there — & I felt as if my spirit would when it left my frame be received & sustained by a beneficient & gentle power" (*Journals*, 2: 562). Months later, another journal entry (1 June 1840) indicates Shelley's belief that we are part of a great design or drama: "God & good Angels guard us! Surely this world, stored outwardly with shapes & influences of beauty & good is peopled in its intellectual life by myriads of loving spirits that mould our thought to good — influence beneficially the course of events & minister to the destiny of Man — Whether the beloved dead make a portion of this company I dare not guess — but that such exist — I feel — far off when we are worldly — evil — selfish— drawing near & imparting joy & sympathy when we rise to noble thoughts & disinterested action (*Journals*, 2: 565). Shelley's characters who desire to be heroes of their own dramas are far from disinterested. Instead, their egocentricity insists that all the world's action revolve around them. Furthermore, they rebel against the authority of a higher power, be it God or Fate, to assign roles and to direct the drama.

The Renaissance dramatists used the *theatrum mundi* motif to represent a synthesized harmony among the individual, the state, and the universe; Shelley, however, employed it to criticize a Romantic individualism that distorts her characters' perceptions of the world and creates disorder in both the public and private spheres of their existence. Her characters explicitly and consciously use theater as an analogy for life, but they extend the comparison when they perceive and perform their lives as a series of dramatic events played out on the world's stage. As playwrights of and actors in the dramatic narration or re-enactment of their lives, they are unable to attain order or a sense of self within the larger spheres because they deny the metaphoric relationship between the world and stage. For them, the world is literally a stage: as a battlefield for Castruccio's and Richard/Perkin Warbeck's political quests as heroic conquerors; as a laboratory for Victor Frankenstein to create a new species that would honor him and bring him fame; as a Romantic landscape for Falkner to play the dashing hero whose actions lead to tragedy. The world-as-stage perception results in disorder; regarding their actions as theatrical performances, the characters ultimately glorify their egos or impose masks that prevent self-knowledge. Shelley herself understood the disabling power of invention if "the mind is no longer a mirror in which outward events may reflect themselves, but becomes itself the painter & creator" (*Journals*, 2: 438). When the boundary between the illusory world and the actual physical one is blurred or erased, the effects, as her characters ruefully discover, can be devastating.

A common convention of Elizabethan drama that Mary Shelley modified to intensify the world-as-stage motif in her fiction is the play-within-the-play, credited to Thomas Kyd, who employed it in *The Spanish Tragedy* (1592) to create an intricate framework of players and observers.[7] Mary Shelley did not specifically record having read Kyd, but she would have been aware of the convention via Shakespeare, Ben Jonson, Francis Beaumont, John Fletcher, and the Spanish playwright, Pedro Calderón de la Barca, all of whom she did read. Especially popular in revenge tragedies, the convention offers another perspective on the world as stage — that of the revenger-hero/protagonist. If the dramatist's play is a representation of his or her view of the world, then the play-within-the-play becomes what Charles and Elaine Hallett term a "self-created illusory world" to allow the hero/protagonist to present his view of the world as he feels it should be or to enable him to effect revenge.[8] For Hamlet, unsure of the validity of the Ghost's story, drama becomes the means by which appropriate action can be taken; as he says, "The play's the thing / Wherein I'll catch the conscience of the King."[9] Mary Shelley refigured the convention in her fiction for a similar effect. Victor Frankenstein's tale as recorded by Robert Walton, Mathilda's and Falkner's epistles, and Lionel Verney's chronicle exemplify Shelley's adaptation of this dramatic convention to warn about the dangers of subjectivity and obsessive individualism. Her characters echo the sentiments of William Godwin's Caleb Williams, who rhetorically asks, "Why should my reflections perpetually centre upon myself? Self, an overweening regard to which has been the source of my errors."[10] As variations on the play-within-the-play, these tales, letters, histories, or performances reveal how the characters position themselves as directors, playwrights, and actors, and how, fully conscious of their own theatricality, they present dramatic reconstructions of their lives and of the world according to their perceptions.

The internal play also intensifies the artificiality of the dramatic form by adding another layer of theatricality, creating a metadrama, or a "drama about drama; it occurs whenever the subject of a play turns out to be, in some sense, drama itself" (Hornby, 31). Lionel Abel, in his collection of essays, *Metatheatre: A New View of Dramatic Form,* examines the relationship between metadrama and character:

> The plays I am pointing at do have a common character: all of them are theatre pieces about life seen as already theatricalized. By this I mean that the persons appearing on the stage in these plays are there not simply because they were caught by the playwright in dramatic postures as a camera might catch them, but because they themselves knew they were dramatic before the playwright took note of them. What dramatized them originally? Myth, legend, past literature, they themselves. They represent to the playwright the effect of dramatic imagination before he has begun to exercise his own; on the other hand, unlike figures in tragedy, they are aware of their own theatricality.[11]

A character's awareness of his or her theatricality: Mathilda constructs her memoirs into a drama, re-enacting events as she writes them; Lionel Verney cannot look at the world around him without perceiving it as a stage on which he wishes to play the hero; Monina de Faro (*Perkin Warbeck*) assumes disguise after disguise to redirect Perkin's "drama" according to the Yorkists' dream. Not only are Shelley's characters aware of their own theatricality, but they also succeed in magnifying it to shape their stories and actions into dramatic form.

During a period of instability or reform, the play-within-the-play convention is "reflective and expressive of its society's deep cynicism about life. When the prevalent view is that the world is in some way illusory or false, then the play-within-the-play becomes a metaphor for life itself" (Hornby, 45-46). In Elizabethan drama, this convention and the *theatrum mundi* motif function as an analogy to provide the characters and audience a means by which to order their respective worlds and thus make sense of their individual roles in a cosmic drama. Indeed, the Renaissance world rapidly changed as it distinguished itself from the medieval one. Humanism and the Reformation profoundly affected people's perception of both secular and religious hierarchy. The heliocentric theory of the solar system in Copernicus's *De Revolutionibus* (1543) debunked Ptolemy's geocentric one, and the notion that the earth, and by extension humanity, was not the center of the universe was indeed unsettling to even the most enlightened thinkers. Kepler's time and motion studies displaced medieval ones; alchemy gave way to chemistry; and the four humours succumbed to biology. By 1662, with the founding of the Royal Society and its promotion of Baconian empiricism, the medieval view of the world and nature had been not only demystified, but also soundly rejected.

Like the Renaissance, the Romantic period experienced a significant reorientation of religious, social, political, and scientific attitudes. The American and French Revolutions, the Reign of Terror, Britain's war with France, expanding industrialism, reform movements, and challenges to traditional class structure — all of these events created doubt, skepticism, uncertainty, and even an *angst* that the Romantics experienced and articulated in their literature. Attuned to these political and social changes, Mary Shelley found the *theatrum mundi* motif and the play-within-a-play convention effectual thematic and structuring devices to depict characters who also struggle to find their place in the drama of life. Because of external or internal upheaval, her characters attempt to understand their relationship to the world and their self-assigned parts within it through role-playing and theatrics.

Thus, not only did the *theatrum mundi* motif furnish the Renaissance playwrights with a structure for their plays, as Stroup has demonstrated, but it also, notes Wendy Sanford, provided the people as a whole with "effective metaphors for man trying to meet and to order the forces that challenged him on earth and in the cosmos."[12] Indeed, perceiving the world as a stage and adopting roles are part of human nature. If kept within boundaries, such invention can indeed be beneficial, as it was for the Renaissance character. Creating an imaginary world is productive as a "special strategy — a dream, ideal, fantasy, a created vision — which the individual devises to give life meaning."[13] These illusions allow one to escape the mundane, to indulge a fantasy, and to construct an ideal world: "In life we long for order and to know the purpose of our existence, which somehow we are not able to identify. In moments of despair we accuse reality of being as chaotic and incoherent as only a madman's dream can be: yet in spite of this we keep turning out individual scenarios for our lives. Often these are convoluted, altered, and modified, yet we never give up on them. A day without even a tiny, most trivial, and carelessly drawn up scenario is not worth living."[14]

Imaginary worlds for a temporary escape or to order one's life can be enabling indeed. However, if coupled with intense subjectivity and individualism, the dramatic illusion often supplants the reality of everyday life. Such a reality begins where the illusion or stage leaves off, and one must be conscious of the boundary. Shelley was acutely aware of this distinction between illusion and life. As she wrote in the 1831 introduction to *Frankenstein*, when her "life became busier . . . reality stood in place of fiction"[15]; that is, "reality" and "fiction" (or drama) were perceived by Shelley as distinct. The characters in her novels, however, find themselves unable or unwilling to distinguish art from life and to separate the dramatic illusion from their reality.

Mary Shelley was not the only Romantic writer to incorporate characteristics of drama into a non-dramatic genre. Although the Romantic period tends to be characterized by poetry and fiction, a dramatic sense nevertheless pervades the period's literature.[16] Timothy Webb, in "The Romantic Poet and the Stage: A Short, Sad History," writes that "the dramatic tendency was important to the Romantic poets."[17] Jeffrey Cox concurs: "dramatizing was the central mode of the romantic imagination" and was germane to the lyrical poetry and novels of the period.[18] Many of the Romantics adopted melodramatic techniques in both fiction and poetry because melodrama, Peter Brooks argues, was important to them as a "drama of moral consciousness so that excitement derives from the characters' own dramatized apprehension of clashing moral forces."[19] Melodrama was present in prose narrative as early as Rousseau's 1781 autobiographical *Confessions*, and many nineteenth-century novels incorporate pantomime, a drama "full of gesture, full of significant non-verbal signs that carry a great measure of expression" (Brooks, 75). The Romantic poets also infused traits of melodrama in their poetry and closet dramas. George Steiner asserts that "we cannot understand the Romantic movement if we do not perceive at the heart of it the impulse toward drama . . . . The romantic mode . . . is a dramatization."[20] That dramatizing was the "heart" of the period's literature and of human nature is certainly evident in Shelley's works. Though Shelley chose to write in narrative rather than dramatic form, she portrays characters for whom a dramatic performance was the "central mode" of their imaginative perception of life itself and who insist on playing the part of a tragic actor, an heroic figure, or a romantic hero, superimposing their imitation of reality upon life itself.

The presence of dramatic elements in her fiction perhaps results in part from Mary Shelley's own attempts at writing drama. Shelley authored two mythological plays in 1820, *Proserpine* and *Midas*, the former of which was revised for publication in 1831. As early as 1817, while she was exploring material for an historical romance (which would later become *Valperga*), her husband encouraged her to write a drama: "*Frankenstein* had convinced [Percy] Shelley that she had a gift for drama, and he urged her to try a play, which strongly attracted her."[21] It was at this point that she began a two-year reading program in English, Continental, and Classical drama. In Italy, during the summer of 1818, both of the Shelleys were researching documents for plays they were planning to write. Mary Shelley was gathering notes for a drama on Charles I and was also translating Alfieri's *Myrrha*, a play about father-daughter incest. Although Percy Shelley wanted her to write a play about the Cencis, on whom she had done extensive research, she passed her notes on to her husband who would eventually write his drama, *The Cenci*; she was more interested in continuing the fictional work she had begun based on the historical Luccan prince, Castruccio (Sunstein, 155-164).

In 1824, Mary Shelley did begin a tragedy in blank verse, inspired by seeing Edmund Kean, whom she greatly admired, perform *Richard III* at

Drury Lane. Her journal entry records her enthusiasm: "I saw Kean in Richard — His wonderful looks his tones, his gesture — transported me — I said I would write a tragedy — I began one" (*Journals*, 2: 475). She later showed her draft to William Godwin, her father, who discouraged her attempt at drama: "To read your specimens, I should suppose that you had read no tragedies but such as have been written since the date of your birth. Your personages are mere abstractions, the lines & points of a mathematical diagram, & not men and women" (*Journals*, 2: 475, n. 1). We are unable to judge Godwin's assessment of his daughter's attempt as the play is not extant, and perhaps his reaction resulted from his own prejudice against the dramatic genre.[22] Whether her tragedy, had she completed it, would have had literary merit or not, Shelley later wrote in a letter to Mrs. Gisborne that she regretted not finishing it: "As to a tragedy — Shelley used to urge me — which produced his own [*The Cenci*]. When I returned first to England, & saw Kean, I was in a fit of enthusiasm — and wished much to write for the stage — but my father very earnestly dissuaded me — I think that he was in the wrong — I think myself that I could have written a good tragedy" (*Letters*, 2: 246). Her love for drama and the theater never diminished. She attended many plays upon her return to England in 1823, and in 1838 she assisted Leigh Hunt with his play, *Legend of Florence* (Sunstein, 340). Equally important, she infused her fiction with dramatic characters and theatrical conventions.

Why Mary Shelley chose to continue writing fiction rather than attempting more drama can only be speculated. Certainly, she expressed a desire for playwriting and partially fulfilled that desire by completing her two mythological plays, although both were written for an adolescent audience. Also, Percy Shelley had urged her to undertake drama long before Godwin discouraged her from the genre, and both Claire Clairmont and Maria Gisborne had suggested that she attempt a tragedy (Sunstein, 328). Possibly she was conscious of the disdainful attitude toward theatrical spectacle by the literary elite, such as Coleridge and Hazlitt.[23] The emphasis on spectacle was an anathema to writers who argued that the imagination was stimulated by language more than by elaborate settings, special effects, and costumes. In her study, Janet Ruth Heller details some of the major objections of the Romantics to the theater in their time, such as the oversized buildings that demanded grand gestures and stylized acting.[24] Furthermore, the "star system" presented complications as the actors, rather than the plays or playwrights, were frequently the "box-office" draw: "critics worried about the tendency of an actor's performance to eclipse the playwright's use of language and wit" (30). Charles Lamb, writes Catherine Burroughs, preferred reading a play rather than watching it being performed.[25] Perhaps Shelley chose not to write for the stage, for like the other Romantics, she felt lost in the shadows of the great dramatists of the past.[26] She did express doubts about her ability to write a play: "Even now, after the study she had invested in playwriting, which was to attract her for years, she worried about her competence for drama, and [Percy] Shelley had regularly to 'incite' her, paraphrasing her father's words, 'There is nothing which the human mind can conceive, which it may not execute.' 'Shakespeare was only a human being,' he added, which may further have daunted her" (Sunstein, 156). Whatever the reasons, Shelley chose to write primarily in the narrative form, but with a decidedly theatrical emphasis.

Mary Shelley was not alone in blending the dramatic and the narrative; in fact, the presence of dramatic conventions, or what Joseph Litvak has coined a "trope of theatricality,"[27] pervades eighteenth-century and nineteenth-century literature as a whole. Daniel Defoe, Samuel Richardson, and Henry Fielding employed dramatic elements in their novels, writes David Marshall, to "present their characters as if they were characters in a play; Defoe above all saw his characters as actors who acted out his own position as a spectacle — his own activity of play-acting."[28] John Richetti refers to Richardson's epistolary novel *Clarissa* as a "dramatic narrative" because of its "large theatrical moments," its "operatic grandeur of speech and gesture," and its characters' self-dramatization.[29] Such self-dramatization is enhanced by narratives told in the first-person, a common technique in eighteenth-century fiction, especially with novelists portraying characters who perceived art as life and/or life as art. In Godwin's *Caleb Williams* (1794), the first-person narrator, Caleb, often refers to his life and the world as a theater. Mary Hays, Ann Radcliffe, Mary Wollstonecraft, and Charlotte Dacre are other examples. Perhaps the two most famous characters to confuse "life" in a novel with the "real" world are Charlotte Lennox's Arabella and Jane Austen's Catherine Morland. In *Northanger Abbey* (1818), Catherine anticipates a Udolpho-like experience at the Tilney estate, so much so that she mistakes a laundry list for a mysterious letter from the past. In *The Female Quixote* (1752), Arabella so firmly believes the French romances she reads by La Calprenède and Madeleine de Scudéry are actual histories and conduct books that she interprets the events and people in her life according to those in the romances. In so doing, she historicizes her life. At one point, Arabella instructs her maid Lucy to recount Arabella's history. Lucy innocently asks, "How can I make a History about your Ladyship?"[30] Arabella's reply: "There is no Occasion . . . for you to make a History: There are Accidents enough in my Life to afford Matter for a long one" (Lennox, 121). Lennox's heroine is certainly theatrical or melodramatic in her manners, but more relevant about her character as predecessor to Shelley's works is her sense of ego: she regards her experiences and life as worth the telling to an audience, who in her mind, is eager to hear her story.

The nineteenth-century novel, writes Joseph Litvak, continues to be very theatrical with "spectacles of surveillance" that undercut the "coherent, stable subjectivity" attributed to nineteenth-century fiction.[31] The play

Lovers' Vows that the young Bertrams and Crawfords wish to stage in *Mansfield Park*, Lucy Snowe's dramatic interpretation of events in *Villette*, the enigmatic governess in Henry James's *The Turn of the Screw* — all these examples suggest that the art of theatrics, to varying degrees and for varying purposes, has had a long tradition in both fictional and nonfictional prose. Although Shelley had read Shaftesbury, Defoe, Richardson, Fielding, Radcliffe, and Wollstonecraft, we can only speculate about her awareness of theatricality in their works.[32] The *theatrum mundi* motif, however, was present throughout the narrative as well as the dramatic tradition that Shelley knew.

Furthermore, Mary Shelley found the world-as-stage metaphor instrumental in describing her own life. As her journals and other commentary reveal, Shelley recognized that playing roles is a common and natural tendency. In fact, these writings demonstrate her concern with the same issues that she explores in her fiction. They show us why she sympathized with her drama-creating characters and their excessive sensibility, although she admonished them. Living with Isabella Baxter's family periodically from 1812 to 1814, Shelley found that the lonely Scottish countryside provided her with the atmosphere to "commune with the creatures of [her] fancy" (*Mary Shelley Reader*, 168). She recalled that experience in Scotland when writing the introduction to her 1831 edition of *Frankenstein*, in which, Pamela Clemit observes, Shelley "dramatizes herself as the passive, Radcliffean heroine of her own tale."[33] Shelley certainly, as this passage demonstrates, reveals her own predilection to create imaginary worlds:

> As a child I scribbled; and my favourite pastime, during the hours given me for recreation, was to "write stories." Still I had a dearer pleasure than this, which was the formation of castles in the air — the indulging in waking dreams — the following up trains of thought, which had for their subject the formation of a succession of imaginary incidents. My dreams were at once more fantastic and agreeable than my writings. In the latter I was a close imitator — rather doing as others had done, than putting down the suggestions of my own mind. What I wrote was intended at least for one other eye — my childhood's companion and friend; but my dreams were all my own; I accounted for them to nobody; they were my refuge when annoyed — my dearest pleasure when free. (*Mary Shelley Reader*, 167)

In her journals, Shelley frequently referred to life as drama or fiction. For example, in an entry for 26 October 1824, she mourned the personal tragedies that she had experienced, describing her life as a story: "Such is the alpha & omega of my tale" (*Journals*, 2: 485).

Perhaps the journal entry that best suggests her own view of life as theater is that of 7 August 1829, written a few days after what would have been her dead husband's thirty-seventh birthday. The entry reveals Shelley's profound sense of loss and an understandable indulgence of self-pity: "It is a strange drama — Oneself acting as a permanent Chorus to the shifting scene — How altered is every thing — How enthusiasm, love & hope have disappeared — One storm — one dark wave closed my destiny leaving me a week on the strand — Since then tossed by adversity — the sport of falsehood — the victim of ingratitude, what has been — what is my fate!" (*Journals*, 2: 511). This passage, at midpoint of her writing career, echoes uncannily her fictional works: Shelley's Mathilda frequently describes her life as a "drama," and Richard/Perkin comments on the "shifting scenes" in the "vast theatre" of the English landscape. Life for both Shelley and her characters did indeed seem to them "a strange drama."

As her journals demonstrate, Shelley continued to exercise her ability to construct imaginary worlds that, whether drawn from fancy or memory, exemplified an aesthetic or just order that was absent from her day-to-day existence. Having returned to live in England in 1823, Shelley experienced extreme loneliness, missing the circle of friends in Italy and that country's warm climate. She indulged in daydreams and reveries of what had and what might have been: "I may dream of grand ideas — I may see scenes which may enchant me — I may either think of the past, or the future, such as I would have it — or I will arrange in magnificent procession & gorgeos [sic] array some woundrous [sic] tale of combinations of man's thought & passion — until the real glory may shine around my head & my fellow beings may know" (*Journals*, 2: 470).

Not only does this entry reveal Shelley's conscious use of imagination to escape a dreary existence, but it also suggests the egocentric empowerment of invention: "the real glory may shine around my head" is not a humble statement. A month later, she wrote: "Then [at Genoa] my solitary walks and my reveries — They *were* magnificent, deep, pathetic, wild and exalted — I sounded the depths of my own nature . . . I was worth something then in the catalogue of beings: I could have written something — been something" (*Journals*, 2: 471).[34] Full of doubt about her abilities to live up to expectations first as daughter of Wollstonecraft and Godwin and then as wife of Percy Shelley, she often resorted to self-pity and revisionist memories in her journal. As she struggled to support herself and her son, Percy Florence, Shelley lamented her mentor-husband's absence and believed that England lacked the artistically nurturing climate of Italy: "Although so utterly miserable at Genoa, yet what reveries were mine as I walked on the road and looked on the changing aspect of the ravine — the sunny deep & its boats — the promontories clothed in purple light — the starry heavens — the fireflies — the uprising of spring — then I could think — and my imagination could invent & combine, and self become absorbed in the grandeur of the universe I created — Now my mind is a blank — a gulph filled with formless mist" (*Journals*, 2: 476). These entries illustrate that Shelley did what her characters do so often: she immersed herself in her own world, "the grandeur of the universe I created." They also, notes Pamela Clemit, offer a romantic revisioning of life before Percy Shelley's death (142). This tendency to create or reconstruct is especially noticeable in Shelley's first-person narratives — *Frankenstein*, *Mathilda*, and *The Last Man*. What the three narrators of these works do, essentially, is compose a dramatic autobiography; and, as Janice Carlisle notes, an autobiography "is, almost by definition, a form that strives to accommodate fact and desire, circumstances as they actually occurred and the longing that they — or oneself — had been somehow different."[35] Shelley understood well how one's desire that events might have been different can color one's interpretation of the past, perception of the present, and anticipation of the future.

In refiguring the *theatrum mundi* in her fiction, Mary Shelley also incorporated techniques from the popular theatrical plays of her time, especially the melodrama, perhaps recognizing that the melodrama embodies what Peter Brooks has termed "the theatrical impulse" (xi-xiii). Michael Booth defines melodrama as a "dream world inhabited by dream people and dream justice" and as an "allegory of human experience dramatically ordered, as it should be rather than as it is."[36] Booth's definition suggests that the genre, like the play-within-the-play convention, was concerned with structuring, or restructuring, experience. Shelley was skeptical of this tendency, which endangers one's ability to separate illusion from life. In his philosophical drama *Life is a Dream* (1635), the Spanish playwright Pedro Calderòn de la Barca explores this very matter.[37] After being imprisoned in a cave, Segismundo is freed to live his life as the prince he is. However, he becomes tyrannical and revengeful, and Basilio, the king and Segismundo's father, warns him that "Before [revenge] happens thou wilt sleep again / Where all that has occurred to thee will seem, / Like all this world's realities, a dream" (Calderòn de la Barca, 53). True to his word, Basilio again imprisons the prince, who is convinced that all was a dream. Shelley refigures Calderòn's thematic device: whereas the prince believes that reality was a dream, Shelley's characters believe that their dream (drama) is reality, and they subsequently create their own dream world. Victor Frankenstein and Robert Walton have grand visions of their discoveries' benefits; Mathilda creates an image of a loving, devoted father to replace the real one who abandoned her at birth; Richard/Perkin Warbeck dreams of reclaiming his "rightful heritage"; Falkner plays the hero to "rescue" Alithea from an abusive husband. Mary Shelley would agree with Peter Brooks that the "romantic imagination strives toward making of life the scene of dramatic conflict and clash, of grandiose struggle represented in hyperbolic gestures" (81). Her characters, in their literal interpretation of the world as a stage, do precisely what Brooks describes: for them, life is a "dramatic conflict and clash." The melodrama's emphasis on self-dramatization and its suggestion of a world as it "should be rather than as it is" are two of the genre's key characteristics that Mary Shelley borrowed to depict her characters' view of life as they struggle to assert their individualism on the world's stage.

In addition to melodramatic rhetoric, Shelley's protagonists also rely on the *tableau* and spectacle, important features of Romantic drama. *Tableaux* were one link between melodrama and the sister art of painting: at the end of dramatic scenes, there is "a resolution of meaning in *tableau*, where the characters' attitudes and gestures, compositionally arranged and frozen for a moment, give, like an illustrative painting, a visual summary of the emotional situation" (Brooks, 48). Catherine Burroughs attributes the stylized acting of the period "emphasized a series of transforming 'poses' and idealized stage 'pictures' over spontaneity and inspiration" (111). In *Victorian Spectacular Theatre 1850-1910*, Michael Booth examines the theater's steady movement toward more and more spectacle and observes that theater, art, and fiction seemed to merge as *tableaux* became popular in the fiction of Scott, Dickens, and Thackeray.[38] We need only recall Elizabeth Lavenza's death scene, Lionel Verney's observance of Raymond's siege of Constantinople, or Falkner's desperate gaze at the sea in which Alithea has drowned to appreciate the function of a textual *tableaux* as a dramatic visual device in Mary Shelley's fiction.

Furthermore, Shelley borrows melodrama's emotional language, its emphasis on spectacle, and its exaggerated acting style to enable her characters to maximize the theatricality of their dramatic presentations, especially when accompanied with an "acting style" of elevated language and elaborate gesture. Such theatrics heighten and draw attention to the characters' self-perceived roles as heroes or heroines. Often, their speech reflects the rhetoric found in the genre: "The search for a dramaturgy of admiration and astonishment needs a rhetoric that can infuse the banal and ordinary with the excitement of grandiose conflict. Melodramatic rhetoric implicitly insists that the world can be equal to our most feverish expectations about it. . . . To figure such a world, rhetoric must maintain a state of exaltation, a state where hyperbole is a "natural" form of expression because anything less would convey only the apparent (naturalistic, banal) drama, not the true (moral, cosmic) drama" (Brooks, 40). To voice their soliloquies and dialogue in common language would do little justice to the drama these characters have created. Throughout Shelley's novels, lines resound with melodramatic rhetoric: "Hear you not the rushing sound of the coming tempest? Do you not behold the clouds open and destruction lurid and dire pour down on the blasted earth? See you not the thunderbolt fall, and are deafened by the shout of heaven that follows its descent?" Despite the nightmarish reality of the plague, the intensity of these lines, spoken by Lionel Verney of *The Last Man*, suggests a soliloquy more akin to a Gothic melodrama than to an historical account of humanity's last days.

In addition to melodrama, the Gothic drama was a source for Shelley's depiction of theatrical characters. Gothic plays are credited with influencing the Romantics' development of the Gothic villain into the melancholy

or guilt-ridden Romantic or Byronic hero.[39] The drama also featured theatrical stage setting and spectacle along with lighting and set designs that
were technically and artistically improved to emphasize the genre's thematic concerns with the darkness of one's acts or soul.[40] It relied on setting
conventions to symbolize the physical and mental state of the characters.
As a result, the stage settings were often "the motivating force in a scene"
(Evans, 21). Two such examples, as Paul Ranger notes, are the bridge over
waterfalls or precipices, which signified mutability, and the labyrinthine
interior, which represented the Romantic concern with oppression of the
human spirit. In *Valperga*, for example, Shelley uses such familiar stage settings to highlight particular scenes: the waterfall and precipice near
Valperga indeed suggest mutability, for the setting is a significant backdrop
to both a delightful afternoon for Castruccio and Euthanasia and a dark
night of deceit and betrayal. Shelley's characters and narrators know well
the effect of setting and how to maximize a scene or *tableau* from their
lives, as Mathilda demonstrates in her careful staging of a proposed joint
suicide with Woodville. They manipulate setting and atmosphere and
describe them in the theatrical language of Gothic melodrama.

During this time, theater architects and directors were also redesigning
the stage itself, in part to accommodate changing tastes of theater-goers. In
Theatre in the Age of Kean, Joseph Donahue details alterations that greatly
affected the actors' movements on the stage and the audience's involvement
with the play and their relationship to the performers.[41] One such modifi-
cation was the elimination of proscenium doors in the early nineteenth century, a change that "signals the theatre's turn from a presentational style of
performance, based on acknowledged artifice, to one based on representation, on the illusion of actual life" (Donahue, 180-181). If then drama were
indeed experiencing early characteristics of the realism that would sweep
the theatrical world by the mid- to late-nineteenth century with Ibsen and
Chekhov among others, Mary Shelley may quite likely have been aware of
this gradually developing trend, attending the theater as frequently as she
did. Furthermore, as she employed theatrical metaphors and conventions
to depict characters' dramatic sensibility, this early nineteenth-century
trend that challenged the boundary between stage and audience enabled
her to capitalize on a similar confusion for her characters. If theater can
become "realistic," then "real life" can become theatrical. As Victor
Frankenstein, Mathilda, Lionel Verney, and others fashion their lives into
theatrical performances and their tales into dramatic narratives, they too
reflect a representational style of acting and stage setting to demonstrate
not only the "illusion of actual life," but also the reality of illusion.

That Mary Shelley should have used such theatricality in her fiction is
less strange than may be supposed. Not only does it enhance the dramatic
perceptions of her characters, but it also reflects Shelley's own experience
of theater. As a young girl, she often went to plays with her father; such an

outing, writes Emily Sunstein, was "a treat so 'exquisite' that she could not eat beforehand" (Sunstein, 41). The interest that Godwin had inspired was continued by Leigh Hunt, who often accompanied her to the theater when the Shelleys were in London. Especially when she returned to London after Percy Shelley's death, Shelley frequented the opera and theater as much as possible. Unlike some of her contemporaries, she appeared to have no reservations about attending the theater and viewing various productions. Emily Sunstein describes such an outing that Shelley made in August 1824 to see Carl Maria von Weber's *Der Freischutz*, whose "Gothic stage effects and 'stream of wild harmony'" impressed the young widow (Sunstein, 259). Despite her limited finances, Shelley attended the theater often by procuring free tickets from her friend John Howard Payne, an American playwright, and she used the advantage to see as many types of plays as possible.

And many types she could have indeed seen. Drama during Mary Shelley's time offered a variety of tragedy, melodrama, comedy, pantomime, and opera.[42] Consumerism had fully replaced aristocratic patronage, and the theater was a literary marketplace that, according to Marilyn Gaull, was driven on "principles antithetical to art."[43] Although revivals of Renaissance and eighteenth-century plays were exceedingly popular, there were also many original theatrical productions and closet dramas by contemporary playwrights.[44] Wordsworth did not publish his Gothic drama *The Borderers* (originally written in 1796) until 1842; however, Shelley read plays by Coleridge, Byron, Percy Shelley, and the Scottish playwright Joanna Baillie. Coleridge's *Remorse*, a revision of his 1797 *Osorio*, was staged at Drury Lane in 1813. Byron, who was an active theater-goer, wrote several closet dramas, including *Manfred* (1817), *Sardanapalus, A Tragedy* (1821), *Cain* (1821), among others. Mary Shelley knew most of Byron's works quite well and even wrote out a fair copy of his play, *The Deformed Transformed*, for which she expressed great admiration in a letter to the poet: "You could not have sent me a more agreable [sic] task than to copy your drama, but I hope you intend to continue it, it is a great favourite of mine" (*Letters*, 1: 285).[45] She had, of course, read Percy Shelley's *The Cenci* (1819) and *Prometheus Unbound* (1820). Among the original productions written for the stage were Joanna Baillie's plays. One of them, *Orra* (1812), is a tragedy on the passion of fear and sensibility. The eponymous heroine plays out her fears from stories she has been told. Manipulated by family and peers, Orra falls prey not only to their machinations, but also to her own excessive sensibility by failing to exert reason and by insisting on re-enacting the fictional events regarding the "haunting" of Brunier's Castle. Several of Shelley's characters bear remarkable likeness to Orra: Mathilda, who dreams of searching for her father as Shakespeare's Rosalind did for hers; Beatrice, who unquestioningly believes she has inherited a prophetic gift; and Richard/Perkin, who accepts the dramatic role of heir to the throne of England.

Also popular during Shelley's time were original dramatic works by established Gothic novelists, such as Horace Walpole's *The Mysterious Mother* (1768) and Matthew Gregory Lewis's *The Castle Spectre* (1797). Other novelists who wrote Gothic drama included Thomas Holcroft and Charles Robert Maturin. Many plays were adaptations of published novels. During Shelley's life, all six of Ann Radcliffe's novels were staged. Even Shelley's first novel, *Frankenstein*, was adapted for the theater.[46] Shelley saw *Presumption*, the first dramatic version, in the theater upon her return to England following her husband's death, and she was amazed to find herself so famous and her first novel so admired (*Letters*, 1: 378). Furthermore, she was familiar not only with Gothic drama and fiction, but also with its many antecedents, including German Romanticism by way of August von Kotzebue and Johann Friederich von Schiller, both of whom she read in 1814-1816.[47]

Associated with the life-as-theater motif is the predilection to indulge an egocentric vision that intensifies subjectivity and directs the gaze inward, producing a destructive rather than an enabling sensibility. Novelists and dramatists of this time explored characters who journey deeply within themselves and who assert that reality is "located in the interplay of mind and world through imagination, no longer in a fixed exterior 'general nature'"; as a result, the emphasis is on the "perceiving self and creative imagination" (Bate, 9). The consequence of such subjectivity is what Mario Praz has described as the "Romantic Agony," a quest for self-knowledge that takes one to such internal depths that a voyage out becomes impossible.[48] The subjectivity and egocentricity of Mary Shelley's characters bear striking parallels to such fictional and dramatic figures as Coleridge's Don Ordonio, Radcliffe's Schedoni, Lewis's Matilda and Ambrosio, Byron's Manfred, and Percy Shelley's Cenci family. In her novels, Shelley questions the benefit of this "perceiving self" because of the self-centered subjectivity that often ensues. Whether the dramatic tendencies of Shelley's characters feed their subjective sensibility or vice versa, the combination of illusory worlds and subjectivity is always problematic if the characters become fixated with or consumed by that mental drama and inward gaze. As Jeffrey Cox has noted, the Romantic tragic drama is concerned with selfhood, but that the protagonist does not attain a sense of wholeness of self because the cosmic structuring that traditional heroes relied upon is gone; therefore, the hero creates his own vision (20-21). In *Perkin Warbeck*, the narrator comments upon this self-created vision and the obsessive nature of these role-playing characters: "Winter crept on into spring, and spring ripened into summer, and still the various actors in this tragic drama were spending their lives, their every thought and heart's pulsation, on one object."[49] That object is their obsession — to return Richard/Perkin to the throne, to play out their drama, and to rewrite history.

The Gothic genre provided Shelley with a literary tradition for her psychological exploration of characters' subjectivity.[50] Gothic fiction in the early nineteenth century was still in its heyday as a distinctly recognizable genre, primarily because of the surface characteristics for which it is so famous: the supernatural, an atmosphere of gloom and decay, mystery, persecuting villains and innocent heroines/heroes, and exotic or medieval settings. These elements, gathered together by Horace Walpole in *The Castle of Otranto* (1764) and refined by later writers, have tended to define the genre and often account for its generally poor reception among some literary critics who dismiss it as popular fiction with little redemptive merit because of its lack of realism and morality, its weak development of character, and its excesses of emotion, violence, and sex.[51]

However, as Mary Shelley and others who continued the tradition realized, the Gothic was, and is, more than just a formulaic compilation of rattling chains, heroines in distress, and haunted castles. One of its central concerns is human nature's confusion in delineating between binary opposites, such as sense/sensibility, private/public, self/other, reality/illusion, good/evil. It challenges the boundaries of these dichotomous spheres as it explores the ambiguous and subjective definition of them. As David Punter notes, Gothic writers are "those who bring us up against the boundaries of the civilised, who demonstrate to us the relative nature of ethical and behavioural codes and place over against the conventional world a different sphere in which these codes do not operate, or operate only in distorted forms" (405). Although Shelley eliminated many of the surface accouterments of the Gothic, she made full use of its focus on character sensibility and subjectivity, understanding that at the "heart" of the Gothic is "an anxiety about the boundaries of self" (Delamotte, viii). Furthermore, the genre's attention to the two separate and gendered spheres of home/private and work/public enabled Shelley to address the problems her characters encounter when they subordinate their private life to their public one.[52]

One of the Gothic's many sources or influences was the eighteenth-century aesthetic of sensibility found in the works of writers such as Jean-Jacques Rousseau, Samuel Richardson, Laurence Sterne, and Henry Mackenzie, all of whom Mary Shelley had read.[53] According to Janet Todd, sensibility is "an innate sensitiveness or susceptibility."[54] Usually presented as the dichotomous partner of reason, sensibility, continues Todd, is "the faculty of feeling, the capacity for extremely refined emotion and a quickness to display compassion for suffering" (*Sensibility*, 7). This "faculty of feeling" is typically associated with a benevolent man whose selfless concern for others and whose belief in the inherent goodness of humanity descend from the ideas in the third Earl of Shaftesbury's *Characteristics* (1711-1713). However, by 1816, when Mary Shelley began writing

Frankenstein, earlier novelists working within the Gothic tradition, such as Ann Radcliffe, Mary Wollstonecraft, William Godwin, and Charlotte Dacre, had already begun exploring the negative consequences of sensibility and what happens when feeling and passion are no longer tempered by benevolence or controlled by reason. These Gothicists, or "Dark Romantics," voice a concern about sensibility's debilitating effects in characters who incline toward extreme subjectivity and become isolated in their struggle with evil. For these writers, the quest for an ideal is questionable as their characters become caught up in a "drama of the mind" and are absorbed in a search for absolutes in an ambiguous world.[55] Positive Romanticism, writes Robert D. Hume, "assumes the ultimate existence . . . of clear answers" while the Gothic or Dark Romanticism "remains darkened by the necessary ambiguities of its conclusions."[56] Gothic novelists such as Radcliffe and Godwin, who profoundly influenced Mary Shelley, relied on a terror rather than a horror aesthetic, downplaying sensationalism to focus on the psychology of characters faced with moral incertitude.[57]

Mary Shelley chose to follow this dark Gothic or Romantic tradition to depict characters whose sensibility leads to a self-centered vision of themselves as actors in a world that to them is a stage on which to perform their lives. The balance of reason and passion and the acquisition of self-knowledge are the desired goals for the genre's characters. However, extreme subjectivity and sensibility jeopardize these goals by blurring the boundaries between illusion and reality: Horace Walpole's Isabella (*Castle of Otranto*) cannot let the labyrinthine passages of Otranto affect her imagination or she will become an easy target for Manfred's desire; Ann Radcliffe's heroines must exert objectivity and reason, not only to account for the apparent supernatural events they witness, but also to thwart the villain's plans and to escape from his oppression. Matthew Gregory Lewis's Agnes (*The Monk*), chained in catacombs with rotting corpses (including that of her infant), and Mary Wollstonecraft's Maria (*Maria, or the Wrongs of Woman*), imprisoned in an insane asylum, must fight to maintain sanity and to prevent slipping into a sleep in which they "dream no more."[58] However, neither dank dungeons nor remote castles test the reason of Mary Shelley's characters; rather self-created delusions do. Mathilda and Victor Frankenstein see themselves as tragic victims of circumstance; Castruccio is the warrior-prince restoring his kingdom; Cornelia Lodore plays the fashionable-society-matron; Falkner is the romance hero determined to save the heroine in distress. These characters imprison themselves by giving full rein to a self-centered passion that leads them on an inward journey to an illusory world whose codes are at odds with the actual one in which they live.

Role-playing often functions as a psychological device for enabling characters to sympathize with and understand others. Sympathy, which David Marshall associates with theatricality, is "the capacity to feel the sentiments of someone else"; it is a "correspondence of feelings between people."[59] (*Surprising Effects*, 3). An effect of benevolence and outwardly directed sensibility, sympathy is essentially what George Eliot called fellow-feeling. However, Mary Shelley's self-obsessed characters seldom achieve a true sympathy or fellow-feeling. Caught up in performing their chosen roles and victimized by their egocentric sensibility, they are unable to sympathize with others. Victor Frankenstein can feel only his own grief and fear, no one else's; Lord Raymond and Castruccio cannot understand their lovers' rejections of them because they are obsessed with their own emotions and desires. Immersed in their roles, these characters are unable to detach themselves to empathize with others.

Gothic fiction stressed a balance between reason and passion, between sense and sensibility. Although the Gothic is often regarded as an antithesis to Neo-classicism's affirmation of reason,[60] the genre's novelists asserted Alexander Pope's adage: "On life's vast ocean diversely we sail, / Reason's the Card, but Passion is the Gale."[61] Mary Shelley echoes this line in *The Last Man*: Lionel Verney ruefully writes that his father "left his bark of life to be impelled by these winds [wit and imagination], without adding reason as the rudder, or judgment as the pilot for the voyage."[62] Shelley recognized that Gothic writers did not glorify or condone emotional excess; instead they warned of an extreme sensibility and subjectivity that gave in to a passion or an obsession. Novelists as diverse as Mary Hays, Charlotte Dacre, Ann Radcliffe, Eliza Fenwick, William Godwin, and Mary Wollstonecraft address this tendency in characters unable or unwilling to see things as they are. Although each of these writers explored the disastrous effects of subjectivity and sensibility for different purposes, the common link between their novels and those of Mary Shelley is that extreme sensibility can lead one to create an illusion, be it an image or story, and to enact or perform that illusion literally according to one's desire and perception of life. If the actual world is unheroic or unjust, then characters create an illusory one in which they cast themselves as the heroes who can right the wrong.

A second related problem with playing roles is the inevitable tension between public and private life. Romantic women playwrights, such as Joanna Baillie, recognized the potential of private or domestic life as matter for the stage. As Catherine Burroughs notes, Romantic women writing about and for the stage "reveal their awareness that the private sphere is inherently theatrical" (12). For example, Joanna Baillie advocated a "theory of theater [that] argues for seeing the theatrical potential of those experiences that often go unperformed due to their private associations" (Burroughs, 12). This publicizing of the personal is a productive one as it presents a feminine view and experience not usually represented by male writers, and certainly Baillie's theory can be seen as educational and socially relevant. However, what if the motivation for public performances of private experiences were misdirected or self-serving? In her works, Shelley addressed two variant and non-gendered facets of the public/private conflict.

First, private experiences should not be displayed upon the public stage for personal gratification at the expense of others. Both David Marshall and Joseph Litvak explore the effect of public theatricality on the private domain in their studies of various writers. Marshall notes that Shaftesbury warns authors of autobiographical works that some things should remain private and that there should be no public stage for the inner self. What concerned Shaftesbury is that the "outer character, as a role designed for others, would place one upon the stage of the world where one would forget one's 'true part' and keep the regard of spectators in view" (Marshall, *Figure*, 57).

Second, the public arena should not be privileged over the domestic one. Mary Shelley's fiction also advocates that not only should the private be separate from the public, as Shaftesbury advocates, but that it should be equally valued by both genders. Anne K. Mellor, in *Mary Shelley: Her Life, Her Fiction, Her Monsters,* suggests that Shelley "offered a more life-supporting ideology grounded on a new conception of the bourgeois family as ideally egalitarian."[63] "The loving family," writes Mellor, "embodies an ethic of disinterested care that is the necessary foundation of a healthy body politic" (*Mary Shelley*, 215). However, Shelley's characters lose touch with the private or domestic sphere that she believed is essential to completeness and fulfillment of self and, by extension, of society at large. A foray into subjective illusion destabilizes or destroys the private sphere of the characters' existence. Those characters who succumb to passion and obsession, or those who are made victims of others' such failings, find that achieving or maintaining a domestic life is impossible. The Gothic stresses the need to balance these two spheres. As Kate Ferguson Ellis has shown in *The Contested Castle,* the site of tension and anxiety in these novels is usually centered in the domestic realm.[64]

The cultural milieu of the period was not conducive to a balance between the private and public spheres, unless those spheres were gendered: private–female; public–male. The notion of separate spheres, so much a part of Victorian literature, had been steadily gaining strength throughout the eighteenth century with the rise of industrialism, capitalism, and the middle class. Despite the late seventeenth-century and early eighteenth-century rationalist philosophy that advocated education for women, most females were still enclosed within the domestic domain as helpmates for their husbands, as educators of their children, and as virtuous moral consciences to the body politic.[65] Even Romanticism itself presented problems for the woman writer, who found a self-centering philosophy at odds with society's image of the "proper lady and the woman writer."[66]

Mary Shelley, like some of her more radical predecessors in the 1790s, such as Hays, Wollstonecraft, and Fenwick, addressed society's gendering of private and public "roles." Although Shelley did not publicly advocate political reform, she was not ideologically conservative on women's issues.[67] In 1830, she even proposed to John Murray that she write a biography of famous women (*Letters*, 2: 115). Although that project never materialized, Shelley quietly practiced what she strongly believed in: freedom for those oppressed by the "social system." Furthermore, in her novels, she emphatically articulated society's need to respect equally the domestic and the public regardless of gender. The strongest and most admirable female characters are those who balance both spheres by rejecting and rebelling against a gender distinction between private and public worlds. Safie of *Frankenstein*, Katherine of *Perkin Warbeck*, and Euthanasia of *Valperga* are just such figures who move within both spheres and attempt to create a place for themselves within each. What many critics have overlooked is a theme that Shelley reiterates time and again in her fiction: that it is the private sphere, for both men and women, that grounds one in reality. Her predecessors having already argued for women's active presence in the public sphere, Shelley takes another tack by inverting the issue and asserts the importance of the domestic sphere for men. Robert Walton, Victor Frankenstein, Castruccio, Lord Raymond, Richard/Perkin, Falkner — all forgo or deny the importance of the private and domestic life by placing undue emphasis on their public stage performances; thus they are unable to achieve fulfillment in either the private or the public role. Realizing, as Woodville does in *Mathilda*, that the domestic is co-equal with the public sphere, not secondary to it, is essential in stabilizing any tendency toward obsessive individualism and in balancing a subjectivity that if inwardly directed can produce a self-constructed theatrical world that either rejects the private or publicizes it.

Yet even Mary Shelley was tempted to theatricalize her own life. The following 1823 journal entry illustrates that she could easily move from narrating her emotions to dramatizing them: "I go on from day to day & know that I am unhappy — know that I desire death only as the sole relief to my misery — but suddenly I awake — it is as a change from narrative to a drama — I feel the prison walls close about me — I feel in every trembling nerve that life has nought but bitterness for me — that young — I can hope no more. enjoy no more — a palpable darkness surrounds me, & I on [a] narrow pinacle of isolated rock, stand shuddering" (*Journals*, 2: 452). A "change from narrative to a drama": a change from merely recounting one's life story to acting or re-enacting it. Life indeed becomes a drama for her characters, a drama that blurs boundaries between illusion and reality, that centralizes the self at the expense of others, and that endangers domestic space.

Chapter 2 Notes

1. Paula R. Feldman and Diana Scott-Kilvert have compiled Mary Shelley's reading list and included it in Volume 2 of their edition of *The Journals of Mary Shelley* (Oxford: Clarendon Press, 1987), 631-684. Unless otherwise noted, all references to Shelley's reading are from Feldman's and Scott-Kilvert's list.

2. Thomas Heywood, *An Apology for Actors* (New York: Scholars' Facsimiles and Reprints, 1941).

3. Thomas Middleton, *A Game at Chess*, ed. T. H. Howard Hill. The Revels Plays (Manchester: Manchester University Press, 1993), V.ii.19.

4. Ben Jonson, *The New Inn*, ed. Michael Hattaway. The Revels Plays (Manchester: Manchester University Press, 1989). I.iii.128-31. Feldman and Scott-Kilvert record that both Shelleys read Shakespeare's works in 1814. Mary Shelley specifically read *As You Like It* in 1815, *Henry IV* in 1820, *Macbeth* in 1818, and Jonson's *The New Inn* in 1820. There is no record of Shelley's having read Middleton or Heywood; however, the *theatrum mundi*'s presence in the plays we know she read would have been sufficient for her to have recognized its function and purpose.

5. Thomas B. Stroup, *Microcosmos: The Shape of the Elizabethan Play* (Lexington: University of Kentucky Press, 1965), 32; hereafter cited in text. Although associated with Renaissance drama, the *theatrum mundi* motif did not originate with Shakespeare or his contemporaries. Stroup quotes Democritus, a fifth century B.C. writer, who wrote, "The world's a stage, life a play. / You come, you look, you go away" and traces the motif through Plotinus to the English Renaissance. Mary Shelley was familiar with the Greek and Roman dramas as well as the English sixteenth- and seventeenth-century ones.

6. Mary Shelley, *The Journals of Mary Shelley 1814-1844*, ed. Paula R. Feldman and Diana Scott-Kilvert (Oxford: Clarendon Press, 1987), 2: 448; hereafter cited as *Journals* and noting volume number.

7. Richard Hornby, *Drama, Metadrama, and Perception* (Lewisburg: Bucknell University Press, 1986), 35; hereafter cited in text. Hornby notes that the play-within-the-play convention is a Renaissance innovation (35). See also Fredson Thayer Bowers' *Elizabethan Revenge Tragedy: 1587-1642* (Gloucester: Peter Smith, 1959) for background on Kyd's contribution to this convention; hereafter cited in text.

8. Charles A. Hallett and Elaine S. Hallett, *The Revenger's Madness: A Study of Revenge Tragedy Motifs* (Lincoln: University of Nebraska Press, 1980), 10; hereafter cited in text.

9. William Shakespeare, *Hamlet*, II.ii.612-13, in *The Riverside Shakespeare* (Boston: Houghton Mifflin, 1974).

10. William Godwin, *Caleb Williams*, ed. David McCracken (New York: W. W. Norton, 1977), 325; hereafter cited in text.

11. Lionel Abel, *Metatheatre: A New View of Dramatic Form* (New York: Hill and Wang, 1963), 60-61.

12. Wendy Coppedge Sanford, *Theater as Metaphor in Hamlet* (Cambridge: Harvard University Press, 1967), 5; hereafter cited in text.

13. Anthony Abbott, *The Vital Lie: Reality and Illusion in Modern Drama.* (Tuscaloosa: University of Alabama Press, 1989), 4; hereafter cited in text.

14. Slawomir Mrozek, "Theatre versus Reality," *New Theatre Quarterly* 12 (1992): 302.

15. Mary Shelley, *The Mary Shelley Reader*, ed. Betty T. Bennett and Charles E. Robinson (New York: Oxford University Press, 1990), 168; hereafter cited in text as *Mary Shelley Reader*.

16. Michael Booth, *Prefaces to English Nineteenth-Century Theatre* (Manchester: Manchester University Press, 1980), 2; hereafter cited in text. Booth describes the period's drama as a gap between the richness of the eighteenth century's and the innovation of the late nineteenth's: "The student of drama usually takes a colossal leap over the dark abyss yawning dangerously between Sheridan and Shaw, and lands thankfully on the other side" (2).

17. In *The Romantic Theatre*, ed. Richard Allen Cave (Totowa: Barnes and Noble, 1986), 13; hereafter cited in text.

18. Jeffrey Cox, *In the Shadows of Romance: Romantic Tragic Drama in Germany, England, and France* (Athens: Ohio University Press, 1992), x; hereafter cited in text. Cox takes exception to Michael Booth's assessment of Romantic drama. He questions applying norms of prior drama to Romantic drama and judging the latter inferior because by so doing, he claims, critics overlook the significance of the plays and their part in literary history.

19. Peter Brooks, *The Melodramatic Imagination* (New Haven: Yale University Press, 1976), 5-6; hereafter cited in text.

20. George Steiner, *Death of Tragedy* (New York: Knopf, 1961), 108; hereafter cited in text.

21. Emily Sunstein, *Mary Shelley: Romance and Reality* (Boston: Little, Brown, 1989), 138; hereafter cited in text.

22. In his preface to *Cloudesley* (1830), Godwin privileges the fiction writer over the historian and the dramatist: "The writer collects his information of what the great men on the theatre of the world are reported to have said and done, and then endeavours with his best sagacity to find out the explanation; to hit on that thread, woven through the whole contexture of the piece" *(Mary Shelley Reader,* 372). One wonders if Godwin were conscious of the irony in using the *theatrum mundi* metaphor in this passage or if he were remembering his own unsuccessful attempt at drama. His play *Antonio, or the Soldier's Return* was performed at Drury Lane on 13 December 1800 to a decidedly unenthusiastic crowd. As William St. Clair in *The Godwins and the Shelleys* notes, "*Antonio* was remembered for having been coughed off stage at its first and only night" (Baltimore: Johns Hopkins University Press, 1989), 232.

23. Indeed, spectacle was very much in demand by the general theater-going populace. Coleridge and Percy Shelley both felt that many theatrical plays were immoral, corrupting the audience who lacked discriminating taste and who preferred plays that were "louder, gaudier, and longer" than ever; see Frank Rahill, *The World of*

Melodrama (University Park: Penn State University Press, 1967), 112; hereafter cited in text. Byron also denounced much of the staged drama of the period and even joined the Drury Lane committee working for drama reform.

24. See Janet Ruth Heller's *Coleridge, Lamb, Hazlitt, and the Reader of Drama* (Columbia: University of Missouri Press, 1990). According to Heller, the Romantic critics' complaints were part of a long tradition of concern with theatrical staging of drama. As far back as the Renaissance, many dramatists desired their works published because the reading audience was more likely to appreciate them than was the viewing audience. Interestingly, Heller's observation about actors overshadowing the play itself is analogous to Mary Shelley's critique of characters whose performances "eclipse" actual life.

25. Catherine Burroughs, *Closet Stages: Joanna Baillie and the Theater Theory of British Romantic Women Writers* (Philadelphia: University of Pennsylvania Press, 1997), 11-12; hereafter cited in text.

26. See Jonathan Bate's study, *Shakespeare and the English Romantic Imagination* (Oxford: Clarendon, 1986). Bate suggests that the lack of actable literary drama during the Romantic period is due in part to the formidable shadow that Shakespeare cast (2); hereafter cited in text.

27. See *Caught in the Act: Theatricality in the Nineteenth-Century Novel* (Berkeley: University of California Press, 1992).

28. *The Figure of Theater: Shaftesbury, Defoe, Adam Smith, and George Eliot.* New York: Columbia University Press, 1986), 78; hereafter cited in text.

29. John Richetti, "Richardson's Dramatic Art in *Clarissa*," *British Theatre and the Other Arts, 1660-1800*, ed. Shirley Strum Kenny (Washington: Folger Shakespeare Library, 1983), 288-308; hereafter cited in text.

30. Charlotte Lennox, *The Female Quixote*, ed. Margaret Dalziel (London: Oxford University Press, 1970), 121; hereafter cited in text,

31. *Caught in the Act: Theatricality in the Nineteenth-Century Novel* (Berkeley: University of California Press, 1992), xi-xii; hereafter cited in text.

32. Austen began *Northanger Abbey* in 1798 although it was not published until 1818. There is no conclusive evidence that Mary Shelley had read any of Austen's novels. She read Radcliffe's *The Italian* in 1814 and *The Mysteries of Udolpho* in 1815, Richardson's *Clarissa* and *Pamela* in 1816, Fielding's *Amelia* in 1817 and *Joseph Andrews* in 1818. According to Emily Sunstein, the moral philosopher Lord Shaftesbury, whose ideas were often reflected in eighteenth-century fiction, was one of Shelley's favorite writers by 1819 (188).

33. Pamela Clemit, *The Godwinian Novel: The Rational Fictions of Godwin, Brockden Brown, Mary Shelley* (Oxford: Clarendon Press, 1993), 142; hereafter cited in text.

34. Following Percy Shelley's death, Mary Shelley shared the rental of a palazzo with Leigh and Marianne Hunt at Genoa until her return to England the following spring.

35. Janet Carlisle, "The Face in the Mirror: *Villette* and the Conventions of Autobiography," in *Critical Essays on Charlotte Brontë*, ed. Barbara Timm Gates (Boston: G. K. Hall, 1990), 266; hereafter cited in text.

36. *English Melodrama* (London: Herbert Jenkins, 1965), 14; hereafter cited in text.

37. Shelley read Calderòn's play in 1820; both she and Percy Shelley admired his works greatly.

38. *Victorian Spectacular Theatre 1850-1910* (Boston: Routledge and Kegan Paul, 1981); hereafter cited in text.

39. Bertrand Evans, *Gothic Drama from Walpole to Shelley* (Berkeley: University of California Press, 1947), 4; hereafter cited in text. For a thorough treatment of the development of this type, see Peter L. Thorslev's *The Byronic Hero* (Minneapolis: University of Minnesota Press, 1962); hereafter cited in text.

40. See Paul Ranger's study, *"Terror and Pity reign in every Breast": Gothic Drama in the London Patent Theatres, 1750-1820* (London: The Society for Theatre Research, 1991).

41. Joseph Donahue, *Theatre in the Age of Kean* (Totowa: Rowman and Littlefield, 1975); hereafter cited in text.

42. See Frank Rahill's *The World of Melodrama*, Michael Booth's *English Melodrama*, and Bertrand Evans' *Gothic Drama from Walpole to Shelley* for detailed background on this period's theatrical drama.

43. Marilyn Gaull, *English Romanticism: The Human Context* (New York: W. W. Norton, 1988), 13; hereafter cited in text.

44. The theatrical plays were stageable, and they were also, with a few exceptions, the plays that contemporary critics, such as Coleridge, Hazlitt, and Lamb, despised. In contrast to these theatrical works of spectacle that dominated the theater are the literary plays or closet dramas made popular by Byron and Shelley.

45. Mary Shelley was quite likely influenced by Byron's drama for her 1830 tale, "The Transformation." See *Mary Shelley: Collected Tales and Stories*, ed. Charles E. Robinson (Baltimore: Johns Hopkins, 1976), 381.

46. See Steven Earl Forry's study of these plays in *Hideous Progenies: Dramatizations of Frankenstein from Mary Shelley to the Present* (Philadelphia: University of Pennsylvania Press, 1990). Forry includes the several of the plays' texts following his critical overview

47. In *Gothic Drama from Walpole to Shelley*, Evans argues that significant precursors to Gothic drama were John Home's *Douglas* (1756), which Shelley had read in 1817; Hall Harston's *The Countess of Salisbury* (1765); Andrew MacDonald's *Vimonda* (1787); and Francis North's *Kentish Barons* (1790). Clara F. McIntyre, however, suggests that Renaissance drama was the direct influence. See her articles "Later Career of the Elizabethan Villain-Hero," *PMLA* 40 (1925): 874-880 and "Were the `Gothic Novels' Gothic?" *PMLA* 36 (1921): 645-667. Elizabethan tragedy indeed incorporated what we now recognize as Gothic settings and elements: labyrinthine castles, murder, mystery, ghosts, and the hero/heroine/villain triad.

48. See Praz's study, *The Romantic Agony*, 2nd ed (London: Oxford University Press, 1951).

49. Mary Shelley, *The Fortunes of Perkin Warbeck*, 3 vols. (Reprint, Norwood Editions, 1976), 213; hereafter cited in text as *Perkin Warbeck*.

50. Generally the Gothic period is dated from 1764 (with Walpole's novel, *The Castle of Otranto*) to 1820 (with Charles Robert Maturin's *Melmoth the Wanderer*). However, David Punter, in *The Literature of Terror* (London: Longman, 1980) and Eugenia DeLamotte, in *The Perils of the Night* (New York: Oxford University Press, 1990), have shown that the Gothic genre extended well beyond 1820, infusing the works of canonical writers like the Brontës, Dickens, Collins, Poe, Hawthorne, Melville, Henry James, Faulkner, and Flannery O'Connor, among others. See also Edith Birkhead's *The Tale of Terror* (1921; reprint, New York: Russell and Russell, 1963); Ernest Railo's *The Haunted Castle*, (New York: E. P. Dutton and Colk 1927); Devendra P. Varma's *The Gothic Flame*, (1957; reprint, New York: Russell and Russell, 1966); and Montague Summers' *The Gothic Quest* (1938; reprint, New York: Russell and Russell, 1964). All references noted hereafter cited in text.

51. Much of the early negative reception was directed to the numerous Minerva Press imitators of Walpole, Sophia Lee, Charlotte Smith, Radcliffe, and Lewis. Dr. Nathan Drake in his 1798 *Literary Hours; or, Sketeches Critical and Narrative* (New York: Garland Press, 1970) had nothing but praise for the genre. However, some periodicals, such as the *Critical Review*, were seldom complimentary even to the most skilled novelists. The Gothic has been more positively re-evaluated by recent critics, such as David Punter, Eugenia DeLamotte, Kate Ferguson Ellis, Elizabeth MacAndrew, to name a few.

52. See Kate Ferguson Ellis's *The Contested Castle: Gothic Novels and the Subversion of Domestic Ideology* (Urbana: University of Illinois Press, 1989) for a well-argued study on the notion of separate spheres in eighteenth-century Gothic fiction; hereafter cited in text.

53. Shelley's journals indicate that she read Rousseau's *Julie, ou la Nouvelle Héloise* (1761) and *Emile* (1762), Richardson's *Clarissa* (1747-8) in 1815, Sterne's *Sentimental Journey* (1767), and MacKenzie's works in 1821.

54. *Sensibility* (London: Methuen, 1986), 7; hereafter cited in text.

55. G. R. Thompson, "Introduction: Romanticism and the Gothic Tradition," in *The Gothic Imagination: Essays in Dark Romanticism*, ed. G. R. Thompson (Pullman: Washington State University Press, 1974), 1-10; hereafter cited in text.

56. "Gothic versus Romantic: A Revaluation of the Gothic Novel," *PMLA* 84 (1969): 288-289; hereafter cited in text.

57. Ann Radcliffe's distinction between terror and horror is still the standard: "Terror and horror are so far opposite, that the first expands the soul, and awakens the faculties to a high degree of life; the other contracts, freezes, and nearly annihilates them. I apprehend that neither Shakespeare nor Milton by their fictions, nor Mr. Burke by his reasoning, anywhere looked to positive horror as a source of the sublime, though they all agree that terror is a very high one" (qtd. in Radcliffe's introduction to *The Mysteries of Udolpho*, ed. Bonamy Dobrée [London: Oxford University Press, 1979], xi); hereafter the novel is cited in text.

58. Wollstonecraft's echo of Hamlet's line is from *Maria, or the Wrongs of Woman* (New York: W. W. Norton, 1975), 33.

59. *Surprising Effects of Sympathy: Marivaux, Diderot, Rousseau, and Mary Shelley* (Chicago: University of Chicago Press, 1988), 3; hereafter cited in text.

60. See Robert Kiely's *The Romantic Novel in England* and David Richter's "Reception of the Gothic Novel in the 1790s" in *The Idea of the Novel in the Eighteenth Century*, ed. Robert W. Uphaus.

61. From "An Essay on Man," Epistle II, ll. 107-108, in *The Poetry and Prose of Alexander Pope*, ed. Aubrey Williams (Boston: Houghton Mifflin, 1969).

62. Mary Shelley, *The Last Man*, ed. Hugh J. Luke, Jr. (Lincoln: University of Nebraska Press, 1965), 5; hereafter cited in text as *Last Man*.

63. *Mary Shelley: Her Life, Her Fiction, Her Monsters* (New York: Routledge, 1989), xii; hereafter cited in text.

64. According to Ellis two patterns exist. One is the "feminine Gothic," which depicts the heroine/protagonist trying to recapture the domestic sphere that has been contaminated or usurped by a villain, making the home a prison rather than a sanctuary. This pattern can be seen in *Valperga* as Euthanasia is torn between her love for Castruccio and his threat to her Tuscan estate. The second pattern is the "masculine Gothic," which presents the point of view of the villain/protagonist who is on the outside, in exile, with no home or no hope of that domestic haven. *Frankenstein*'s creature, Perkin Warbeck, and Falkner exemplify the masculine Gothic. Both of these patterns can be found in Mary Shelley's fiction, as male and female characters come to understand the need to balance the domestic and the public.

65. See Katharine Rogers' study of rationalism and feminism in *Feminism in Eighteenth-Century England* (Urbana: University of Illinois Press, 1982).

66. See Meena Alexander's *Women in Romanticism* (Totowa: Barnes and Noble, 1989) and Mary Poovey's *The Proper Lady and the Woman Writer—Ideology as Style in the Works of Mary Wollstonecraft, Mary Shelley and Jane Austen* (Chicago: University of Chicago Press, 1984).

67. However, many critics have evaluated Shelley as a conservative on women's rights and social place because she did not explicitly advocate women's presence in the public arena. They frequently cite her refusal to write a tract for women's rights as requested by Edward Trelawny. Although Shelley abhorred oppression of any kind, she personally had no wish to enter the political limelight. Perhaps she was ambivalent to the issue, as Emily Sunstein suggests (341-2) and as her 31 October 1838 journal entry reveals (*Journals*, 2: 554). It also may have been her reluctance to attract public attention, given Sir Timothy Shelley's threats to withdraw the limited support he allotted for raising her son, Percy Florence. Yet, perhaps remembering her own experience when she eloped with Percy Shelley, Mary Shelley did indeed support women who were victims of social inequities and whose unconventional lives raised society's collective eyebrow: Claire Clairmont, Mary Diana Dods, Caroline Norton are some notable examples. As she wrote in her journal, "If I have never written to vindicate the Rights of women, I have ever befriended women when oppressed — at every risk I have defended & supported victims to the social system" (*Journals*, 2: 557). See also Katherine Hill-Miller's analysis of Shelley's

feminism in *"My Hideous Progeny"*: *Mary Shelley, William Godwin, and the Father-Daughter Relationship* (Newark: University of Delaware Press, 1995), 203.

Frankenstein: Storytelling as Dramatic Performance

Life's but a walking shadow, a poor player
That struts and frets his hour upon the stage
And then is heard no more; it is a tale
Told by an idiot, full of sound and fury,
Signifying nothing.
— Shakespeare, *Macbeth*

On 28 July 1823, the first dramatization of Mary Shelley's *Frankenstein* was staged at the English Opera House. *Presumption; or, The Fate of Frankenstein*, by Richard Brinsley Peake, enjoyed a successful run, thrilling audiences with the Gothic melodrama's encapsulated version of Shelley's novel: "*Frank*: It lives! I saw the dull yellow eye of the creature open, it breathed hard, and a convulsive motion agitated its limbs. . . . What have I accomplished? the beauty of my dream has vanished! and breathless horror and disgust now fill my heart. For this I have deprived myself of rest and health, have worked my brain to madness; and when I looked to reap my great reward, a flash breaks in upon my darkened soul, and tells me my attempt was impious, and that the fruition will be fatal to my peace for ever" (Forry, 143). Shelley herself saw the play a day after it opened and wrote to Leigh Hunt that she was amazed at her story's popularity and fame (*Letters*, 1: 378). After Peake's dramatic version, at least five more English theatrical adaptations were staged during Mary Shelley's lifetime (Forry, 31).[1] That a popular novel with Gothic roots such as *Frankenstein* should have been adapted for the theater was not unusual in the Romantic period; for example, all Ann Radcliffe's novels were staged, as were fictional works by other Gothic novelists. The exotic settings, the presence (or suggestion) of the supernatural, the theatrical characters and language, and the often taboo themes of Gothic fiction facilitated such stage adaptations. The popular appeal of *Frankenstein* has continued throughout the twentieth-century as well. Numerous Hollywood productions of the novel have enjoyed commercial success.[2] Although most films take liberties with Shelley's story, they have, nevertheless, contributed to the myth's perpetual fame.

The *theatrum mundi* motif is more subtle in *Frankenstein* than in her other first-person narratives, indicating that Mary Shelley was perhaps experimenting with the motif that she would more fully develop in her later fiction.[3] Victor does not define his life as a "tragedy" or "drama" as often as Mathilda does, nor does he refer to the world as a stage with the same frequency as Lionel Verney. However, he does self-consciously narrate his personal history as if it were a literary construct, referring to it as a "tale," a "story," and, at times, a "tragedy." Moreover, Victor employs dramatic devices in his narration to Walton, and the very act of his storytelling becomes a theatrical performance in itself.

Despite the lack of overt dramatic analogies, the novel clearly illustrates Mary Shelley's concern with the dangers of confusing the actual world with an illusory one and of perceiving life as art. In fact, Victor violates these dichotomous boundaries in more drastic ways than do his literary successors in the Shelley canon. He creates, or re-creates, a world and a life — not only with language in the form of a dramatic text, but also with physical body parts in the form of a living being. Victor's imagined world, one in which creatures would "bless [him] as [their] creator and source," nearly comes to fruition within the existing physical world of which Victor is neither creator nor source. With the "birth" of the monster, these two worlds collide with devastating results well beyond his comprehension. Victor's words following Clerval's death– "And whose death is to finish the tragedy?"–suggest that his dream has become a nightmare and his glorious heroic drama has turned into a domestic tragedy.

The situation out of which her novel sprang is well-known to most readers: the ghost story contest among the Shelleys, Lord Bryon, and John Polidori during the summer of 1816, when they, along with Claire Clairmont and Matthew Gregory Lewis, spent rainy evenings at Villa Diodati on Lake Geneva reading Gothic tales and debating the question of vitalism.[4] In the introduction to the 1831 edition of *Frankenstein*, Mary Shelley recounts the germ of her most famous novel: "I busied myself *to think of a story* — a story to rival those which had excited us to this task. One which would speak to the mysterious fears of our nature, and awaken thrilling horror — one to make the reader dread to look round, to curdle the blood, and quicken the beatings of the heart (*Mary Shelley Reader*, 169).[5] Shelley first mentions the novel in her journal entry of 24 July 1816: "I read nouvelle nouvelles and write my story" (*Journals*, 1: 118).[6] She worked on *Frankenstein* fairly regularly throughout the summer and fall of 1816, indicating her effort in the journal with "Write." Shelley worried whether a publisher would accept her work, and both John Murray and Charles Ollier, Percy Shelley's publisher, did indeed reject the manuscript. However, Lackington, Allen and Co. agreed in August 1817 to publish the novel, which appeared on 1 January 1818. One wonders if Shelley had any presentiment of its impact when on New Year's Eve, 1817, she wrote in her journal: "Fran[kens]tein comes" (*Journals*, 1: 189).

Since the novel was unsigned, *Frankenstein*'s "birth" into the literary world prompted mixed reaction and some curiosity. "Upon the whole," wrote Sir Walter Scott in *Blackwood's Edinburgh Magazine*, "the work impresses us with a high idea of the author's original genius and happy power of expression."[7] In April 1818, *The Gentleman's Magazine*'s critic wrote, "This Tale is evidently the production of no ordinary Writer . . . many parts of it are strikingly good, and the description of the scenery excellent."[8] Other reviews not so admiring or polite were those in *The British Critic* (April 1818) and *The Monthly Review* (April 1818). Despite negative comments, often directed more at the moral character of the presumed author and "his" association with William Godwin than at the novel itself, *Frankenstein* was a popular success.[9] By spring Mary Shelley's authorship was recognized, and Victor Frankenstein's "story" was established as a modern myth in its own day.

The novel's richness and complexity invite incredibly diverse approaches. Critics and readers alike have been intrigued by the various ideas and questions *Frankenstein* posits and by the many sources for them.[10] Those critics viewing Victor as a Romantic overreacher trace the novel's debt to the Faustian and Promethean myths, the latter of which Shelley herself acknowledged in the subtitle.[11] Others classify Victor and the creature as Romantic interpretations of Milton's Satan and Adam[12] or as examples of Rousseau's theories.[13] Still other studies have examined the novel's relationship to Coleridge's "The Ancient Mariner,"[14] its position in the Gothic canon,[15] or its reflection of contemporary political and scientific issues.[16] The Romantics seem to invite biographical approaches, and Mary Shelley is no exception. Psychoanalytical and biographical studies often explore the novel's portrayal of motherhood and family.[17] Some recent studies suggest that *Frankenstein* depicts Shelley's rejection of the male Romantic ego and of the radical ideals held by her parents and husband.[18] Such varied perspectives validate the novel's canonical status, and the *theatrum mundi* motif actually highlights many of the novel's elements and themes already explored in these prior studies.

Nearly all the major characters in *Frankenstein* to some degree blur life and art by creating imaginary worlds or by perceiving the physical world as a stage on which to play out their personal dramas. A theatrical imagination holds no danger for Clerval and Elizabeth because they recognize boundaries that prevent the make-believe world from supplanting the actual one. Satisfied with their "real life" roles amidst their family and friends, they do not cast themselves into heroic parts that demand a public spotlight. However, illusory worlds become dangerous when the boundaries are ignored, as Robert Walton and Victor Frankenstein discover when their performances on the stage of life have come to signify nothing close to the dramas they have envisioned..

In *The Figure of Theater*, David Marshall explores authors' concerns "with the theater that exists outside the playhouse: the theatrical relations formed between people who face each other from the positions of actor and spectator, and the play of characters created by a view of the self as a persona, a role, or a representation that can display or conceal or counterfeit the signs of inner feeling" (1). Mary Shelley also explores the tension between actor and spectator in *Frankenstein*. Because of his appearance, the creature is initially denied a relational role in the physical world and is relegated to observing life secretly rather than participating openly in it. However, in Victor's dramatic perception, the creature is cast as a monstrous villain, a part he eventually assumes for lack of one in a satisfying domestic relationship. Desiring to play the hero of an epic masterpiece, Victor finds himself instead the villain of a domestic tragedy. Such performances present Shelley's harshest critique of the egocentric desire to privilege public fame and glory over domestic happiness by contrasting observing characters with acting ones, the latter of whom fail in both their "real life" and assumed roles and ultimately victimize the former.

The dramatic conventions of *Frankenstein* are simultaneously enhanced and complicated by the narrative voices and the novel's structure. In her first major work, Mary Shelley chose to present the action through a first-person narrative, as she would later in *Mathilda* and *The Last Man*. Although a first-person viewpoint naturally invites ambiguity, *Frankenstein* does so particularly as it is not narrated directly to the reader by the central protagonist. Shelley complicates the usual epistolary novel and frame tale structure to emphasize the conflict between acting and observing characters. Typically, the eighteenth-century epistolary novel portrays characters whose method is "writing to the moment," as in Richardson's *Pamela* and *Clarissa* or in Eliza Fenwick's *Secresy*. It can also feature characters who fashion their stories into memoirs long after the events have occurred, as in Mary Hays' *Memoirs of Emma Courtney* and William Godwin's *Caleb Williams*. The frame tale or tale-within-a-tale, a narrative structural pattern similar to the dramatic play-within-the-play, is a common feature in the Romantic novel: Radcliffe's *A Sicilian Romance*, Scott's *The Bride of Lammermoor*, and Maturin's *Melmoth the Wanderer* are but a few examples. In *Frankenstein*, Shelley uniquely blends the characteristics of both these narrative strategies. The creature has told his story to Victor, who then relays his and the creature's stories to Walton, who writes everything, including his own record, in letters to his sister. At the center of the novel is the creature's narration of the De Lacey family (along with Safie's story), and at the outer extremity is Margaret Saville, Walton's sister, the recipient of Walton's letters and the reader of both Victor's and the creature's tales.[19] The layering of teller/actor and listener/audience not only compromises any attempt at objectivity, but also heightens the novel's dramatic quality. Marc A. Rubenstein suggests that the concentric frame structure emphasizes the fact that each participant in a story becomes an observer/listener of another's tale: "the telling of a story — the return to a beginning — involves each narrator as both observer and actor" (194). Indeed, the three major characters — Walton, Victor, and the monster — both observe and act to varying degrees. However, empowerment through acting and writing is granted almost exclusively to Victor and, to some extent, Walton. Only they are able to exert any control over the content: Walton as transcriber, and Victor as author and editor. The creature's story, although centrally positioned, is buried within both Walton's and Victor's stories.

Victor demonstrates his perception that his life is a literary construct by structuring his history into a dramatic narrative, and he emphasizes the theatrical in his very telling of it — which is a performance in itself. He has already rehearsed it for the magistrate in Geneva. Before relating the events to the judge, Victor prefaces the story by saying that he knows who murdered his family and wants to accuse the criminal formally so that he can be apprehended. Promising aid, the magistrate is a willing audience as Victor begins:

> "I thank you," replied I; "listen, therefore, to the deposition that I have to make. It is indeed a tale so strange, that I should fear you would not credit it, were there not something in truth which, however wonderful, forces conviction. The story is too connected to be mistaken for a dream, and I have no motive for falsehood." My manner, as I thus addressed him, was impressive, but calm; I had formed in my own heart a resolution to pursue my destroyer to death; and this purpose quieted my agony, and provisionally reconciled me to life. I now related my history briefly, but with firmness and precision, marking the dates with accuracy, and never deviating into invective or exclamation. (*Frankenstein*, 147)

"Tale," "story," and "my history"–all are telling revelations that Victor perceives his life as a work of art and centers himself, despite the narrative's ultimate purpose to reveal the murderer. However, the magistrate does not react to the narrative as Victor expects an audience to. Understandably, the judge is unprepared for what he hears and raises reasonable questions as to the difficulty of punishing the creature, whose whereabouts are unknown and whose incredible strength may defy capture. Victor dismisses these objections, citing what he believes is the real reason the magistrate does not take immediate action: "But I perceive your thoughts: you do not credit my narrative, and do not intend to pursue my enemy with the punishment which is his desert" (*Frankenstein*, 147).

Why would the magistrate not believe Victor? Of course, the implausibility of the story is a factor, although the magistrate appears to accept Victor's story — at least from what we can determine by Victor's description of this scene. Setting aside the obvious objection, another possibility is the magistrate's lack of sympathy, or more precisely, empathetic involvement because the story is not dramatically told. In the first performance, Victor admits that he related basically the facts to the magistrate. The narrative is brief, reported with "firmness and precision"; dates are accurate;

emotion is controlled. Essentially what Victor has done is to present a scientific and legal case study, a series of facts. There is no human interest, no drama. Although there are the verbal script and the delivery of it to the magistrate, Victor does not join these two elements into what Patrice Pavis identifies as a mise en scène, a "bringing together of text and performance.[20] Granted, under more "normal" circumstances, a judge would desire only the facts in order to prosecute a criminal. But the incredible events of Victor's situation require a dramatic representation to become credible or palatable to ensure audience complicity. His story is ironically paralleled to the creation of the monster: he must make the text "come to life" just as he has done with his creation. He evidently succeeds with Walton, whose resemblances to Victor admittedly predispose him to sympathy. Nevertheless, Walton terms Victor's history a "strange and terrific story," and, unconsciously echoing Victor's own words to the magistrate, he admits that despite the supernaturalness of it, the "tale is connected, and told with an appearance of the simplest truth" (*Frankenstein*, 154). Addressing his sister, Walton shares with her an honest reaction to what he has just heard: "You have read this strange and terrific story, Margaret; and do you not feel your blood congealed with horror, like that which even now curdles mine?" (*Frankenstein*, 154). Although he does not describe Victor's storytelling as such, Walton has in fact witnessed a theatrical performance. His own reactions, and what he assumes will be Margaret's, parallel those of *Presumption*'s theater-goers: to use Mary Shelley's words, "it appeared to excite a breathless eagerness in the audience" (*Letters*, 1:378).

As he relates his narrative to Walton, Victor twice defines his life with theatrical terms. One time, following release from prison after Clerval's murder, Victor hears spectators, who are observing him leave, remark that, "'He may be innocent of the murder, but he has certainly a bad conscience'" (*Frankenstein*, 135). In a dramatic internal soliloquy, Victor asks "whose death . . . is to finish the tragedy? Ah! my father, do not remain in this wretched country; take me where I may forget myself, my existence, and all the world" (*Frankenstein*, 135).[21] Victor's question goes unanswered, but it becomes obvious that he believes his own death will conclude the drama of his life. The second time he uses the term "tragedy" occurs as he and Elizabeth are planning the wedding: "I shut up, as well as I could, in my own heart the anxiety that preyed there, and entered with seeming earnestness into the plans of my father, although they might only serve as the decorations of my tragedy" (*Frankenstein*, 141). Certainly "tragedy" need not always refer to the dramatic genre. Out of context, the word may describe Victor's misfortunes. However, contextualized with the novel's dramatic theme and conventions, Victor's word choice is significant: his life has become a drama, and all other people and events are but "decorations of [his] tragedy."

   Victor frequently interrupts his story to address his listener, Walton. In a digression to Walton about how Alphonse Frankenstein would have disapproved of his son's quest to create life, Victor stops suddenly: "But I forget that I am moralizing in the most interesting part of my tale; and your looks remind me to proceed" (*Frankenstein*, 41). After relating the circumstances surrounding Elizabeth's death, Victor interrupts his story again to comment to Walton: "But why should I dwell upon the incidents that followed this last overwhelming event. Mine has been a tale of horrors; I have reached their *acme*, and what I must now relate can but be tedious to you. Know that, one by one, my friends were snatched away; I was left desolate. My own strength is exhausted; and I must tell, in a few words, what remains of my hideous narration" (*Frankenstein*, 146). Such pauses during Victor's narrative to Walton function much as asides to the audience by a stage actor, and his use of the second person indicates that he is conscious of the listener's presence and sympathetic involvement.

   Victor also finds empowerment in imagination. If he thinks an idea or event possible, then he becomes convinced that it will become a reality. Referring to the creature being the murderer of William, he admits that "No sooner did that idea cross my imagination, than I became convinced of its truth" (*Frankenstein*, 56). Victor's assurance in the accuracy of his thought is not motivated by a Gothic premonition or portent but by his egocentric nature. Furthermore, he cannot fathom a perception other than his own; as he believes or assumes, so does everyone else. For example, because he trusts that Justine is innocent of William's murder, she therefore cannot be found guilty. Victor demonstrates his dramatic, imaginative capacity frequently. When he does not know the facts of a situation, invention substitutes its own version. Although unaware of the details of William's death, Victor tells Walton that "my imagination was busy in scenes of evil and despair" (*Frankenstein*, 57) as he reconstructs the events as he assumes they have been enacted. His choice of the word "scenes" rather than a non-theatrical synonym suggests his dramatic inclination, quite likely fostered not only by his imagination, but also by childhood plays that he, Elizabeth, and Clerval enacted when they were children.

   The play-acting by Clerval, Elizabeth, and Victor emphasizes the *theatrum mundi* motif and distinguishes between inventive theatrics that can be entertaining and beneficial on the one hand or obsessive and detrimental on the other. For Elizabeth and Clerval, the little plays were a source of amusement and may even have provided positive role models. According to Victor, Clerval was the motivating force behind their mini-dramas: "I remember, when he was nine years old, he wrote a fairy tale, which was the delight and amazement of all his companions. His favourite study consisted in books of chivalry and romance; and when very young, I can remember, that we used to act plays composed by him out of these favourite books, the principal characters of which were Orlando, Robin Hood, Amadis, and

St. George" (*Frankenstein*, 28).[22] For Clerval's imaginary capabilities, Mary
Shelley may have drawn upon her own predilection for the "formation of
castles in the air — the indulging in waking dreams — the following up
trains of thought, which had for their subject the formation of a succession
of imaginary incidents" (*Mary Shelley Reader*, 167). Certainly what is significant in this passage is that Clerval purposely dramatizes these fictional
tales. In so doing, he lays the groundwork for Victor's later dramatic perception. In the 1831 edition, Shelley intensified the dramatic motif:
"[Clerval] was deeply read in books of chivalry and romance. He composed heroic songs, and began to write many a tale of enchantment and
knightly adventure. He tried to make us act plays, and to enter into mas-
querades, in which the characters were drawn from the heroes of
Roncevalles, of the Round Table of King Arthur, and the chivalrous train
who shed their blood to redeem the holy sepulchre from the hands of the
infidels"[23] In the revision, the children act out not only plays, but mas-
querades as well. Furthermore, Clerval now writes "many a tale of
enchantment and knightly adventure," not merely "a fairy tale." Note also
that Victor says Clerval "tried to make us act plays," suggesting that Victor
as a youth was not as predisposed to this childhood activity as was his
friend. Also in the 1831 edition, Mary Shelley explicitly chose the *theatrum
mundi* metaphor to describe Clerval: "Meanwhile Clerval occupied himself, so to speak, with the moral relations of things. The busy stage of
life, the virtues of heroes, and the actions of men, were his theme; and
his hope and his dream was to become one among those whose names
are recorded in story, as the gallant and adventurous benefactors of our
species"(*Frankenstein* - 1831, 38). In this passage, Clerval's ego appears to
drive him to desire glory and fame as Victor's does him, and his love for
role play is unquestionable. Yet Victor will be the one to play-act as an
adult and see the world as a stage on which to enact his role of supreme
creator. Why not Clerval, who has obviously demonstrated such an affinity for theatrics as a child? Or Elizabeth, whose propensity for invention is
reminiscent of Mary Shelley's: the world was a "vacancy, which she sought
to people with imaginations of her own" (*Frankenstein*, 28)?

Certainly one reason is the role models the characters choose as children. Elizabeth responds to poetry and the beauty of the natural world: she
"busied herself with following the aerial creations of the poets"
(*Frankenstein*, 28). In the 1831 edition, Shelley added the following to this
line: "and in the majestic and wondrous scenes which surrounded our
Swiss home . . . she found ample scope for admiration and delight"
(*Frankenstein*, 36).[24] Clerval identifies with chilvaric knights, choosing
romance and historical characters whose "virtues" reflect courtly love,
chivalry, and benevolence. Their qualities were still viable and admired,
unlike the theories of the ancient alchemists Victor adheres to. While he
desires to be a "benefactor" to society as does Victor, Clerval enacts a role

that is compatible within society; Victor, in his attempt to be supreme creator, imposes on the world an "unnatural" being that has no place or role. Dismissing such chilvaric heroes and calling Clerval's activities "childish pursuits," Victor inclines toward the natural philosophers who held little interest for the others: "I read and studied the wild fancies of [Paracelsus and Albertus Magnus] with delight; they appeared to me treasures known to few beside myself" (*Frankenstein*, 30). Clerval's literary models were heroes whose actions were noble and benevolent; Victor's "favourite authors" promised him the ability to conjure up ghosts and devils, "the fulfilment of which [he] most eagerly sought" (*Frankenstein*, 30).

A second reason that Clerval and Elizabeth do not suffer the same fate as Victor lies in their sympathetic capabilities. They constantly direct their sensibility toward others and perceive themselves as part of the world rather than dissectors of it or creators of another. Clerval's affinity for tales and stories continues into adulthood and he uses them for beneficial purposes. When Victor is recuperating from his year-long illness following the creation of the monster, Clerval cheers him with invented "tales of wonderful fancy and passion" patterned after Persian and Arabic authors (*Frankenstein*, 52). Clerval reflects a mimetic rather than expressive theory of literature, attuned to the drama of the external world. As he and Victor make their way through Europe and England, Clerval "was alive to every new scene," unlike his friend who was "filled with dreary imaginations" (*Frankenstein*, 114). With images that anticipate the *tableaux* of Keats's urn, Clerval notes not only the grandeur of nature, but also the charm of the village and the duties of the people who live there. He sees himself in harmony with the world; Victor tries to master it. Clerval's inventions complement and embrace nature; Victor's dissect it to recreate it in monstrous form.

Elizabeth also uses imagination to sympathize with others, and she does not allow it to affect her perception of the physical world or herself. She accepts herself for what she is and does not project an image of a character she creates solely for the public; in fact, her "person was the image of her mind" (*Frankenstein*, 28). A nineteenth-century angel-in-the-house figure, Elizabeth extends her sympathy to others, "continually endeavouring to contribute to the happiness of others, entirely forgetful of herself" (*Frankenstein*, 33). Like Clerval, she has a gift for storytelling. Her stories, included in her letters to Victor, feature local gossip and the history of Justine, and they are noticeably less self-centered than Victor's. Her language is commonplace and simple, not melodramatic and grandiloquent. She enjoys relaying the neighborhood small talk about actual people and their day-to-day lives on a domestic rather than public stage. Elizabeth's approach to storytelling in her letters contrasts with Victor's. As she writes to Victor at Ingolstadt, "I dare say you well remember the heroine of my little tale" (*Frankenstein*, 48). The heroine of her "tale" is Justine, not her-

self. In her second letter to Victor, which he reads while returning home
from Ireland with his father, Elizabeth expresses her concern that Victor
may not love her. Yet, she ponders his emotional state rather than her own.
She does not dwell on her own unhappiness, but reassures Victor that
though she loves him, she wants their union only if it is his choice as well.

These letters differ sharply from Victor's. Consider that the audience
learns of Justine's history through Elizabeth's letter. Why has Victor not
related her background earlier when telling about the events and companions of his childhood? Surely Justine, as a member of the household,
deserves mention. Possible answers can be found without and within the
novel's boundaries. Stepping outside the boundaries of the text, one possibility is that Shelley wanted to contrast Elizabeth's sympathetic concern for
others with Victor's egocentric sensibility. A second reason, found within
the text, is that Victor's placement of Justine's history suggests that Justine
becomes important only when she can heighten his role as the guilt-ridden
tragic hero who seemingly mourns her fate. Elizabeth remarks in her first
letter that, following Caroline Beaufort Frankenstein's death, "every one
was too much occupied in their own grief to notice poor Justine"
(*Frankenstein*, 49), the implication being that Justine also mourned. Her
words not only foreshadow Victor's response to Justine's ultimate fate —
which he uses to solicit pity for himself — but also serve as a reminder to
him that his gaze might be more outwardly directed.

Both Clerval and Elizabeth are more closely aligned with the arts than
Victor is; they daydream, create other worlds, and bring fictional romance
characters to life in play. Yet, unlike Victor, they do not lose themselves in
their creations, nor do they violate nature or deity by letting their creations
cross the boundary between the imaginary world and the physical one.
They both possess great capacity for sympathy and emotion. Victor even
notes to Walton that Clerval's "wild and enthusiastic imagination was
chastened by the sensibility of his heart" (*Frankenstein*, 115). However,
that sensibility is not self-centered. Elizabeth and Clerval reach out to others, give of themselves, and value domestic ties; Victor does not. He structures his dramatic narrative to maximize audience sympathy, depicting
himself as both repentant villain and tragic victim.

Despite the few explicit dramatic references, Mary Shelley reveals the
theatricality of Victor's narrative through various elements of drama, such
as stage setting, *tableaux*, and soliloquies. Although the descriptions of the
Swiss, English, and Scottish settings reflect Mary Shelley's personal experiences, they are also indebted to Gothic fiction and melodrama. The sublimity of the alpine glacier at Chamounix, the isolation of both Victor's
solitary apartment and the Orkney islands, the desolation of the graveyard
scenes — all are stock images of the Gothic tradition. With such settings,
Victor invents vivid *tableaux*, freeze-frames of action, that intensify the theatricality of his narrative. Perhaps the most famous *tableau* is the creation

of the monster on that "dreary night of November." The beginning of the creation chapter has incredible visual impact: "I saw the dull yellow eye of the creature open; it breathed hard, and a convulsive motion agitated its limbs. . . . He held up the curtain of the bed; and his eyes, if eyes they may be called were fixed on me. . . . while a grin wrinkled his cheeks. . . . one hand was stretched out, seemingly to detain me" (*Frankenstein*, 42-43). Victor's descriptions of the creature's first actions heighten the horrific unnaturalness of his experiment. He has attained his quest for an ideal of sorts, and, like the knight in "La Belle Dame Sans Merci," he cannot reconcile it with reality. Another significant *tableau* is Elizabeth's death scene, particularly striking if the reader is familiar with John Henry Fuseli's painting, *The Nightmare* (1782).[25] This scene should focus on Elizabeth; however, in Victor's portrayal, the focal subject is not Elizabeth, but his reaction to her fate: "She was there, lifeless and inanimate, thrown across the bed, her head hanging down, and her pale and distorted features half covered by her hair. Every where I turn I see the same figure — her bloodless arms and relaxed form flung by the murderer on its bridal bier. Could I behold this, and live? Alas! life is obstinate, and clings closest where it is most hated. For a moment only did I lose recollection; I fainted" (*Frankenstein*, 144). Victor appropriates Elizabeth's centrality and turns attention from her fate to his reaction to it. In this *tableau*, Victor's image dominates the foreground, directing the observer's gaze to him; Elizabeth's image is relegated to the background, a "mere decoration" for Victor's tragedy. Also note the use of the present tense "I turn I see": as he relates the tale to Robert Walton, Victor is still replaying this vivid scene in his mind.

Victor is also adept in theatrical prose and in adapting a narrative passage to soliloquy form. He frequently uses dramatic, symbolic language, heavy with literary allusion. For example, in the following lines, he presents himself as an Adam figure, who, after the fall, cannot return to Eden or innocence: "some softened feelings stole into my heart, and dared to whisper paradisaical dreams of love and joy; but the apple was already eaten, and the angel's arm bared to drive me from all hope" (*Frankenstein*, 139). Victor's soliloquies best illustrate his theatrical flair with language. One example occurs at the beginning of Victor's hunt for the creature at the graves of his family. Describing the setting with particular care and detail, Victor paints a scene that could become a backdrop for any Gothic drama. Finding himself at the cemetery at dark, everything quiet but the leaves, "the scene," Victor tells Walton, "would have been solemn and affecting even to an uninterested observer. The spirits of the departed seemed to flit around, and to cast a shadow, which was felt but seen not, around the head of the mourner" (*Frankenstein*, 149). Not only does Victor evoke recognizable Gothic elements, but he also creates an eerie *tableaux* that tellingly objectifies him as the subject and narrator. His kinship to dramatic Gothic villains, such as Byron's Manfred and Radcliffe's Schedoni, are evident in the following passage, which also illustrates Victor's skill in creating scenes and performing soliloquies:

> The deep grief which this scene had at first excited quickly gave way to rage and despair. They were dead, and I lived; their murderer also lived, and to destroy him I must drag out my weary existence. I knelt on the grass, and kissed the earth, and with quivering lips exclaimed, "By the sacred earth on which I kneel, by the shades that wander near me, by the deep and eternal grief that I feel, I swear; and by thee, O Night, and by the spirits that preside over thee, I swear to pursue the dæmon, who caused this misery, until he or I shall perish in mortal conflict. For this purpose I will preserve my life: to execute this dear revenge, will I again behold the sun, and tread the green herbage of earth, which otherwise should vanish from my eyes for ever. And I call on you, spirits of the dead; and on you, wandering ministers of vengeance, to aid and conduct me in my work. Let the cursed and hellish monster drink deep of agony; let him feel the despair that now torments me."
> (*Frankenstein*—149)

Victor has certainly improved upon his theatrical delivery; these lines could easily have been spoken on the stage by an actor such as Edmund Kean. They clearly indicate that Victor's dramatic flair has flourished since the factual, precise performance for the magistrate.

In the 1831 edition, Shelley added a lengthy passage to the conclusion of Chapter Eight, following Justine's death. In it, Victor voices remorse for the pain he has caused his family and friends. However, read as a soliloquy, the addition demonstrates Victor's affinity toward the melodramatic and the self-reflexive:

> From the tortures of my own heart, I turned to contemplate the deep and voiceless grief of my Elizabeth. This also was my doing! And my father's woe, and the desolation of that late so smiling home — all was the work of my thrice-accursed hands! Ye weep, unhappy ones; but these are not your last tears! Again shall you raise the funeral wail, and the sound of your lamentations shall again and again be heard! Frankenstein, your son, your kinsman, your early, much-loved friend; he who would spend each vital drop of blood for your sakes — who has no thought nor sense of joy, except as it is mirrored also in your dear countenances — who would fill the air with blessings, and spend his life in serving you — he bids you weep — to shed countless tears; happy beyond his hopes, if thus inexorable fate be satisfied, and if the destruction pause before the peace of the grave have succeeded to your sad torments!
> Thus spoke my prophetic soul, as, torn by remorse, horror, and despair, I beheld those I loved spend vain sorrow upon the graves of William and Justine, the first hapless victims to my unhallowed arts.
> (*Frankenstein*—1831, 89)

Again Victor objectifies himself in this soliloquy, treating himself as a character, as if he were out of himself, observing and narrating what the figure of Victor did and felt. Note the Shakespearean echoes in the language–"my thrice-accursed hands"; "Ye weep, unhappy ones"; "my prophetic soul." Such expressions enhance the theatricality of the passage, not only in the delivery of these lines, but also in the depiction of Victor himself as the tragic villain-hero to whom fate has been unkind.

As he relates the story to Walton, Victor keeps the focus on himself, as evidenced by the *tableaux* that should feature others. Although the creature's story is dutifully included, it is repeated second-hand and enclosed within Victor's narrative. Even the incredible act of creating life is left untold, not only because Victor does not want another to repeat his accomplishment, but also because he does not want the deed itself to upstage the portrayal of his agony as a result of it. His ego urges him to ensure that he is the center of his story. Despite protestations to the contrary, his only concern is for himself, and he resents anyone else who takes center stage from him or who does not lavishly sympathize with him. Victor reveals this self-centeredness several times as he relates his history. When he returns home from Ingolstadt after William's death, Ernest greets him, lamenting his brother's long absence from home and the loss of the child. As Ernest's honest emotions of sympathy give way to tears, Victor chides him: "Do not . . . welcome me thus; try to be more calm, that I may not be absolutely miserable the moment I enter my father's house after so long an absence" (*Frankenstein*, 58). The emphasis on "I" directs Walton's attention to Victor's rather than Ernest's sorrow and reveals Victor's preoccupation with himself. Later when the innocent Justine is about to go on trial, Victor again laments for only himself: "During the whole of this wretched mockery of justice, I suffered living torture" (*Frankenstein*, 60). He offers no comments or sympathy regarding the "torture" Justine surely feels as she awaits execution for a crime she did not commit. While he indeed feels guilt, Victor chooses not to play the benevolent hero's role but the role of the tragic victim of circumstance, who, with only good intent, unknowingly brought such misery to those he loved.

Two other examples of Victor's egocentricity are found in his letter to Elizabeth and in his remembrances of Clerval. Agreeing to their marriage, Victor writes to his future bride, exhorting a demanding promise of her: "I have one secret, Elizabeth, a dreadful one; when revealed to you, it will chill your frame with horror, and then, far from being surprised at my misery, you will only wonder that I survive what I have endured. I will confide this tale of misery and terror to you the day after our marriage shall take place; for, my sweet cousin, there must be perfect confidence between us" (*Frankenstein*, 142). "Perfect confidence" indeed! Victor has demonstrated very little care about what Elizabeth has suffered these many years. Furthermore, he knows full well he will never have to tell her the secret because he believes that the creature's threat to be with him on his wedding night will eliminate the need for such a confidence. Victor's ego fuels his belief that the creature will attack him, not his bride; as a result, Elizabeth is an easy target for the creature's revenge.[26] William, Justine, Clerval, and Elizabeth are the innocent victims, yet Victor would have us believe it is he, more so than they, who deserves our sympathy.

Relating a detailed description of his and Clerval's journey to England, Victor gives an apparently tribute to Clerval, alternating between directly addressing his lost friend and referring to him in the third person. However, as with most elegies, this one reveals more about the author than the subject: "Clerval! beloved friend! even now it delights me to record your words, and to dwell on the praise of which you are so eminently deserving. He was a being formed in the 'very poetry of nature.' His wild and enthusiastic imagination was chastened by the sensibility of his heart. . . . Pardon this gush of sorrow; these ineffectual words are but a slight tribute to the unexampled worth of Henry, but they soothe my heart, overflowing with the anguish which his remembrance creates. I will proceed with my tale" (*Frankenstein*, 115-16). Victor begins with Clerval as the focus, but by the time he is ready to return to his "tale," the audience's attention is on Victor, not his subject. The melodramatic language, "Pardon this gush of sorrow," attempts to elicit audience sympathy for him, not for Clerval.

In perceiving the world as a stage on which to impose his own production of life, Victor creates a tension between the public image he desires and the domestic space he occupies. Unlike Elizabeth and Clerval, he is not satisfied with merely playing the chivalrous hero of a romance or history; rather, he strives to be conqueror and ultimate creator in the role of the scientist who can discover and dissect one of life's greatest mysteries in order to reconstruct it according to his vision. "What glory," he tells Walton, "would attend the discovery, if I could banish disease from the human frame, and render man invulnerable to any but a violent death" (*Frankenstein*, 30). Discovering the secret of life's origin, he makes a feeble attempt to mask his pride while actually grandstanding: "I was surprised that among so many men of genius, who had directed their inquiries toward the same science, that I alone should be reserved to discover so astonishing a secret" (*Frankenstein*, 38-39). As he debates over whether to create a human-like being or one of a "simpler organization," he decides the former: "my imagination was too much exalted by my first success to permit me to doubt of my ability to give life to an animal as complex and wonderful as man" (*Frankenstein*, 39). Victor is not satisfied with merely possessing the knowledge of endowing life; he must enact it, abandoning home and family to do so. However, he finds that his self-created role mirrors the familial relationship that he has rejected.

While at Ingolstadt, Victor fails to stay in touch with his family, despite their letters to him. Curiously, it is only when Victor considers returning home upon completion of his schooling that "an incident happened" to keep him at Ingolstadt. Absolving himself of direct responsibility by using the passive voice almost exclusively, Victor tells Walton how he, Victor, "was led" to undertake the task of creating life. Once he begins work on the creature, he forgets home and family entirely. Although Victor later tells Walton that neglecting family was detrimental, at the time he gave them little thought, obsessed with the act of creation: "I knew well therefore what would be my father's feelings; but I could not tear my thoughts from my employment, loathsome in itself, but which had taken an irresistible hold of my imagination. I wished, as it were, to procrastinate all that related to my feelings of affection until the great object, which swallowed up every habit of my nature, should be completed" (*Frankenstein*, 41). Continuing to isolate himself in a "solitary chamber, or rather cell, at the top of the house, and separated from all the other apartments by a gallery and staircase," Victor pursues his obsession: "Engaged heart and soul," he forgets "friends who were so many miles absent" and becomes "insensible to the charms of nature" (*Frankenstein*, 41).

Victor's insistence that he loves his family rings a bit hollow when one closely examines his autobiographical account. Despite his protestations to the contrary, Victor is not a family man; in fact, he is quite willing to forgo his family to satiate his obsession. Although initially he expresses misgivings about leaving home and the "old familiar" faces for Ingolstadt, he is quite excited at the prospect of acquiring knowledge and leaving a life that had been "remarkably secluded and domestic" (*Frankenstein*, 34). Victor admits to Walton that he desired to explore beyond the back garden of home: "I had often, when at home, thought it hard to remain during my youth cooped up in one place, and had longed to enter the world, and take my station among other human beings" (*Frankenstein*, 34). He may well have said "to make my entrance upon the stage," for the public spotlight and the fame and approbation that can accompany it are indeed his goals. Victor leaves home a second time, embarking for England to fulfill his promise to the creature. He observes that he "was delighted with the idea of spending a year or two in change of scene and variety of occupation, in absence from my family" (*Frankenstein*, 113). Although one reason for going abroad is to create the female, another is to escape the entrapment Victor feels at home. Requesting permission from his father to leave, he pleads to be allowed "to travel and see the world before I sat down for life within the walls of my native town" (*Frankenstein*, 113). "Walls" suggest an impenetrable enclosure that keeps in as much as it keeps out. Who can achieve fame and glory penned in a domestic sphere? Greatness, fame, and glory lie in the public arena, on the great stage of life.

Victor does not consider one obvious ramification of his experiment: his actions produce a parent-child relationship like the very one from which he has been trying to escape. Victor uses the metaphor of family to describe his project: "A new species would bless me as its creator and source; many happy and excellent natures would owe their being to me. No father could claim the gratitude of his child so completely as I should deserve theirs" (*Frankenstein*, 40). By populating the world with another species or "family," Victor believes that he will not only go down in the history books, but he will also establish himself as a god, a "modern Prometheus" — the ultimate role in the drama of life. Mary Shelley was surely aware that Victor would evoke feelings of compassion in a literary generation familiar with the Romantics' sympathetic presentations of Promethean/Faustian figures.[27] However, Victor's reaction to the creature's birth indicates that he cannot play the part of an archetypal father figure. His quest for glory, honor, and fame has led to a familial relationship that he cannot sustain. Failing in his heroic role, Victor chooses to play the tragic victim, both of circumstance and hubris.

Victor Frankenstein is not the only character whose sensibility encourages a self-centered perspective. In his quest for the secrets of the North Pole, Robert Walton quite literally attempts to appropriate the world as a stage on which to enact his life-long dream of discovering the magnetic secret of the North Pole. Having early loved the sea, Walton turned from it at his dying father's request. He discovered poetry and so became a poet, living in a "Paradise of [his] own creation" (*Frankenstein*, 16). However, Walton abandoned the art. Although one reason was his inheriting money to finance a sea expedition, the other was his fear that he could not take center stage in annals of poetic history: "I imagined that I also might obtain a niche in the temple where the names of Homer and Shakespeare are consecrated" (*Frankenstein*, 16). The obsessions to be a hero and to play the lead role in a great drama were primary motives for Walton to leave home and poetry. Walton prepares diligently for the role, enduring hardships and various apprenticeships. Before setting sail from St. Petersburgh, he tries to justify his actions: "And now, dear Margaret, do I not deserve to accomplish some great purpose?" (*Frankenstein*, 17). Mirroring Victor's self-centeredness, Walton clearly belittles those who do not pursue heroic fame and public greatness: "My life might have been passed in ease and luxury; but I preferred glory to every enticement that wealth placed in my path" (*Frankenstein*, 17). In Walton's eyes, the domestic role is unquestionably inferior to the public one.

Walton's ambition is emphasized more strongly in the 1831 edition. He writes to Margaret, "But success *shall* crown my endeavours. Wherefore not? thus far I have gone, tracing a secure way over the pathless seas: the very stars themselves being witnesses and testimonies of my triumph. Why not still proceed over the untamed yet obedient element? What can stop the determined heart and resolved will of man?" (*Frankenstein*—1831, 23). Like Victor, Walton is a performer who desires an audience and fame–"witnesses and testimonies of my triumph." Although Walton is eager to share his drama with his sister, Margaret Saville is not a satisfactory audience for the would-be hero. He desires a companion: "I bitterly feel the want of a friend," he laments to Margaret, evidently dismissing her because of her gender (he has made it clear that he wants a male friend) and his crew perhaps because of maritime hierarchy. Walton quite unconsciously reveals the reason for this need: he, as actor, needs applause, an audience to appreciate his efforts. Perhaps Margaret, not entirely sympathetic with his dream, cannot provide instant gratification for his success. Therefore, Walton needs a friend there, to witness his act, "to participate in [his] joy" (*Frankenstein*, 18). In the 1831 edition, Shelley more strongly develops the parallels between Victor and Walton. Walton joyfully tells Margaret of Victor's apparent interest in Walton's goal: "I [Walton] was easily led by the sympathy which he evinced, to use the language of my heart; to give utterance to the burning ardour of my soul; and to say, with all the fervour that warmed me, how gladly I would sacrifice my fortune, my existence, my every hope, to the furtherance of my enterprise. One man's life or death were but a small price to pay for the acquirement of the knowledge which I sought; for the dominion I should acquire and transmit over the elemental foes of our race" (*Frankenstein*—1831, 28). In both editions, Walton feels that he has found a sympathetic companion in Victor, one who will applaud his greatest role ever as a discoverer of the magnet's secret. Walton even shares his "little history" with Victor, a repeat of the exposition he has given to Margaret in the first letter. Also, both characters use similar language of melodramatic and elevated prose that suggests theatrical artifice rather than genuine understanding.

However, Walton never has the opportunity to enact his drama. Victor's cautionary tale, the danger of the ice, and the fears of the crew force him to abandon his dream and return to England. Not only does he not have his own story to tell, but Victor's tale literally occupies the space reserved for Walton's. Walton realizes that he has been transformed from actor to spectator just like Margaret, who is the audience for all these actions. Although Walton transcribes the story, Victor retains editorial privilege: "Frankenstein discovered that I made notes concerning his history: he asked to see them and then himself corrected and augmented them in many places" (*Frankenstein*, 155). Despite the centrality and primacy of Victor's narration, Walton attempts to de-marginalize his own dramatic narrative. His concern about the dangers of the crushing ice, his pretentious anxiety over Margaret's worry for his welfare, his behavior to the crew, his agonizing over a final decision — all these actions suggest Walton's insistence that there is another story besides Victor's to tell, that the curtain cannot drop without his chance in the spotlight. However, Walton is denied his glory with not only the crew's decision to return, but also with the unexpected appearance of the creature himself, whose exit into the darkness closes the play. Walton's drama is never realized; it is silenced, and he is denied a performance as an heroic conqueror of nature's secrets.

The other character desirous to make an entrance on the world's stage is the creature. However, unlike his creator or Walton, the creature does not seek fame or glory; he merely quests for an accepted role in domestic society. Victor spurns all familial domestic ties; the creature desires just one. Victor is able to participate in the drama of life; the creature is able only to observe, denied any role to play. Rejected by his creator and spurned by all who see him, he is not only a social outcast, but also an actor with no stage, no script, no fellow characters. As Martin Tropp notes, "the Monster hangs suspended in the tension between the self and world, the imaginary and the concrete, illusion and reality" (*Frankenstein*, 48). Abandoned by his father figure, the creature searches for some bond with humans, but he is shunned because of his appearance. Denied participation, he becomes an observer, watching carefully the human action of the De Lacey family. The view of the family through the chink in his rustic hovel suggests the stage setting of a domestic drama with the window frame acting as a proscenium arch or door: "On examining my dwelling, I found that one of the windows of the cottage had formerly occupied a part of it, but the panes had been filled up with wood. In one of these was a small and almost imperceptible chink, through which the eye could just penetrate. Through this crevice, a small room was visible, white-washed and clean, but very bare of furniture. . . . It was a lovely sight, even to me, poor wretch! who had never beheld aught beautiful before" (*Frankenstein*, 80). The creature dramatizes the De Lacey family's actions, expertly describing their day-to-day movements, dialogue, and emotions. The family members are unaware that they are "performing" before an observer who wants nothing more than to participate with them: "I longed to join them," the creature tells Victor, "but dared not. . . . for the present I would remain quietly in my hovel, watching, and endeavouring to discover the motives which influenced their actions" (*Frankenstein*, 81). The only way the creature can participate is secretly. Likening himself to an "invisible hand," he supplies firewood and brings food.

Being an observer, however, is not enough. He wants to interact, and he even creates a little scenario of how to play the introduction scene: "I formed in my imagination a thousand pictures of presenting myself to them, and their reception of me. I imagined that they would be disgusted, until, by my gentle demeanour and conciliating words, I should first win their favour, and afterwards their love" (*Frankenstein*, 85). He hesitates because he has seen his reflected image and understands that his appearance separates him from the others. When he presents himself to the De Laceys, the creature is rejected, despised, and feared.[28] He feels this rejection more profoundly than he did Victor's immediately after his creation. Understanding the sense of family and love by observing the De Laceys, the creature now recognizes the loss of such a union. In a sense, the De Laceys have created him, or more accurately, molded the existing form; the creature says to the blind father, "you raise me from the dust by this kindness" (*Frankenstein*, 97).

After relating the account of the De Lacey family, the creature tells Victor that he wants nothing more than to be a part of the drama of human existence: "Such was the history of my beloved cottagers. It impressed me deeply. I learned, from the views of social life which it developed, to admire their virtues, and to deprecate the vices of mankind. As yet I looked upon crime as a distant evil; benevolence and generosity were ever present before me, inciting within me a desire to become an actor in the busy scene, where so many admirable qualities were called forth and displayed" (*Frankenstein*, 94). "An actor in the busy scene": the creature's words anticipate Mary Shelley's own language several years later following Percy Shelley's death: "How many tears & spasms of anguish this solitude has cost me lies buried in my memory — formed to feel pleasure in society — in intercou[r]se with person of wit & genius & the busy scene of life" (*Journals*, 2: 555). The above passage from the novel is significant in that it reflects the creature's desire for acceptance. Isolated as an observer, he wants to be a part of life and to employ his natural benevolence. The creature does not want to spend his existence in a hovel, unknown and unwanted, his only connection to domestic life through a chink in the wall. He wants a purpose, a part to play. This longing for a role and familial ties results in his demand that Victor make him a mate, a promise Victor makes but does not keep.

After the creature's last hope for domestic happiness is destroyed, Victor and the creature begin an elaborate exchange of roles. As Pamela Clemit notes, "Mary Shelley builds on Godwin's use of the pursuit to destabilize moral values: in the complex equivocations of *Frankenstein*, the abandoned creature returns to challenge his monstrous father, and the pair act out a drama of enticement and threat that leads to widespread social destruction" (144).[29] Victor becomes the helpless victim as his family is destroyed before him, and the creature assumes the role of villainous revenger. Just as the creature hunted down Victor to plead for the creation of a female companion, so Victor later hunts down the creature to close the scene of this nightmarish play forever. Also, they echo each other's words: "I, like the arch fiend, bore a hell within me" (*Frankenstein*, 101), moans the creature to his creator; "I bore a hell within me" (*Frankenstein*, 65), claims Victor to Walton, after relating Justine's story. At first each identifies himself as well-intentioned; then they both identify themselves with Satan; later, they name each other as the devil or a monster. Just as Victor refers to himself as "author of unalterable evils" in reference to the crea-

ture's birth and action, so the creature warns Victor that he will be author
of Victor's fate should his creator not listen to his story: "On you it rests,
whether I quit for ever the neighbourhood of man, and lead a harmless life,
or become the scourge of your fellow-creatures, and the author of your
own speedy ruin" (*Frankenstein*, 75). At Victor's deathbed, the creature has
almost fully assumed the victimized villain role that Victor played so well.
Looking at his creator, the creature exclaims more to himself than to
Walton, "'That is also my victim! . . . in his murder my crimes are con-
summated; the miserable series of my being is wound to its close!'"
(*Frankenstein*, 161). Although he perceives himself inextricably entwined
with Victor, the creature still finds association with the only other personages available to him: those in literary texts, particularly Milton's *Paradise
Lost*: "When I call over the frightful catalogue of my deeds, I cannot
believe that I am he whose thoughts were once filled with sublime and transcendant [sic] visions of the beauty and the majesty of goodness. But it is
even so; the fallen angel becomes a malignant devil. Yet even that enemy of
God and man had friends and associates in his desolation; I am quite
alone" (*Frankenstein*, 163). The boundaries between creator and creation,
between father and son, blur to indistinction. Victor's dream to star in a
heroic drama and the creature's dream to play in a domestic one turn into
surrealistic nightmares as they find themselves the actors in a tragedy or
melodrama.

The tendency to view life as art and art as life intensifies for the creature
when he discovers works by Plutarch, Milton, and Goethe. He reads all the
books as "true" accounts and identifies with the personages in them, especially those of Adam and Satan in *Paradise Lost*. Even his daydreams
reflect his connection to literary figures: "some times I allowed my
thoughts, unchecked by reason, to ramble in the fields of Paradise, and
dared to fancy amiable and lovely creatures sympathising with my feelings.
. . . But it was all a dream; no Eve soothed my sorrows, nor shared my
thoughts; I was alone" (*Frankenstein*, 97). Although he is denied access to
the human stage, the creature is aware that his experiences can be constructed into a tale or history, just like Werter's or Adam's or the historical
figures in Plutarch's work. Pleading for audience with Victor, he refers several times to his life as a story: "Listen to my tale," "listen to me," "Hear
my tale; it is long and strange" (*Frankenstein*, 75). Even the introduction
to the creature's story is melodramatic, and the setting on the glacier in the
hut recalls the sterile and isolated attic laboratory in which the creature
was brought to life. Victor writes: "seating myself by the fire which my odious companion had lighted, he thus began his tale" (*Frankenstein*, 76).

For Victor, he and the text are as one, a concept with literary precedent.
Referring to Samuel Richardson's characters, Pamela and Clarissa, William
Ray writes that the novels, or the characters' letters, "link both selfhood
and social identity with the deliberate textualization of self."[30] The parallel

of Victor's two creations — the creature and the dramatic text — intensifies Victor's desired role of creator/author and his desperate wish to dominate life itself. Victor explicitly refers to the creature as a text: "I had been the author of unalterable evils; and I lived in daily fear, lest the monster whom I had created should perpetrate some new wickedness" (*Frankenstein*, 68). When Victor realizes that Walton is recording his dramatic tale, he exercises editorial privilege to ensure its accuracy. Walton writes to Margaret: "Frankenstein discovered that I made notes concerning his history: he asked to see them, and then himself corrected and augmented them in many places; but principally in giving the life and spirit to the conversations he held with his enemy. "Since you have preserved my narration," said he, "I would not that a mutilated one should go down to posterity" (*Frankenstein*, 155). In Sir Walter Scott's novel *Rob Roy*, the first-person narrator, Frank Osbaldistone, expresses concern that "the tale told by one friend, and listened to by another, loses half its charms when committed to paper."[31] "Charms" are not what Victor feels may be lost in Walton's transcription. His emendations, Walton tells us, are directed primarily to the exchanges between him and the creature, and it is not unreasonable to assume that Victor wants to ensure that he is sympathetically portrayed in Walton's narrative. The adjective "mutilated" in the above passage is significant. Victor has already created one mutilation — the creature, or his "abortion" as he calls it.[32] Failing in his role as supreme creator of a living being, he takes precautions, fearing that this creation, this "hideous narration," will also take on a life of its own beyond his control. The novel certainly seemed to. For the 1831 edition, Shelley referred to it as her "hideous progeny"; it became a modern myth almost immediately upon its publication and ensured Shelley's membership in the Romantic canon. Perhaps Victor's tale took on its own life as well. We will never know how Margaret Saville reacted to Walton's letters and the bizarre tales contained within them — unless we employ invention ourselves and extend the novel's boundaries. It is possible that had Margaret passed the letters on, Victor's story would at least have lived on as literature, if not as a scientific or psychological case study. Such a scenario would have pleased Victor, for it would have guaranteed his fame in history books for many generations to come. However, it is also possible, that, judging the content of the letters too horrific for public view, she burned them in the fireplace, as the creature lit his own funeral pyre — obliterating Victor's only recourse to fame and demonstrating the mutability of textual as well as corporeal existence.

Chapter 3 Notes

1. Forry provides the scripts for *Presumption* and the others: *Another Piece of Presumption* (1823), also by Peake; *Frank-in-Stream; or, The Modern Promise to Pay* (1824), playwright unknown; *Frankenstein; or the Man and the Monster* (1826), by Henry M. Milner; *The Monster and Magician; or, The Fate of Frankenstein* (1826), by John Atkinson Kerr; and *Frankenstein; or, the Model Man* (1849), by Richard and Barnabas Brough. At least fifteen dramas based on *Frankenstein* appeared throughout France and England from 1823 to 1826.

2. For background on the many twentieth-century media depictions of the novel, see also Martin Tropp, *Mary Shelley's Monster: The Story of "Frankenstein"* (Boston: Houghton Mifflin, 1976) and Donald Glut, *The Frankenstein Legend: A Tribute to Mary Shelley and Boris Karloff* (Metuchen: Scarecrow Press, 1973); both references hereafter cited in text.

3. Shelley made a number of changes regarding *theatrum mundi* references in the 1831 edition. However, the emendations do not suggest a conscious effort to emphasize the motif more in the later edition than in the 1818 one. For example, one of Elizabeth's references is deleted, but Clerval's penchant for playacting is more fully explored. I note relevant changes between the two texts in this chapter.

4. In "The First *Frankenstein* and Radical Science," (*TLS* 9 April 1993: 12-14), Marilyn Butler provides background on the debate between materialism and spiritualized vitalism, suggesting that the 1818 edition reflected these contemporary opposing views.

5. Unless otherwise noted, citations from the novel will be based on the 1818 edition from *The Mary Shelley Reader* and hereafter cited as *Frankenstein*.

6. "nouvelle nouvelles" refers to *Nouveaux contes moraux et nouvelles historiques* (1802), by Madame de Genlis. The work is a collection of stories, one of which is a tale of Pygmalion and Galatea. For detail on Shelley's interest in de Genlis, see Burton Pollin's "Philosophical and Literary Sources of *Frankenstein*," *Comparative Literature* 17 (1965): 97-108.

7. Sir Walter Scott, "Remarks on *Frankenstein; or the Modern Prometheus: A Novel*," *Blackwood's Edinburgh Magazine* 2 (March 1818): 620.

8. Review of *Frankenstein*, by Mary Shelley, *The Gentleman's Magazine* 8 (April 1818): 334.

9. Reviewers and readers assumed the author was a male, and many attributed it to Percy Shelley, perhaps because the novel was dedicated to Godwin

10. See the following for detail regarding the various sources for the novel: George Levine, "The Ambiguous Heritage of *Frankenstein*," in *The Endurance of Frankenstein*, ed. George Levine and U. C. Knoepflmacher (Berkeley: University of California Press, 1979); Burton R. Pollin, "Philosophical and Literary Sources of *Frankenstein*."

11. See the following: Chris Baldick, *In Frankenstein's Shadow: Myth, Monstrosity, and Nineteenth-Century Writing* (Oxford: Clarendon Press, 1987); Harold Bloom, "*Frankenstein*, or the New Prometheus," *Partisan Review* 32 (1965): 611-618;

Paul Cantor, *Creature and Creator: Myth-making and English Romanticism* (Cambridge: Cambridge University Press, 1984); and Joseph Gardner, "Mary Shelley's Divine Tragedy," *Essays in Literature* 4 (1977): 182-197.

12. See the following: Sandra Gilbert, "Horror's Twin: Mary Shelley's Monstrous Eve" in *The Madwoman in the Attic*, ed. Sandra Gilbert and Susan Gubar (New Haven: Yale University Press, 1979), 213-247; Milton Mays, "*Frankenstein*, Mary Shelley's Black Theodicy," *Southern Humanities Review* 3 (1969): 146-153; Leslie Tannenbaum, "From Filthy Type to Truth: Miltonic Myth in *Frankenstein*," *Keats-Shelley Journal* 26 (1977): 101-113; and Philip Wade, "Shelley and the Miltonic Element in Mary Shelley's *Frankenstein*," *Milton and the Romantics* 2 (1976): 23-25.

13. See the following: James O'Rourke, "'Nothing More Unnatural': Mary Shelley's Revision of Rousseau," *English Literary History* 56 (1989): 543-569 and David Marshall, *The Surprising Effects of Sympathy: Marivaux, Diderot, Rousseau, and Mary Shelley*.

14. See the following: Sarah Webster Goodwin, "Domesticity and Uncanny Kitsch in 'The Rime of the Ancient Mariner' and *Frankenstein*," *Tulsa Studies in Women's Literature* 10 (1991): 93-108 and Mary Lowe-Evans, *"Frankenstein": Mrs. Shelley's Wedding Guest* (New York: Twayne Publishers, 1975).

15. See Kate Ferguson Ellis, *The Uncontested Castle*; Eugenia de Lamotte's *Perils of the Night*; Elizabeth MacAndrew, *The Gothic Tradition in Fiction*; David Punter, *The Literature of Terror*; Hartley Spatt, "Mary Shelley's Last Men: The Truth of Dreams" *Studies in the Novel* 7 (1975): 526-537); and Mary K. Patterson Thornburg, *The Monster in the Mirror* (Ann Arbor: UMI Research Press, 1987).

16. See Fred Botting, "*Frankenstein* and the Language of Monstrosity" in *Reviewing Romanticism,* ed. Philip Martin and Robin Jarvis (London: Macmillan, 1992); Marilyn Butler, "The First Frankenstein and Radical Science"; Wilfred Cude, "Mary Shelley's Modern Prometheus: A Study in the Ethics of Scientific Creativity," *Dalhousie Review* 52 (1972): 212-225; and Samuel Holmes Vasbinder, *Scientific Attitudes in Mary Shelley's Frankenstein* (Ann Arbor: UMI Research Press, 1984).

17. See Richard Dunn, "Narrative Distance in *Frankenstein*," *Studies in the Novel* 6 (1974): 408-417; John Dussinger's Kinship and Guilt in Mary Shelley's *Frankenstein*," *Studies in the Novel* 8 (1976): 38-55; Anne K. Mellor, *Mary Shelley: Her Life, Her Fiction, Her Monsters*; Ellen Moers, "The Female Gothic" in *The Endurance of Frankenstein*; Marc A. Rubenstein, "'My Accursed Origin': The Search for the Mother in *Frankenstein*," *Studies in Romanticism* 15 (1976): 165-194; Janet Todd, "Frankenstein's Daughter: Mary Shelley and Mary Wollstonecraft," *Women and Literature* 4 (1976): 18-27; William Veeder, *Mary Shelley and Frankenstein: The Fate of Androgyny* (Chicago: University of Chicago Press, 1986) and Paul Younguist, "*Frankenstein*: The Mother, the Daughter, and the Monster," *Philological Quarterly* 70 (1991): 339-359

18. See Meena Alexander, *Women in Romanticism* (Totowa: Barnes and Noble, 1989), and Jane Blumberg, *Mary Shelley's Early Novels* (Iowa City: University of Iowa Press, 1993).

19. See Joyce Zonana's "'They will prove the truth of my tale': Safie's Letters as the Feminist Core of Mary Shelley's *Frankenstein*," *Journal of Narrative Technique* 21 (1991): 170-184. Zonana reads the novel as an eco-feminist tract against male appropriation of female spirit and body through Safie's letters, which lie at the virtual center of the novel and are never reproduced or violated. In "Mary Shelley's Last Men: The Truth of Dreams," Hartley Spatt notes that, of the fictional characters, Margaret Saville is the final reader/observer.

20. "From Text to Performance," in *Performing Texts*, ed. Michael Issacharoff and Robin F. Jones (Philadelphia: University of Pennsylvania Press, 1988), 87.

21. Mary Shelley revised this passage in the 1831 edition and deleted the dramatic reference. The revision suggests that Victor is more proactive, intent on ending "the existence of the monstrous Image," than reactive, passively waiting for the drama to conclude.

22. Although Orlando is a conventional name for a romance hero (see, for example, Charlotte Smith's *The Old Manor House*), the probable reference is to Ariosto's character in *Orlando Furioso* (1532), which Mary Shelley recorded reading 26 May 1818 through 19 July 1818, well after the publication date of *Frankenstein* (1 January 1818). However, she may have been familiar with the romance via her father or Percy Shelley, who read it April 1815. John Hoole's 1783 translation of Ariosto's work was popular with early nineteenth-century readers including Scott and Southey. The legend of Robin Hood was included in Thomas Percy's *Reliques* (1765, with revised editions until 1794). Although Mary Shelley did not specifically record reading a version of Robin Hood once she began a journal, it is likely that the legend of Sherwood Forest's famous outlaw-hero was familiar to her. Southey published an abridged version of the romance *Amadis of Gaul* in 1803, and Shelley records in her journal that she read it during January and February of 1817. The legend of St. George, like Robin Hood, was probably well-known by most British children.

23. Mary Shelley, *Frankenstein; or the Modern Prometheus*, 1831 edition, ed. James Kinsley and M. K. Joseph (Oxford: Oxford University Press, 1969), 37; hereafter cited in text as *Frankenstein - 1831*.

24. In this 1831 revision, Shelley more sharply contrasts Elizabeth's love of nature and outwardly directed sensibility with Victor's lack of both: while Elizabeth pondered the "magnificent appearances of things," Victor "delighted in investigating their causes" (36).

25. Fuseli depicts a lifeless young woman dressed in white sprawled across an unkempt bed with an incubus sitting atop her and a eerie horse in the shadows. Her head hangs off the bed, and her arms are dangling on the floor. Dark shadows contrast with the light cast on the foregrounded woman. Shelley was familiar with this work; Fuseli was a friend of both Wollstonecraft and Godwin

26. Readers have often been puzzled as to why Victor could not understand that the creature's pattern of inflicting revenge was to destroy all who were dear to Victor. I argue that, because of his ego, Victor could only conceive himself as the target or the center of the drama; William Veeder suggests that Victor had created the monster "to enact his murderous will against his family" (151).

27. Anne Mellor posits that Percy Shelley felt Victor was a victim (*Mary Shelley*, 63).

28. Mr. De Lacey, the blind father, accepts him freely and converses with him; it is the sighted family members who attack the creature.

29. The character reversals and chase scenes in the novel parallel those in Godwin's *Caleb Williams*. Falkland, comfortably established on his manorial estate, is pursued by Caleb, who has discovered Falkland's haunting secret of the past. Caleb is then, in turn, pursued by Falkland, who seeks to destroy the man who possesses that secret.

30. *Story and History* (Cambridge: Basil Blackwell, Inc., 1990), 133; hereafter cited in text.

31. Sir Walter Scott, *Rob Roy*, ed. Edgar Johnson (Boston: Houghton Mifflin Co., 1956), 1.

32. According to Anne Mellor, Percy Shelley coined the term "abortion" for the monster, for whom, Mellor claims, he had very little sympathy (*Mary Shelley*, 62).

Mathilda: Life as Theatrical Production

> This whole creation is essentially subjective, and the dream is the the-
> ater where the dreamer is at once scene, actor, prompter, stage man-
> ager, author, audience, and critic.
>
> — Carl Jung, *General Aspects of Dream Psychology*

"**I**f the world is a stage and I merely an actor on it my part has been strange, and alas! tragical": so writes the eponymous heroine of Mary Shelley's 1819 novella, *Mathilda*.[1] Although the *theatrum mundi* motif pervades all of Shelley's fiction, nowhere is it more explicit than in this work. The above paraphrase from Shakespeare's *As You Like It* is one of many dramatic references or conventions that Shelley's first-person narrator employs in writing her epistolary memoir and cautionary tale. Indulging an excessively introspective sensibility, Mathilda constructs her autobiography as a dramatic tragedy that reveals an egocentric view of life as a stage on which she, a tragic actress, performs the leading role as an incest victim.[2] Not only is she an actress, but she is also the "prompter, stage manager, author, audience, and critic" as well.

Mary Shelley wrote *Mathilda* in the summer and fall of 1819. In her 4 August 1819 journal entry, she records "Write," which most scholars agree refers to "The Fields of Fancy," the original introductory frame tale to Mathilda's personal narrative. From 4 August to 12 August, she worked daily on the novel, and by 12 September 1819, she recorded in her journal, "Finish copying my tale" (*Journals,* 1: 296). Shelley asked the Gisbornes to take the copy to her father, who acted as her literary agent, when the Gisbornes returned to England in May 1820. However, Godwin did not submit the manuscript for publication because, Maria Gisborne claimed, he found its topic "disgusting and detestable" (*Maria Gisborne Journals,* 44). The novella remained unpublished until 1959, when Elizabeth Nitchie's edition first made the texts of both *Mathilda* and Shelley's initial draft, "The Fields of Fancy," available to students and scholars.

Only fairly recently has the novella generated critical attention, much of which offers psychoanalytical and/or biographical readings, and certainly with justifiable cause.[3] *Mathilda*, like Shelley's other fiction, indeed has roots in her experiences and relationships. The work was composed during a troubled period in her marriage following the deaths of her two children, one-year old Clara in November 1818 and three-year old William in June 1819. The losses severely strained the Shelleys' marriage, and Mary Shelley's despondency was further aggravated by Godwin's seeming lack of sympathy for his grandchildren's deaths. Shelley begins her third Journal on 4 August 1819 with a bitter recollection of their recent tragedies: "We have now lived five years together & if all the events of the five years were blotted out I might be happy — but to have won & then cruelly have lost the associations of four years is not an accident to which the human mind can bend without much suffering" (*Journals*, 1: 293).[4] Shelley's self-conscious reflections on her own "tragedies" during the time of the work's composition and Mathilda's self-pitying narration indeed invite a psychoanalytical and/or biographical approach. Terence Harpold, for example, declares it a "profoundly autobiographical work," and Anne K. Mellor describes it as an account of her "deepest and most ambivalent feelings toward her father."[5] Although intriguing, psychobiographical approaches often do not explore *Mathilda*'s literary merits and do tend to identify the narrative voice as Mary Shelley's, thereby assuming that the overtly self-reflexive and hyperbolic style is hers. Unquestionably, the novella's intense emotion derives in part from Shelley's own, just as the power of Byron's *Manfred* or Brontë's *Jane Eyre* has roots in each author's experiences and imagination. However, we must, as Audra Dibert Himes writes, "demarcate the ground between Mary Shelley and Mathilda. Treating Mary Shelley as an author function allows us to focus more clearly on Mathilda as the scriptor of *Mathilda*."[6] Moving beyond Shelley's authorial presence and reading the work as her first-person narrator's memoir, then the theatrical rhetoric and intense subjectivity clearly reflects Mathilda's artistic sensibility rather than Shelley's. Such an approach calls us to re-evaluate judgments of *Mathilda* as "poor fiction . . . a simplistic, finally sentimental response to [Mary Shelley's] involved ties to husband and father" or as a work "devoid of the professionalism which characterizes Shelley's important novels."[7] The novella is neither simplistic nor lacking in professionalism; instead, it reveals Mary Shelley's careful craftsmanship in creating a character who constructs her life into a dramatic text depicting the dangers of a debilitating confusion of life with art and reality with illusion.

The entirety of the text is a memoir composed by Mathilda, a twenty-year-old woman near death, whose subjectivity encourages her inclination to view herself as the center of life. This sensibility ultimately directs her to perceive the world as a stage, her life as a theatrical production, and herself as an actress in that production, as her echo of Jaques' lines indicate: "if the world is a stage and I merely an actor on it my part has been strange, and alas! tragical" (*Mathilda*, 254). Mathilda's conscious use of theatrical metaphors evidences her inability or unwillingness to deal with reality, and the account she gives of her life reflects a self-indulgent theatricality. In her opening lines, she refers to the memoir as a "tragic history"; later, she writes "I am a tragedy" (*Mathilda*, 175 and 233 repectively). As Mathilda nears the end of her epistle, she perceives not only the letter, but also her entire existence as a dramatic text: "This was the drama of my life which I have now depicted upon paper. . . . Now my tears are dried; the glow has faded from my cheeks, and with few words of farewell to you, Woodville, I close my work; the last that I shall perform" (*Mathilda*, 245).

The theatrical motif in the above passage recalls that found in *Frankenstein*: the emphasis on life as a performance and dramatic text. Stepping outside the boundaries of Mathilda's memoir for a moment, we can indeed place Mary Shelley's use of such overtly theatrical references within a tradition of narrative fiction.[8] For example, William Godwin's haunted and hunted protagonist Caleb Williams employs the same metaphor in the opening line of his epistolary memoir: "My life has for several years been a theatre of calamity" (*Caleb Williams*, 3). In *Memoirs of Emma Courtney*, Mary Hays' heroine perceives her life as a literary construct: "And is this all of human life — this, that passes like a tale that is told? Alas! it is a tragical tale."[9] As with Shelley's other fiction, *Mathilda's* theatrical conventions can be positioned within a dramatic tradition as well as a narrative one. Shelley's protagonist employs melodramatic language and theatrical metaphors in a similar fashion to what Daniel Watkins has observed of characters in Romantic drama. In *A Materialist Critique of English Romantic Drama*, Watkins explores the relationship between power and language, specifically how characters manipulate the power of discourse or become victims of such manipulation.[10] Frequently, Watkins argues, the end result is that the story is privileged above life: "Rather than experience providing the basis for . . . assessments of linguistic expression, stories come to provide the basis for . . . assessments of experience" (14).[11] What occurs, essentially, is a conflation of "experience" or reality and "linguistic expression" or storytelling, a conflation that Mathilda creates as she records her dramatic autobiography. She not only manipulates language, but, more dangerously, is manipulated by it. For Mathilda, life and theater are no longer distinct concepts: the world is a stage, and life is dramatic production.

Returning again to Mathilda's memoir, we can trace the narrator's dramatic perception of life in part to an acutely introspective sensibility that had been cultivated in years of near-solitary existence on an isolated Scottish estate. Her only companion, a nurse, left when Mathilda was seven, and her guardian aunt, who forbade her to play with neighboring children, possessed a cold restraint that denied the emotional nurturing crucial for a child to develop self-confidence and stability. About her aunt, Mathilda writes, "I believe that without the slightest tinge of a bad heart she had the coldest that ever filled a human breast: it was totally incapable of any affections. She took me under her protection because she considered

it her duty" (*Mathilda*, 182). The aunt does not take an active part in raising her niece, who is consigned to a distant room. Despite being abandoned
and ignored, Mathilda believes herself to be the "offspring of the deepest
love" and exhibits "the greatest sensibility of disposition" (*Mathilda*, 183).
She loves animals and revels in the outdoors, treasuring "all the changes of
Nature; and rain, and storm, and the beautiful clouds of heaven [that]
brought their delights with them. When rocked by the waves of the lake
[her] spirits rose in triumph as a horseman feels with pride the motions of
his high fed steed" (*Mary Shelley Reader*, 184). In many respects, Mathilda
is a Wordsworthian child of nature: she hikes through the mountains, rows
a skiff on the lake, and gathers flowers by a stream.[12] She also indulges her
imagination the way many children do, discovering literature and theatrics
as a source of entertainment and then immersing herself in stories and daydreams through role-play and invention. However, without playmates or
mentors, she has no one to direct or moderate sensibility, and, as she
matures, she continues to possess a child-like egocentric view of life.

Introspective sensibility draws Mathilda deeper and deeper into a self-
created world that, unlike reality, fulfills her dreams. As a child, Mathilda
views art as life; as a young adult, she views life as art. The concept of art
as life was a convention of sensibility: "there is an assumption that life and
literature are directly linked, not through any notion of mimetic depiction
of reality but through the belief that the literary experience can intimately
affect the living one. So literary conventions become a way of life."[13]
Literary conventions indeed become a "way of life" for Mathilda; more
dangerously, life becomes a literary experience, specifically a drama, as she
perceives literature first as entertainment and then as a mode by which to
live. Her longing for companionship leads her to the books in her aunt's
library. There, she reads, among others, Shakespeare, Milton, and Livy, all
of whom substitute for "human intercourse." To escape her loneliness, she
journeys into a world of fancy and fictional characters. Imaginative daydreams that are harmless to most children's development soon evolve into
a confusion of illusion and reality for Mathilda, and she begins to equate
art and life: "I brought Rosalind and Miranda and the lady of Comus to
life to be my companions, or on my isle acted over their parts imagining
myself to be in their situations. Then I wandered from the fancies of others
and formed affections and intimacies with the aerial creations of my own
brain — but still clinging to reality I gave a name to these conceptions and
nursed them in the hope of realization" (*Mathilda*, 185). In this passage,
the choice of texts is significant, revealing much about the narrator's character. Unlike Mathilda, whose father first abandons and then incestuously
desires her, *The Tempest*'s Miranda has a loving and caring parent,
Prospero, who carefully (albeit overbearingly) ensures his daughter's protection and her eventual happiness in marriage. The Lady in Milton's
masque, *Comus*, has two brothers who retrieve her after her abduction.

Rosalind, the spunky heroine of *As You Like It*, disguises herself as a boy, Ganymede, in order to search for her beloved father, banished from his land, and she orchestrates the eventual union between the tongue-tied Orlando and herself. Longing for her father, Mathilda sees herself as a dramatic Rosalind, dreaming of how she too will adopt disguise to find him: "My favourite vision was that when I grew up I would leave my aunt, whose coldness lulled my conscience, and disguised like a boy I would seek my father through the world" (*Mathilda*, 185).

Mathilda's childhood dreams and longings are natural and understandable, given her lonely situation. Mary Shelley recognized the human tendency to indulge imaginary fancies, as she herself often did as a young girl. Recall again the passage she wrote in the preface to the 1831 edition of *Frankenstein*, where she described her enjoyment in "the indulging in waking dreams — the following up trains of thought" (*Mary Shelley Reader*, 167). Whereas Shelley understood the distinction between "imaginary incidents" and actual life, Mathilda does not; she "nurse[s]" these conceptions "in the hope of realization" (*Mathilda*, 185). Stimulated by sensibility, Mathilda's predilection for fusing illusion and life, evident at an early age, intensifies as she grows older. Before she meets her father upon his return, Mathilda comments that she has been only an observer of life, not an actor in it: "The earth was to me a magic lantern and I [a] gazer, and a listener but no actor; but then came the transporting and soul-reviving era of my existence: my father returned and I could pour my warm affections on a human heart; there was a new sun and a new earth created to me" (*Mathilda*, 245). A "new sun and a new earth": essentially, Mathilda has created a world for herself, a world that centers her and her father and one in which they will blissfully exist as she has always imagined they would. That world, however, is shattered, along with Mathilda's long-held hopes for happiness. Her recourse is to perceive her life as a tragic play that, fostered by her sensibility, accords her a starring role as a victim of fate. By the time she constructs her memoir/letter to Woodville, Mathilda's fusion of life and art is complete: "I am, I thought, a tragedy; a character that [Woodville] comes to see act: now and then he gives me my cue that I may make a speech more to his purpose: perhaps he is already planning a poem in which I am to figure. I am a farce and play to him, but to me this is all dreary reality: he takes all the profit and I bear all the burthen" (*Mathilda*, 233). Mathilda protests that her life is a "dreary reality" and that it is Woodville who sees her as a play; however, she transfers to Woodville her own perception of her existence, for it is she, not he, who refers to life as a drama. Planning a double suicide, she is careful to arrange the setting for what she describes as "the last scene of my tragedy" (*Mathilda*, 235).

Such frequent use of theatrical metaphors reveal Mathilda's perception of life as a performance that can be constructed into a dramatic text. Furthermore, as a performer, she requires an audience, and although she claims to direct the memoir to Woodville, she expects others to read her history: "I do not address [these thoughts] to you alone because it will give me pleasure to dwell upon our friendship in a way that would be needless if you alone read what I shall write. I shall relate my tale therefore as if I wrote for strangers. . . . Others will toss these pages lightly over: to you, Woodville, kind, affectionate friend, they will be dear" (*Mathilda*, 176). In chapter IX, Mathilda introduces Woodville in the third person, rather than addressing him directly: "The name of my friend was Woodville. I will briefly relate his history that you may judge how cold my heart must have been not to be warmed by his eloquent words and tender sympathy" (*Mathilda*, 223). The second person address, "you," indicates that Mathilda is directing her drama to an audience beyond her friend. Had her letter been a mere explanation of her grief to Woodville, she could have ended it at this point. Granted, Mary Shelley must include Woodville's background for the benefit of the reader. However, Mathilda chooses to include him in her dramatis personae to highlight her role as a tragic heroine and to provide her audience with a sense of closure to her drama.

Mary Shelley further emphasizes Mathilda's penchant for the dramatic through the revised structure of the novel. Originally Shelley planned that the story of Mathilda, like that of Victor Frankenstein, would be set within a frame tale. Initially entitled "The Fields of Fancy," this early draft introduces the frame tale's first-person narrator, who is mourning the loss of loved ones.[14] A spirit, Fantasia, transports the narrator to the Elysian fields where she meets a Socratic instructor, Diotima, who counsels grieving and guilt-ridden individuals by stressing the need for friendship and self-knowledge. As the narrator listens to Diotima speak to a group, she notices a young woman, Mathilda, who later relates her sad history. Shelley's decision to abandon the frame tale structure that she effectively employed in *Frankenstein* suggests that perhaps she wished to spotlight her protagonist and heighten the novella's dramatic quality by allowing Mathilda to recount her life to the audience directly. The *theatrum mundi* motif in her first novel illustrates the dramatic potential of storytelling; in *Mathilda*, it becomes the mode by which one's life is perceived. The revision recalls Shelley's own words later recorded in her journal: "[life] is as a change from a narrative to a drama" (*Journals*, 2: 452), and it suggests that Shelley recognized that the novel's new structure reinforces her character's perception of life as theater.

Mathilda's dramatic tendency is also evidenced by the structure of her narrative and by the arrangement of its events, patterned after a traditional five-act play. Chapters one and two comprise Act I, an exposition including the pre-plot history of Mathilda's parents and her own childhood up to her father's return. The rising action of Act II (chapters three and four) portrays Mathilda's meeting her father and their life together in London. Chapters five through eight form Act III, with the climax of her father's confession of his incestuous love and his apparent suicide. The falling action of Act IV (chapters nine through eleven) includes her move to the solitude of the heath, her friendship with Woodville, and the failed dual suicide. The last chapter, Act V or the *denouement*, provides the obligatory summary of the action with a recounting of each memorable event and its date. The epilogue is a fitting finale for an individual fully aware of theatrical manipulation: "Farewell, Woodville, the turf will soon be green on my grave; and the violets will bloom on it. There is my hope and expectation; your's are in this world; may they be fulfilled" (*Mathilda*, 246). These are indeed melodramatic lines to accompany the final curtain.

In a first-person narrative, the telling of events and the description of characters depend upon how the narrator perceives them and how she chooses to adjust factual information to suit her purpose. Mathilda's self-dramatization clearly demonstrates her manipulation of character, setting, and language — essentially her proficiency as a playwright. For example, she embellishes the facts of her parents' lives and their personalities with dramatic skill. Although she has most likely learned about her parents from both her aunt and father, Mathilda recreates this knowledge of their childhood, courtship, and marriage with carefully selected details and with a purposeful arrangement that one would expect of a playwright or novelist. The language that Mathilda employs confirms her skill: "Diana had torn the veil which had before kept him in his boyhood"; "Diana filled up all his heart"; and "It was through her beloved lessons that he cast off his old pursuits and gradually formed himself to become one among his fellow men" (*Mathilda*, 179). The passions of Mathilda's sensibility find voice in her choice of language and reveal her "role" as playwright as well as tragic actress.

Living in her own imagination as a child, Mathilda constructs an ideal image of her father, an image that she preserves into adulthood and that disastrously deconstructs when reality shatters the illusion. She envisions how he will act, what he will say, how he will feel. Authors of both Gothic fiction and novels of sensibility in the late 1700s explored how sensibility affects characters who create or re-create events and personages (self and other) according to an image. For some characters, the construction happily correlates with reality. In *Maria or the Wrongs of Woman* (1798), Mary Wollstonecraft's heroine creates an image of a man based on his own marginal annotations in books lent to her.[15] Reading these notes, Maria constructs the character of Darnford before even seeing or meeting him, and "fancy, treacherous fancy, began to sketch a character, congenial with her own, from these shadowy outlines" (Wollstonecraft, *Maria*, 34). She creates an image to suit her perception of what that individual should be: "Every glance afforded colouring for the picture she was delineating on her heart" (Wollstonecraft, *Maria*, 39). Maria is fortunate; the real Darnford corresponds to the ideal. For other characters, however, this version of the

Pygmalion theme proves detrimental, as in the case of Mary Hays' heroine, Emma Courtney, who becomes obsessed with a man, Augustus Harley, by gazing at his portrait: "I accustomed myself to gaze on this resemblance of a man, in whose character I felt so lively an interest, till, I fancied, I read in the features all the qualities imputed to the original by a tender and partial parent" (*Emma Courtney*, 59). Emma soon invests Harley with attributes that she desires him to have, but which he does not possess. Her obsession prevents her from accepting the "real" Harley for who he is. The danger of such wish-fulfillment is that imaginative speculation creates an illusion of an object that often has little relationship to its reality.

Mary Shelley employs the same technique to voice this theme in *Mathilda*. Long before the father returns to England, Mathilda essentially constructs his image from a picture, a letter, and some history: "the idea of [my] unhappy, wandering father was the idol of my imagination. I bestowed on him all my affections; there was a miniature of him that I gazed on continually; I copied his last letter and read it again and again" (*Mathilda*, 185). This image possesses the ideal qualities she desires. She repeats his words recorded in the letter; she dreams that she will be his "consoler" and "companion"; and she determines that he will love her, for the image that the lonely child constructed could not do otherwise. Mathilda actually composes a mini-drama portraying a sentimental reunion of father and daughter: "My favourite vision was that . . . disguised like a boy I would seek my father through the world. My imagination hung upon the scene of recognition; his miniature, which I should continually wear exposed on my breast, would be the means and I imaged the moment to my mind a thousand and a thousand times, perpetually varying the circumstances. Sometimes it would be in a desert; in a populous city; at a ball; we should perhaps meet in a vessel; and his first words constantly were, 'My daughter, I love thee!' What extatic moments have I passed in these dreams" (*Mathilda*, 185). This passage reveals the young Mathilda's adeptness at creating what she desires and in constructing a dramatic scene. Irony adds to the drama as her father's words, "My daughter, I love thee," foreshadow the later scene when he confesses his incestuous love and proclaims, "My daughter, I love you" (*Mathilda*, 201). Note the language in this passage: "vision," "imagination," "image," "dreams." Mathilda's word choices demonstrate her insistence on recreating events and characters as she wishes them to be, not as they necessarily are. Also, Mathilda chooses the dated, poetic "thee" in her scenario; the father uses "you," the standard pronoun and less stylized. Distorted though her perceptions may be, she employs language with a purpose and is well aware of its impact upon the audience.

As she structures the events of her drama, Mathilda is very conscious of setting's significance as backdrop to the action and characters. Frequently she breaks from the narrative portion of her memoir to set up a scene or *tableau* to intensify the dramatic effect. Perhaps the two most memorable scenes that Mathilda orchestrates to her full advantage are those of her proposed joint suicide with Woodville and of her meeting with her father for the first time. Envisioning a romantic and melodramatic denouement comparable to a Renaissance tragedy, Mathilda painstakingly prepares the suicide scene in chapter XI:

> I planned the whole scene with an earnest heart and franticly set my soul on this project. I procured Laudanum and placing it in two glasses on the table, filled my room with flowers and decorated the last scene of my tragedy with the nicest care. . . . Now all was ready and Woodville came. I received him at the door of my cottage and leading him solemnly into the room, I said: My friend, I wish to die. I am quite weary of enduring the misery which hourly I do endure, and I will throw it off. What slave will not, if he may, escape from his chains? Look, I weep. (*Mathilda*, 235)

This passage indicates that Mathilda deliberately constructs her story as a drama and that she was aware at the time the event occurred of the dramatic impact her "last scene" would have. Her use of theatrical terms and her painstaking arrangement of props illustrate her skill at stage setting. Even the first sentence of her greeting to Woodville demonstrates her ability to maximize the effect of a single line: "My friend, I wish to die." What better way to elicit the full attention of her audience, who is Woodville, for that scene.

The other example occurs when Mathilda is sixteen. Upon hearing that her father has returned to England and will be coming for her, Mathilda is understandably excited and is unable to express "the tumult of emotions" within her. She can "only relieve [her] transports by tears, tears of unmingled joy" (*Mathilda*, 186). The day he is to arrive, Mathilda still fantasizes about him: "At day break I hastened to the woods; the hours past on while I indulged in wild dreams that gave wings to the slothful steps of time, and beguiled my eager impatience" (*Mathilda*, 186). Returning, she loses her way despite her familiarity with her surroundings: "My father was expected at noon but when I wished to return to meet him I found that I had lost my way . . . in the intracacies [sic] of the woods, and the trees hid all trace by which I might be guided. I grew impatient, I wept, and wrung my hands but still I could not discover my path" (*Mathilda*, 186-87). This delay, intentional or not, increases Mathilda's intense anticipation, heightens her sensibility, and adds to the dramatic effect that she has envisioned upon meeting her father for the first time. An inherent sense of the theatrical dictates the action of the scene, and Mathilda's skill as both actor and director reveals itself in her use of setting to optimize the effect of her "entrance" when she finally discovers the way home:

> It was past two o'clock when by a sudden turn I found myself close to the lake near a cove where a little skiff was moored — It was not far

from our house and I saw my father and aunt walking on the lawn. I
jumped into the boat, and well accustomed to such feats, I pushed it
from shore, and exerted all my strength to row swiftly across. As I
came, dressed in white, covered only by my tartan rachan, my hair
streaming on my shoulders, and shooting across with greater speed
tha[n] it could be supposed I could give to my boat, my father has often
told me that I looked more like a spirit than a human maid. I
approached the shore, my father held the boat, I leapt lightly out, and
in a moment was in his arms. (*Mathilda*, 187)

This scene is self-consciously but exceptionally well-played. Despite the
spontaneity and passion, Mathilda completely controls the action and
atmosphere of the dramatic meeting. Her flair for theatrics may seem
strangely juxtaposed to the solitary and unworldly existence that she has
led. Yet it stems from her familiarity with literature and from her powers
of sensibility, which can either create imaginary characters to delight a
child in play or obsess a young woman with a world of illusion, a world
capable of destroying her.

Mathilda's *tableaux*, or freeze-frame moments, enhance the melodramatic quality of her narrative. In the climactic pursuit of her father through
the thunderstorm, Mathilda spies an oak tree. Making full use of this dramatic setting, she writes, "Once, overcome by fatigue, I sunk on the wet
earth; about two hundred yards distant, alone in a large meadow stood a
magnificent oak; the lightnings shewed its myriad boughs torn by the
storm" (*Mathilda*, 213). Inspired by the scene, she tries her hand at
prophecy, an important element in tragedies and the Gothic; addressing her
servant, she says, "'Mark, Gaspar, if the next flash of lightning rend not
that oak my father will be alive'" (*Mathilda*, 213). The tree is indeed struck
in the next instant: "I had scarcely uttered these words than a flash
instantly followed by a tremendous peal of thunder descended on it; and
when my eyes recovered their sight after the dazzling light, the oak no
longer stood in the meadow" (*Mathilda*, 213). An artist could easily trans-
pose this scene into a dramatic landscape painting focusing on the rent tree
and the blinded heroine. Another example occurs as Mathilda closes her
drama. She sets the scene for her soliloquy, creating a *tableaux* that intensifies her words: "I rose and walked slowly to the window; the wide heath
was covered by snow which sparkled under the beams of the sun that shone
brightly through the pure, frosty air: a few birds were pecking some crumbs
under my window. I smiled with quiet joy; and in my thoughts, which
through long habit would for ever connect themselves into one train, as if
I shaped them into words, I thus addressed the scene before me" (*Mathilda*,
243). Again, she provides detail of the surroundings from the bright sun to
the little birds. The window itself is symbolic: she is inside, a prisoner of
her sensibility, looking out on the tranquillity of nature. But the window

also provides a proscenium frame for the focal object of this *tableau*: Mathilda.

Cognizant of the power of setting to enhance the dramatic effect of an event, Mathilda strategically selects the places where actions will occur. When she decides to discover the reason for her father's altered behavior, she deliberately chooses an Edenic-like wood, whose peaceful surroundings, like its Biblical and Miltonic predecessors, sharply contrast to the temptation scene that will occur. The season is the end of spring when "the woods were clothed in their freshest verdure, and the sweet smell of the new mown grass was in the fields" (*Mathilda*, 198). Mathilda painstakingly describes the details so that we may visualize the setting as she perceived it: the tree trunks are "slim and smooth" and "wound round by ivy whose shining leaves of the darkest green contrasted with the white bark"; the grass "was mingled with moss" and "covered by the dead leaves of last autumn"; the leaves were "gently moved by the breeze;" and the sky appeared through the leaves' "green canopy" (*Mathilda*, 198). She manipulates the action and setting as skillfully as a stage director would: "I chose therefore the evening . . . I invited him to walk with me . . . I seated myself with him on a mossy hillock" (*Mathilda*, 198). Once again, Mathilda imposes herself upon the scene. The purpose here is to discover the father's secret; therefore, the spotlight should be on the father. However, the repetition of "I" clearly indicates that although Mathilda assumes the role of director, she also appropriates center stage. Ranita Chatterjee notes this contrast in the confessional scene as Mathilda dominates the discourse: "It is Matilda who is determined to gain her father's confidence and thus know the reasons for his sudden coldness toward her" (141).

In the above as well as in other passages, the pronoun "I" maintains the focus on the subject, Mathilda. Its prevalence in a personal narrative is expected, but Mathilda uses it excessively. In one short paragraph in chapter four, she writes "I" eleven times; in another, ostensibly about her father and her, nine times (*Mathilda*, 193 and 190, respectively). Poor writing on Mary Shelley's part? No; rather Shelley knew full well how to let her character reveal her own subjectivity. Mathilda cannot refrain from directing attention away from another character and toward herself. After meeting Woodville, she provides background on her new friend for the reader of her drama. However, immediately upon revealing Woodville's untimely loss of his fiancee Elinor, she turns the occasion to lament her own fate: "In two months Elinor would be twenty one: every thing was prepared for their union. How shall I relate the catastrophe to so much joy . . . . But why should I repine at this? Misery was my element, and nothing but what was miserable could approach me; if Woodville had been happy I should never have known him. And can I who for many years was fed by tears, and nourished under the dew of grief, can I pause to relate a tale of woe and death?" (*Mathilda*, 225-26). Mathilda's question at the end of this passage reflects not only her inability to sympathize with another who experienced loss of a loved one, but also her fear that his story may upstage her own.

The memoir's poetic and stylized language is frequently hyperbolic and emotionally charged, enhancing the text's theatricality. Mathilda describes the pages of her letter as "precious memorials of a heart-broken girl," and she envisions that Woodville's "tears will fall on the words that record [her] misfortunes" (*Mathilda*, 176). Recalling the happiness of their relationship, she relies on personification and poetic pronouns for effect: "O, hours of intense delight! Short as ye were ye are made as long to me as a whole life when looked back upon through the mist of grief that rose immediately after as if to shut ye from my view. Alas! he were the last of happiness that I ever enjoyed" (*Mathilda*, 190). Remembering her father's sudden and unexplained silence, she writes: "But days of peaceful melancholy were of rare occurrence: they were often broken in upon by gusts of passion that drove me as a weak boat on a stormy sea to seek a cove for shelter; but the winds blew from my native harbour and I was cast far, far out until shattered I perished when the tempest had passed and the sea was apparently calm" (*Mathilda*, 193). Such metaphorical excesses reflect Mathilda's style, not Mary Shelley's.[16] This heightened, poetic language, full of elaborate images, similes, and metaphors, demonstrates Mathilda's love for the dramatic. Her aunt is "as a plant beneath a thick covering of ice; I should cut my hands in endeavouring to get at it" (*Mathilda*, 183). Love is "a ghost, ever hovering over my father's grave" and "woe had stampt its burning words telling me to smile no more" (*Mathilda*, 215). Mathilda describes herself as "tender as the sensitive plant, all nerve" and as having "been hardened to stone by the Medusa head of Misery (*Mathilda*, 222 and 223 respectively). She not only has "learned the language of despair," but she is despair: "a strange being am I, joyous, triumphant Despair" (*Mathilda*, 236).

In a passage that suggests madness as much as it reveals stylized language, Mathilda writes a soliloquy that, if performed, would draw an audience to the edge of their seats:

> There was too deep a horror in my tale for confidence; I was on earth the sole depository of my own secret. I might tell it to the winds and to the desart heaths but I must never among my fellow creatures, either by word or look give allowance to the smallest conjecture of the dread reality: I must shrink before the eye of man lest he should read my father's guilt in my glazed eyes: I must be silent lest my faltering voice should betray unimagined horrors. Over the deep grave of my secret I must heap an impenetrable heap of false smiles and words: cunning frauds, treacherous laughter, and a mixture of all light deceits would form a mist to blind others and be as the poisonous simoon to me. (*Mathilda*, 216)

The controlled repetition of "I must" enhances the melodramatic quality of this passage, revealing Mathilda's command of language to evoke pathos. The irony in this passage is not lost on the reader. Mathilda protests that she can never reveal her father's secret, that she must be silent. Why, then, this letter, this tragic memoir of events which she claims she must carry to her grave? Because Mathilda's dramatic presentation of her father's incestuous love elevates her to a tragic heroine like those of Renaissance and Romantic tragedies, such as Webster's Duchess of Malfi and Percy Shelley's Beatrice Cenci, and so engages the reader's sympathy.

The dramatic effect of Mathilda's narrative is also highlighted by frequent tense changes. At several points, Mathilda jumps from past to present tense to address the reader much as an actor gives an aside to the audience. For example, in chapter IV, Mathilda recounts in the past tense her father's sudden change toward her and then introduces a scene using present tense: "There are many incidents that I might relate . . . but I will mention one" (*Mathilda*, 192). In concluding this chapter, Mathilda again addresses the audience. Referring to her father's unexplained behavior, she writes, "But still do I flatter myself that this would have passed away" (*Mathilda*, 197). She also uses the present tense to re-enact emotions or events as she relates them in her letter. Telling how she pondered her father's confession, she repeats the curse she uttered three years earlier in the present tense:

> To this life, miserable father, I devote thee!—Go!—Be thy days passed with savages, and thy nights under the cope of heaven! Be thy limbs worn and thy heart chilled, and all youth be dead within thee! Let thy hairs be as snow; thy walk trembling and thy voice have lost its mellow tones! Let the liquid lustre of thine eyes be quenched; and then return to me, return to thy Mathilda, thy child, who may then be clasped in thy loved arms, while thy heart beats with sinless emotion. Go, Devoted One, and return thus! — This is my curse, a daughter's curse: go, and return pure to thy child, who will never love aught but thee. (*Mathilda*, 204)

Later, Mathilda writes, "Oh never, never, may I see him again. . . . The mutual link of our destinies is broken" (*Mathilda*, 205). Although such tense shifts are standard conventions of first-person narratives, they also illustrate Mathilda's command of theatrical language and gesture as well as her consciousness that her history is a dramatic construct. Use of the present tense dramatizes these "lines," which are patterned after soliloquies so common in melodrama and Renaissance tragedies. As she concludes her letter, Mathilda cannot resist another soliloquy, the lengthiest of her drama: "I salute thee, beautiful Sun, and thou, white Earth, fair and cold! . . . I am about to leave thee" (*Mathilda*, 243). She continues the farewell speech for three paragraphs, investing it with melodramatic rhetoric rich in metaphor and stylized imagery: "thou, oh, Sun! hast smiled upon, and borne your part in many imaginations that sprung to life in my soul alone, and which will die with me"; "One of these fragile mirrors, that ever doted on thine image, is about to be broken, crumbled to dust"; and "Receive then the grateful farewell of a fleeting shadow who is about to disappear" (*Mathilda*, 243-244). In these soliloquies, Mathilda assures us that she can act — or overact — the part as well as any contemporary actress on the London stage.

Mathilda's narrative contains many allusions to literature, classical mythology, and the Bible. These references reinforce the text as a conscious literary construct, and they provide thematic coherence, demonstrating Mary Shelley's "role" as the ultimate creator of the text. Certainly Mathilda's line "if the world is a stage and I merely an actor on it" solidifies the theatrical metaphor. The allusion to Alfieri's *Myrrha* foreshadows the father's incestuous love, very unlike the romance and courtly love tradition of Spenser's *Faerie Queene*, which Mathilda reads to her father and which, we may assume, represents Mathilda's understanding of love.[17] The excerpt from Wordsworth's Lucy poem strengthens the young Mathilda's image as a child of nature. Twice Mathilda identifies with Dante's Matilda: once as a child and then again before she dies. In the *Purgatorio*, Canto XVIII, Matilda stands by a fountain from which flow Lethe on one side and Eunoi on the other. Lethe erases remembrance of sin; Eunoi recalls good deeds. Unfortunately, Shelley's Mathilda is unable to drink from either side of Dante's fountain: she can neither forget the self-inflicted blame for her father's death nor believe she has lived a worthwhile life. Mathilda compares herself to Proserpine, "who was gaily and heedlessly gathering flowers on the sweet plain of Enna, when the King of hell snatched her away to the abodes of death and misery" (*Mathilda*, 192). She associates her suffering with Job's (216) and later identifies with Cain: 'the mark of misery would have faded from my brow" (*Mathilda*, 241).

Dreams and madness, also staples of tragedy, melodrama, and the Gothic, are present in Mathilda's drama. Before her father leaves for the second time, Mathilda dreams about her pursuit of him almost exactly as it would occur the next day. Whether she indeed had such a dream or is adding to the dramatic effect of her memoir as she writes it, the prophetic vision adds a touch of unearthliness common in Gothic literature. Mathilda's tragedy also suggests that its heroine experiences madness. After reading her father's farewell letter to her, Mathilda thinks "there was madness in the thought" of her father as a lover. She calls him cruel to drown himself in the sea, for it adds "madness to [her] despair" (*Mathilda*, 214). Later, Mathilda is depressed because the weather prohibits Woodville from visiting her; still she expects him to come: "He would well know that this drear sky and gloomy rain would load my spirit almost to madness" (*Mathilda*, 234). In perhaps one of her more reasoned moments, she writes that the suicide scheme was "madness."

An even more significant reference to madness occurs after her father's suicide when she is still in London. For her the city is a "a prison, a wiry prison from which you can peep at the sky only" (*Mathilda*, 218). This passage describes the "frantic nature of [her] sensations" and depicts Mathilda's conscious and artistic control of language in a remarkable emotional moment: "I was often on the verge of madness. Nay, when I look back on many of my wild thoughts, thoughts with which actions sometimes endeavoured to keep pace; when I tossed my hands high calling down the cope of heaven to fall on me and bury me; when I tore my hair and throwing it to the winds cried, 'Ye are free, go seek my father!' . . . when I have recollected all this I have asked myself if this were not madness" (*Mathilda*, 218). Having so convincingly described herself as one in the throes of madness and passion, Mathilda suddenly becomes "sane" and detached, and in one of her asides to the audience, she says, "Do not mistake me; I never was really mad. I was always conscious of my state when my wild thoughts seemed to drive me to insanity, and never betrayed them to aught but silence and solitude" (*Mathilda*, 219). Others, Mathilda says, never perceived her as mad, only as "a poor girl broken in spirit." Mathilda deftly displays her need to control her mental confusion and turmoil with her abrupt movement from apparent madness to apparent sanity. Whether she is truly mad or not is a subject for another essay. What is relevant here is that Mathilda's employing the literary convention of madness demonstrates her consciousness of her life as art.[18] As Polonius remarks of Hamlet's behavior, "though this be madness, / Yet there is method in't." Madness, or the suggestion of it, also implies the magnitude of Mathilda's break with reality, a fissure caused by her extreme sensibility.

The danger of such an inner-directed sensibility is a dominant theme in late eighteenth-century literature, especially the Gothic. As William Walling notes, "*Mathilda* is concerned primarily with one of the most prevalent themes in English literature since the rise of the novel in the eighteenth century — the exploration of the conflict between the individual sensibility and the demands upon it implicit within the context of social existence."[19] Walling's observation links *Mathilda* to a narrative tradition with which Shelley was well acquainted. By the 1790s, the Gothic novel had established itself as a psychological genre for its exploration into the dark side of sensibility that often resulted in a debilitating subjectivity devoid of reason and altruism.[20] The novelists warned against a debilitating subjectivity that directed the gaze inward, that inflamed passion, and that ignored reason. Perhaps the best description of such a sensibility is found in the following excerpt from Ann Radcliffe's *The Mysteries of Udolpho* (1794), which Shelley read in 1815, a year before beginning *Frankenstein*. On her deathbed, the speaker Signora Laurentini confesses her past crimes and rues the consequences of her self-centered passions:

Beware of the first indulgence of the passions; beware of the first! Their
course, if not checked then, is rapid — their force is uncontroulable —
they lead us we know not whither — they lead us perhaps to the com-
mission of crimes, for which whole years of prayer and penitence cannot atone!–Such may be the force of even a single passion, that it
overcomes every other, and sears up every other approach to the heart.
Possessing us like a fiend, it leads us on to the acts of a fiend, making
us insensible to pity and to conscience. And, when its purpose is
accomplished, like a fiend, it leaves us to the tortures of compassion,
remorse, and conscience. Then, we awaken as from a dream, and perceive a new world around us. . . . Remember, sister, that the passions
are the seeds of vices as well as of virtues, from which either may
spring, accordingly as they are nurtured. Unhappy they who have never
been taught the art to govern them."[21]

Laurentini's words voice the concern of a generation of late eighteenth-century novelists: a lack of guidance, a narrow education, and an undisciplined, passionate nature can lead to self-destruction. If unchecked by
reason and if inwardly rather than outwardly directed, such a sensibility
can result in self-indulgence, isolation, and a confusion of reality and illusion that frequently leads to madness and suicide.

Of course, neither *Mathilda* nor these Gothic novels suggest that their
authors regarded sensibility or introspection as an inevitable precursor to
self-destruction. In fact, Shelley's novella demonstrates through Mathilda's
aunt that a lack of sensibility often results in a cold, dispassionate nature,
an equally unenviable state. When moderated by reason and benevolence,
introspection generally encourages compassion and enlightened self-
knowledge, which Shelley exemplifies by Woodville, who has come to the
heath to recover from his loss and who engages in self-exploration as part
of the healing process. However, he does not resort to Mathilda's self-pity
and is able to remain sympathetic toward others' needs and problems. Not
having learned to moderate her passion with reason or sympathy,
Mathilda, on the other hand, is either unwilling or unable to benefit from
emotional and psychological soul-searching. Recognizing the consuming
effect of her sensibility, Woodville tells Mathilda, "do not despair. That is
the most dangerous gulph on which you perpetually totter" (*Mathilda*,
240). Initially he is able to moderate Mathilda's extreme melancholia,
encouraging her to emerge from the throes of her sensibility. His words, she
writes, "had magic in them, when beginning with the sweetest pity, he
would raise me by degrees out of myself and my sorrows until I wondered
at my own selfishness" (*Mathilda*, 232). However, when he leaves to care
for his ailing mother, she cannot remain "out of [her]self" and once again
slips into histrionic self-pity.

Mathilda's penchant for the theatrical may have been inherited from her
father. The parallels between them suggest that it is no coincidence both

can play tragic victims so well. The depiction of the father resonants with theatrical qualities, as he gives full rein to a self-centered, introspective sensibility which becomes, to use Syndy Conger's description, "no longer a means to any other end . . . but an end in itself."[22] Unchecked by reason and discipline, sensibility warps his sense of reality, shatters his relationship with Mathilda, and ultimately leads to both of their deaths. Diana's dying after Mathilda's birth devastated the father: "From the moment of my mother's death until his departure [my aunt] never heard him utter a single word: buried in the deepest melancholy he took no notice of any one; often for hours his eyes streamed tears or a more fearful gloom overpowered him" (*Mathilda*, 180). However, Diana's death becomes a vehicle to indulge an extreme sensibility that transformed understandable grief into the maudlin self-pity revealed in his departing letter to his sister. He begins with "Pardon me . . . for the uneasiness I have unavoidably given you"–as if his abandonment of Mathilda were but a minor consequence out of his control. He continues with Werther-like melodrama, "I must break all ties that at present exist. I shall become a wanderer, a miserable outcast— alone! alone!" (*Mathilda*, 180). His last words regarding Mathilda were "Take care of her and cherish her: one day I may claim her at your hands; but futurity is dark, make the present happy to her" (*Mathilda*, 181). If he so desires and is able, he "may" assume his role as her father. His selfish actions destroy the family unit and deny Mathilda a childhood conducive to fostering the virtues of sensibility. Mathilda indulges her grief in a similar manner after her father has drowned at sea: "since his death all the world was to me a blank except where woe had stampt its burning words telling me to smile no more" and "warm tears once more struggled into my eyes soothing yet bitter; . . . I sank once more into reverie" (*Mathilda*, 215-16). She, too, breaks all ties, by feigning her death so that her London relatives do not look for her and by seeking out a desolate cottage on a Northern English heath "to find that solitude which alone could suit one whom an untold grief is seperated [sic] from her fellow creatures" (*Mathilda*, 216).

We could justly argue that the father's portrayal is controlled by Mathilda, whose depiction of him would enhance her own role as tragic heroine. Still, there are other parallels. Both lack parental guidance and both indulge their theatrical tendencies. In his childhood, the father had neither proper supervision nor a broad classical education. His own father died early, and his mother brought him up "with all the indulgence she thought due to a nobleman of wealth" (*Mathilda*, 176). In school, "he discarded books; he believed that he had other lessons to learn than those which they could teach him" (*Mathilda*, 177). Novels, however, he read eagerly. Unfortunately, they stimulated his awareness "of the existence of passions" and "produced a strong effect on him who was so peculiarly susceptible of every impression" (*Mathilda*, 178). His reading did not provide him with a sense of history or philosophy which might, perhaps, have strengthened his powers of reason and provided a larger view of the world. Perhaps Mary Shelley was echoing her mother's warning about the possible dangers of fiction as expressed in *A Vindication of the Rights of Woman*.[23] Indeed, the father's character illustrates the same flaw as that found in many characters in eighteenth-century and Romantic works. Figures as diverse as Charlotte Lennox's Arabella, Richard Brinsley Sheridan's Lydia Languish, and Charlotte Dacre's Cazire depict their authors' warning that art may lead to a distorted perception of the actual world and human behavior if one fails to recognize the boundary between the illusory world and the actual one, between the stage and life itself.[24]

Left to "act for himself," Mathilda's father developed a "character [that] became strongly and early marked and exhibited a various surface on which a quick sighted observer might see the seed of virtues and of misfortunes" (*Mathilda*, 176-77). He never acquired the self-discipline necessary to moderate his inherently passionate nature with reason. His sensibility became introspective and led to self-indulgence and egoism. Despite his "unbounded generosity," he never subordinated his own desires to others' needs, and his excessive spending was frequently "careless extravagance . . . to satisfy passing whims" (*Mathilda*, 177). The father's self-centered attitude obliterated the disinterest and objectivity required to balance an egocentric sensibility. For all his self-absorption, he never developed a sense of self. Outwardly, he appeared assured and confident; inwardly, he was unsure and frightened: "By a strange narrowness of ideas he viewed all the world in connexion only as it was or was not related to his little society. He considered queer and out of fashion all opinions that were exploded by his circle of intimates, and he became at the same time dogmatic and yet fearful of not coinciding with the only sentiments he could consider orthodox. To the generality of spectators he appeared careless of censure; but . . . [he] never dared express an opinion or a feeling until he was assured that it would meet with the approbation of his companions" (*Mathilda*, 177-78). This passage also reveals the father's own sense of theatricality, at least according to Mathilda's perception. He is obviously the actor for the spectators, an actor who is well-attuned to the audience's demands, altering his performance to suit them. The father's sense of life as a dramatic performance for others functions as a mask that prohibits self-knowledge. This seemingly minor fact of the father's background illustrates how carefully Mary Shelley crafted *Mathilda*: she warns that playing for the crowd can result in a loss of self-identity and will.

Mathilda and her father are both sharp contrasts to Diana and Woodville; while the former pair epitomize sensibility's disabling effects, the latter pair depict its enabling ones. Diana was everything that her husband was not. She was pragmatic in her approach to life, and despite inexperience in the "mysteries of life and society," she possessed understanding of "a deeper kind and laid on firmer foundations" than his. She had the virtues of sensibility with none of its debilitating qualities: she was humble, with "a firm reliance on her own integrity and a belief in that of others" (*Mathilda*, 178-179). She also embarked on a different reading program than did her husband: she "read no novels"; however, she was well-versed in traditional Greek, Roman, and English literature and history (*Mathilda*, 178-179). As a novelist herself, Shelley certainly does not advocate avoiding novels or any other art form and indeed uses this narrative genre as a vehicle to educate her audience. Nevertheless, *Mathilda* does demonstrate how insidiously art and illusion may supplant life and reality for characters reluctant or unable to reconcile their fate in the "real" world.

Despite tragic experiences, Woodville maintains his touch with reality and remains a viable part of society. He mirrors Diana in that his actions are benevolent, not obsessive, and he represents sensibility's ideal in balancing passion and reason. Even his name suggests a union of nature and society: "wood" and "ville." Like the father, Woodville lost his lover, Elinor. Though he grieves for her, his sensibility is not self-indulgent. His focus is on others, not himself. When he tells Mathilda the story of Elinor's death, Elinor is the subject, not he. Mathilda's father thought of Diana's death only in respect to himself. Although Woodville retreats to a solitary place "peacefully [to] indulge his grief" and to leave "any spot where he had seen here or where her image mingled with the most rapturous hopes," the escape is temporary. his understanding He does not wallow in self-pity or alienate himself from his mother or society. As soon as his mother needs him, he goes to her.

Woodville is not a self-reflexive actor on the stage of life, one who plays only to an audience or who attempts to rewrite the drama to suit his desires. He accepts himself for who he is and does not interpret or create events according to his own subjectivity. Mathilda delineates the differences between him and her father: "He was younger, less worn, more passionless than my father and in no degree reminded me of him," and Woodville is as "a poet of old whom the muses had crowned in his cradle" (*Mathilda*, 228 and 223 respectively). Unlike the father who read only novels, Woodville was educated in the classics. As a result, "no error could pervert" his understanding and "no dross [could] tarnish" his mind. Most important, he does not see himself as the center around which all else revolves: "He mingled in society unknowing of his superiority over his companions, not because he undervalued himself but because he did not perceive the inferiority of others" (*Mathilda*, 224). Although he possesses sensibility, he has no "arrogance or vanity." His sense and reason counter the negative effects of sensibility.

Mathilda does describe Woodville with divine adjectives: "To bestow on your fellow men is a godlike attribute — So indeed it is and as such not one fit for mortality;–the giver like Adam and Prometheus must pay the penalty

of rising above his nature by being the martyr to his own excellence"
(*Mathilda*, 224). However, Woodville never rises above his nature; he does
not play God as Victor Frankenstein does or recreate the world or his life
as he would wish it to be. Instead of constructing others according to his
vision, he accepts them for who they are. His sense of "other" rather than
self is most apparent in his rational rejection of the dual suicide that
Mathilda proposes:

> I have powers; my country men think well of them. Do you think I sow
> my seed in the barren air, and have no end in what I do? Believe me, I
> will never desert life until this last hope is torn from my bosom, that in
> some way my labours may form a link in the chain of gold with which
> we ought all to strive to drag Happiness from where she sits. . . . But
> if I can influence but a hundred, but ten, but one solitary individual, so
> as in any way to lead him from ill to good, that will be a joy to repay
> me for all my sufferings . . . if you can bestow happiness on another; if
> you can give one other person only one hour of joy ought you not to
> live to do it? And every one has it in their power to that. (*Mathilda*,
> 237-38)

Although he has suffered loss, Woodville sees the positive aspects of life.
He would say the glass was half-full; Mathilda would say, half-empty. For
Woodville, goodness is its own reward, and evils should be "punished as
all things evil ought to be punished, not by pain . . .but by quiet obscurity,
which simply deprives them of their harmful qualities" (*Mathilda*, 229).
This philosophy reflects a man whose feelings are governed by benevolent
reason.

Woodville and Mathilda are a study in opposites. She desires to know
her father's secret because, in her egocentric view, she is convinced that she
can help him: "you must," she says to him, "permit me to win this secret
from you" (*Mathilda*, 199). As in *Frankenstein*, Mary Shelley once again
alludes to the dangers of a quest for knowledge that crosses some vaguely
defined boundary. Mathilda's persistence in ferreting out her father's secret
of his incestuous love for her leads to the confession that violates both her
and her father's private self. This violation transgresses moral and social
codes and destroys not only the constructed image but the individual as
well. Guilt-ridden and devastated over her father's death, Mathilda believes
that she has been the cause of it. Although the father's final letter to her
indicates that he plans to wander the continents, she interprets his words
as a death wish and so assumes the drowning was a suicide. Her assumption is a valid one, given her father's history of irresponsibility regarding his
actions. However, what better way to heighten her tragedy and embellish
the characterization of her drama than to paint the father's death as a suicide because of the crime against his daughter.

In contrast, Woodville desires to help Mathilda because he is genuinely
concerned for her, not because he sees himself as a hero. Unlike her, he

respects privacy, and he does not demand to know the grief and secrets that she is reluctant or unable to share: "I do not ask you disclose them"; "I do not ask you to reveal it"; "do not think that I would intrude upon your confidence"; and "do not tell me why you grieve" (*Mathilda*, 230-31). Just as it appeared that Diana could balance the father's sensibility, so it seems that Woodville can enable Mathilda's. As long as he is with her, Mathilda can emerge periodically from the throes of her sensibility. His words, she writes, "had magic in them, when beginning with the sweetest pity, he would raise my by degrees out of myself and my sorrows until I wondered at my own selfishness" (*Mathilda*, 232). However, once he leaves, she slips into histrionic self-pity. Woodville recognizes the consuming effect of her sensibility and tells Mathilda, "do not despair. That is the most dangerous gulph on which you perpetually totter" (*Mathilda*, 240). He entreats her to have confidence in his sincerity. He offers his friendship and is willing to be the anchor for Mathilda, who perceives herself as "a weak boat on a stormy sea" (*Mathilda*, 193). Despite Woodville's friendship, she is unable to control the despair that ultimately leads to her passive suicide.

The final setting in Mathilda's drama is a lonely house on the heath in Scotland, a location that mirrors the self-imposed isolation and alienation resulting from her disabling sensibility: "In solitude only shall I be myself," she writes (*Mathilda*, 218). Although she claims she is not "misanthropic," Mathilda cannot bear even the sight of other people and so chooses the heath location because she can "wander far without molestation from the sight of [her] fellow creatures" (*Mathilda*, 219). She has too long indulged her sensibility, and not even the genuine care and friendship of Woodville can redirect it. Mathilda began her narrative by referring to her life as a "tragic history" (*Mathilda*, 175) and concludes it by reflecting that her part on life's stage "has been strange, and alas! tragical" (*Mathilda*, 245). In this, her last act and last action, Mathilda sums up the events of her short life in the evocative, melodramatic language that she has perfected: "So day by day I become weaker, and life flickers in my wasting form, as a lamp about to lose its vivifying oil" (*Mathilda*, 246). Haunted and unhappy for most of her life, she now feels peace, knowing that death is near and brings with it a union with her father. Her last words are a fitting epilogue to her drama: "Farewell, Woodville, the turf will soon be green on my grave; and the violets will bloom on it. *There* is my hope and my expectation; your's are in this world; may they be fulfilled" (*Mathilda*, 246). And so the curtain drops, and the drama ends, with the spotlight on the play's leading lady — Mathilda.

Chapter 4 Notes

1. The text for *Mathilda* is from *The Mary Shelley Reader*, Betty T. Bennett and Charles E. Robinson, ed. (New York: Oxford University Press, 1990), 245; hereafter cited in text as *Mathilda*.

2. In his Preface to the *Mary Shelley Reader*, Charles E. Robinson notes that in *Mathilda*, "the reader will encounter a complicated persona who, in a strange state of mind, struggles as a self-conscious actress in a drama about the taboo subject of incest" (vii). My thanks to Robinson, who encouraged me to pursue this observation for this project.

3. Ranita Chatterjee observes the lack of critical attention to the novella as well as she explores the incest theme in her essay, "Mathilda: Mary Shelley, William Godwin, and the Ideologies of Incest," in *Iconoclastic Departures: Mary Shelley After Frankenstein*, ed. Syndy M. Conger, Frederick S. Frank, and Gregory O'Dea (Madison: Fairleigh Dickinson University Press, 1997), 130-149; hereafter cited in text..

4. In a 24 November letter to Marianne Hunt, Shelley reveals her anxiety for her fifth child, the recently born Percy Florence: "I cannot fear yet it is a bitter thought that all should be risked on one yet how much sweeter than to be childless as I was for 5 hateful months—Do not lett [sic] us talk of those five months; when I look back on all I suffered at Leghorn I shudder with horror" (Letters 1: 114). Contextualized with her other entries and letters, this passage suggests the toll her children's deaths had on her.

5. Harpold, "'Did you get Mathilda from Papa?': Seduction Fantasy and Circulation of Mary Shelley's *Mathilda*" *Studies in Romanticism* 28 (1989): 49-67, and Mellor, *Mary Shelley: Her Life, Her Fiction, Her Monsters* (New York: Routledge, 1989), 193; hereafter cited in text.

6. "'Knew shame, and knew desire': Ambivalence as Structure in Mary Shelley's *Mathilda*," in *Iconoclastic Departures: Mary Shelley After Frankenstein*, 116.

7. Quotations are cited from the following two studies, respectively: William Veeder, *Mary Shelley and Frankenstein: The Fate of Androgyny*, 217, and Jane Blumberg, *Mary Shelley's Early Novels* (Iowa City: University of Iowa Press, 1993), 225, n. 20; hereafter cited in text.

8. For detailed studies on theatrical conventions in fiction, see David Marshall, *The Figure of Theater: Shaftesbury, DeFoe, Adam Smith, and George Eliot* (New York: Columbia University Press, 1986); Joseph Litvak, *Caught in the Act: Theatricality in the Nineteenth-Century Novel*; John Richetti, "Richardson's Dramatic Art in *Clarissa*" in *British Theatre and the Other Arts, 1660-1800*, ed. Shirley Strum Kenny (Washington: Folger Shakespeare Library, 1983), 288-308; and Nina Auerbach, *Private Theatricals: The Lives of the Victorians* (Cambridge: Harvard University Press, 1990); all references hereafter cited in text.

9. *Memoirs of Emma Courtney* (London: Pandora, 1987), 198. Hays was a close friend of both William Godwin and Mary Wollstonecraft. It is not known whether Shelley had read this novel; however she was aware of Hays' work and admired her,

closing an 1836 letter to her with, "your name is of course familiar to me as one of those women whose talents do honor to our sex" (*Letters*, 2: 269-270). For a critical overview of Hays, see M. Ray Adams, *Studies in the Literary Backgrounds of English Radicalism* (Lane: Franklin and Marshall Press, 1947); Katharine Rogers, "The Contribution of Mary Hays" *Prose Studies* 10 (1987): 131-142; and Janet Todd, *The Sign of Angellica: Women, Writing and Fiction, 1660-1800* (London: Virago, 1989); references hereafter cited in text.

10. Watkins, *A Materialist Critique of English Romantic Drama* (Gainsville: University Press of Florida, 1993).

11. Although Watkins is here referring specifically to those characters in Wordsworth's *The Borderers*, this observation is applicable to many Romantic dramatic figures.

12. See Meena Alexander's *Women in Romanticism* (Totowa: Barnes and Noble, 1989), 160-66, which suggests the influence of Wordsworth's Lucy poems on the characterization of Mathilda.

13. Janet Todd, *Sensibility* (London: Methuen, 1986), 4.

14. The first chapter of the "Fields of Fancy" draft is found in Elizabeth Nitchie's edition of *Mathilda* (Chapel Hill: University of North Caroline Press, 1959), 90-104.

15. *Maria, or the Wrongs of Woman* (New York: W. W. Norton, 1975); hereafter cited in the text.

16. For example, contrast Shelley's effectively concise prose in her nonfiction, such as the biographical entries in the *Lives of the Most Eminent Literary and Scientific Men of Italy, Spain, and Portugal* and *Lives of the Most Eminent Literary and Scientific Men of France*. Also, her characters and narrators who reject a literal *theatrum mundi* view of life, e.g., Katherine Gordon of *The Fortunes of Perkin Warbeck* and the narrator of *Lodore*, do not resort to such melodramatic language.

17. Mary Shelley began translating *Myrrha* in 1818. Alfieri's play is often spelled "*Mirra*" as well. For more background on the influence of Alfieri's work on *Mathilda*, see Judith Barbour's "'The meaning of the tree': The Tale of Mirra in Mary Shelley's *Mathilda*" in *Iconoclastic Departures: Mary Shelley After Frankenstein*, 98-114.

18. In "The Performing Self: Psychodrama in Austen, James and Woolf," Lynda S. Boren notes a similar attribute of James' governess in *The Turn of the Screw*. The governess is reflected only in her own drama, the story itself: "The form her madness takes is that of a drama, a fantasy she creates and which places her center stage, the heroine of a tragedy laced with sexual innuendoes" (19).

19. William Walling, *Mary Shelley* Twayne English Author Series. (New York: Twayne Publishers, 1972), 111.

20. See G. R. Thompson's "Introduction: Romanticism and the Gothic Tradition" and Robert D. Hume's "Exuberant Gloom, Existential Agony, and Heroic Despair: Three Varieties of Negative Romanticism" in *The Gothic Imagination: Essays in Dark Romanticism* ed. G. R. Thompson (Pullman: Washington State University Press, 1974), 1-10 and 109-127, respectively.

21. Ann Radcliffe, *The Mysteries of Udolpho*, Bonamy Dobrée, ed (London: Oxford University Press, 1970), 646-647; hereafter cited in text.

22. Introduction. *Sensibility in Transformation*, ed. Syndy McMillan Conger (Rutherford, NJ: Fairleigh Dickinson University Press, 1990), 13.

23. Mary Wollstonecraft argues that novels often impede intellectual reasoning and promote an "overstretched sensibility"; see *A Vindication of the Rights of Woman*, ed. Charles W. Hagelman, Jr. (New York: W. W. Norton, 1967), 105.

24. From Charlotte Lennox's *The Female Quixote*, ed. Margaret Dalziel (London: Oxford University Press, 1970) and Richard Sheridan, *The Rivals*, George H. Nettleton and Arthur E. Case, ed (Carbondale: Southern Illinois University Press, 1969), 789-830; and *Confessions of the Nun of St. Omer* (New York: Arno Press, 1972), respectively.

The Last Man: Autobiography as Drama

My soul, sit thou a patient looker-on;
Judge not the play before the play is done;
Her plot hath many changes; every day
Speaks a new scene; the last act crowns the play.
— Francis Quarles, *Respice Finem*

As in *Frankenstein*, the tension in Mary Shelley's fourth major work, *The Last Man* (1826), derives from a frustrated observer who desires to be an actor and a hero. The first line of the above epigraph epitomizes the condition of such an observer, Lionel Verney, the narrator of this novel. In *Mathilda*, the eponymous heroine asserts that she is the quintessential actor of a drama; in *The Last Man*, Lionel Verney proves himself to be the quintessential observer of one. After several attempts to play the hero in the drama of human existence, Lionel can only command the spotlight as the last man writing his dramatic autobiography. The cruel irony, however, is that as the last man on the world's stage, he has no audience to appreciate his textual "performance."

The germ of the story can be dated as early as fall 1823. In a letter on 2 October, Mary Shelley wrote to Leigh Hunt, "I am now busy writing an Article for the London — after which I shall begin a Novel . . . more wild & imaginative & I think more in my way" (*Letters*, 1: 393). According to Emily Sunstein, Shelley worked steadily on the novel through the summer of 1824. She diligently did research, reading about Constantinople and re-visiting Bishopsgate and Eton, all prominent settings in the novel.[1] She also requested from John Cam Hobhouse admission to parliamentary sessions, claiming that, intriguing as the spectacle of the sessions was, she was more interested in studying the setting for *The Last Man*: "I am engaged in a tale which will certainly be more defective than it would otherwise be, if I am not permitted to be present at a debate" (*Letters*, 1: 466). Although she wanted to "take her time to make *The Last Man* her best work yet" (Sunstein, 247), Shelley later referred to it as a "foolish book"[2] and regretted its "state of imperfection in which partly for want of time I was obliged to leave it."[3] The effort of writing the novel, given her emotional and financial situation, seemed to take its toll on her. "You can form no idea of the difficulty of the subject," she wrote to her friend, John Howard Payne, "the necessity of making the scene <general> universal to all mankind and of combining this with a particular interest which must constitute the novel — If I had at the commencement fore seen the excessive trouble . . . I should never have had the courage to begin" (*Letters,* 1: 510). The novel was published on 23 January 1826 by Henry Colburn and, like *Frankenstein,* did not bear her name on the title page; instead, "by the author of Frankenstein" was inscribed.[4]

Critical reception of *The Last Man* was rather unfavorable and at times caustic. *The Monthly Review* considered the novel to be the "offspring of a diseased imagination" (Review of *The Last Man,* 335), and *The Literary Gazette* pronounced it a "sickening repetition of horrors," wondering why Shelley did not entitle it "The Last Woman" (Review of *The Last Man,* 103).[5] Modern critics have been more receptive, perhaps because its theme strikes the post-atomic and AIDS age as a realistic possibility rather than a wild improbability.[6] Muriel Spark, Elizabeth Nitchie, and Ernest Lovell have all praised the novel, and Emily Sunstein judges it Shelley's "most original and impressive fiction" next to *Frankenstein* (269).

As with Mary Shelley's other works, *The Last Man* has generally intrigued critics for its biographical significance. In this *roman à clef,* the characters of Adrian and Lord Raymond are fairly recognizable portraits of Percy Shelley and Lord Byron, respectively. Denied writing a formal biography of her husband by Sir Timothy Shelley, Mary Shelley may have decided upon a fictional portrayal as the next best thing.[7] Shelley herself can be seen in Idris, Perdita, and especially the narrator, Lionel Verney. Without a doubt, Shelley drew upon her own feelings of isolation in her depiction of Lionel: "The Last Man! Yes I may well describe that solitary being's feelings, feeling myself as the last relic of a beloved race, my companions, extinct before me" (*Journals,* 2: 476-477). Uncannily, Shelley recorded this entry on 14 May 1824, the evening before she learned of Byron's death at Missolonghi on 19 April. Subsequent journal entries reveal how desolate and alone she felt with so many who had been dear to her now dead; to infuse Lionel Verney with similar emotions was no coincidence.

However revealing the biographical parallels may be, the novel is significant for its last man theme as well. As William Walling rightly observes, Shelley, "partly through the accident of temperament and experience, partly through the intention of design, undertook an artistic exploration of something far larger than a merely personal reaction to her own individual history" (87). Shelley's *The Last Man* was not the first work to treat such a theme,[8] and Lionel Verney himself seems to recognize that his story is part of a tradition, for he alludes to Daniel Defoe's and Charles Brockden Brown's plague novels in his narrative. However, according to Morton D. Paley, the idea of a last man was considered ludicrous by 1826, perhaps one reason for the novel's weak reception.

A recent approach to the novel explores the treatment of the masculine Romantic ego. Although some critics, such as Hugh M. Lake, read *The Last Man* as a "monument to the life and ideas of [Shelley's] husband," others disagree. Anne Mellor, for example, suggests that the novel reveals "all the guilt and resentment she felt towards her husband and the political ideology he espoused" (*Mary Shelley*, 144). William Veeder offers a differing observation. Adrian, he argues, is not a portrait of Percy Shelley as he was, but as Mary Shelley wanted him to be (75). Veeder's comment is especially relevant to this study, for he alludes to Shelley's own predilection to do what her characters do so often: construct an ideal figure to replace a disappointing or imperfect actual one. As with her first two novels, Shelley employed the *theatrum mundi* metaphor to criticize egocentric characters whose desire to be starring actors on the public stage of life confuses the boundary between illusion and reality and threatens domestic stability. Like Victor Frankenstein, Lord Raymond represents Shelley's indictment of such a sensibility. Lionel Verney, who also longs for the spotlight of center stage, reluctantly finds himself like Walton — on the sidelines of public life, observing and recording rather than acting. He, too, finds an outlet by taking up the pen. Excepting the author's introduction, the entire novel is Lionel Verney's account of the events leading up to his departure for distant shores. Although there is no evidence to discount the truth of the story, all the characters and events are filtered through Lionel's gaze and hence subject to his perceptions and control. Lionel's theatrical references, his depiction of the other characters, and his dramatic rendering of this history demonstrate his desire to act rather than merely to observe, and his narrative reveals a pattern of attempts and failures on the public stage. Having been repeatedly denied the hero's role, Lionel, as the last man, has the last word. Authorship grants him the authority to signify his existence. The attempt, however, is vain: there is no audience, save himself, to read the autobiography he has so industriously — and dramatically — recorded.[9]

Lionel employs the *theatrum mundi* metaphor to describe his and others' actions. Returning to England from Austria out of concern for Adrian's health, Lionel perceives his country as a stage on which he can act out his hopes: "Native England, receive thy child! thou art the scene of all my hopes, the mighty theatre on which is acted the only drama that can, heart and soul, bear me along with it in its development" (*Last Man*, 28). Seeing his sister, Perdita, for the first time since he left for Vienna, he describes the two of them as "full grown actors on this changeful scene" (*Last Man*, 29). Believing that Lord Raymond planned on accepting the Protectorship and marrying Idris, Lionel apprehensively accompanies him to Perdita's cottage, anticipating his sister's devastated reaction. He describes the imagined confrontation in dramatic terms: "this scene oppressed me even to terror. . . . Yes, I will witness the last scene of the drama" (*Last Man*,

45). The scene would not be the last of that drama, however, because Raymond renounces public life — at least for a time — and marries Perdita. This theatrical terminology does not necessarily reflect Lionel's language when these events occurred, but it is undoubtedly an integral staple of his memoirs written much later in Rome.

Another telling example of Lionel's dependence upon the *theatrum mundi* metaphor occurs after the plague begins its assault on England. As Lionel observes a group of Eton students, including his son Alfred, at play, he philosophizes about the roles they will assume in the world: "Here were the future governors of England; the men, who, when our ardour was cold, and our projects completed or destroyed for ever, when, our drama acted, we doffed the garb of the hour, and assumed the uniform of age, or of more equalizing death; here were the beings who were to carry on the vast machine of society; here were the lovers, husbands, fathers; here the landlord, the politician, the soldier, some fancied that they were even now ready to appear on the stage, eager to make one among the dramatis personae of active life" (*Last Man*, 165). Lionel comments that it was not long ago that he felt the same way, noting that though individuals pass on, the species remains: "willingly do I give place to thee, dear Alfred . . . and in the drama you are about to act, do not disgrace those who taught you to enter on the stage, and to pronounce becomingly the parts assigned to you!" (*Last Man*, 165). Not only does Lionel describe life in theatrical terms, but he makes clear that a public role garners fame far superior to any private one. Nevertheless, Lionel does acknowledge the rewards of domestic life, for he has observed the sad fate of Raymond and Perdita and realizes the disastrous possibilities if the public stage overshadows private life. However, Lionel also asserts that those "dramatis personae" in public roles of business, politics, and war will appear in the history books for posterity; those in domestic roles will not.

Lionel increasingly relies upon the *theatrum mundi* metaphor as the plague advances: "the same tragedy was acted on a smaller, yet more disastrous scale"; "tragedies were acted harrowing to the soul"; "these smaller and separate tragedies were about to yield to a mightier interest" (*Last Man*, 188, 193, 213, respectively). As Lionel nears completion of his narrative, the dramatic metaphors intensify greatly, suggesting that Lionel truly perceives his writing effort and the events around him as a theatrical tragedy. He refers to his digression about Merrival the astronomer as a "tragedy" that he will conclude "in a few words" (*Last Man*, 221). As Lionel rides back to Paris, fearing Adrian's situation, he forgets "the sad drama of human misery" (*Last Man*, 294). When the survivors reach Switzerland, he writes that they were "not quite wrong in seeking a scene like this, whereon to close the drama. . . . This solemn harmony of event and situation regulated our feelings, and gave as it were fitting costume to our last act" (*Last Man*, 309). That the plague should cause one to invoke dramatic metaphors is understandable, and Lionel, recording the events in retrospect, is able to make full use of the theatrical allusions for effect. However, these passages reflect just as much Lionel's dramatic sensibility as they do the horrifying results of the plague. For Lionel, his work is not a mere chronicle of events, but a drama of human endeavors and, more specifically, a drama of his own life. As such there is little or no distinction between life and art; they are one and the same.

The novel's *theatrum mundi* motif is intensified by a disturbing scene Lionel witnesses during the throes of the plague in England. The scene occurs, appropriately enough, at the theater during a production of *Macbeth*, and Lionel's inclusion of this episode is a significant example of his critical theory of art and of the world-as-stage motif. In an effort to maintain some normality, Adrian, as Lord Protector, has permitted the London theaters to remain open during the dangerous summer months. Lionel observes that "Tragedies deep and dire were the chief favourites. Comedy brought with it too great a contrast to the inner despair" (*Last Man*, 201). Lionel insists that "it was not in [his] nature to derive consolation from such scenes; from theatres . . . where fictitious tears and wailings mocked the heart-felt grief within . . . from assemblies of mourners in the guise of revellers" (*Last Man*, 201). Drama as representation of life strikes Lionel as hollow and artificial; for him, "reality" is drama and life merged into one entity. One evening, Lionel remembers "witness[ing] a scene of singular interest at one of the theatres, where nature overpowered art, as an overflowing cataract will tear away the puny manufacture of a mock cascade" (*Last Man*, 201). Lionel actually observes two scenes, one outside the theater and one on its stage. The "real life" scene concerns a woman who cannot find her husband; Lionel takes her to the hospital where the man lies dying from the plague. Lionel shudders at the setting, which he describes as a scene of horrors, and imagines his family, then still healthy, lying in those beds.

With this event fresh in his mind, Lionel chances upon a production of *Macbeth* at the Drury Lane Theatre starring the "first actor of the age."[10] Lionel comes in at the start of the fourth act. This act, which features the deaths of Lady Macduff and her children, ironically foreshadows the loss Lionel will eventually experience. Lionel takes great care to describe the realistic setting, so real that the "entrance of Macbeth did not destroy the illusion, for he was actuated by the same feelings that inspired us, and while the work of magic proceeded we sympathized in his wonder and his daring, and gave ourselves up with our whole souls to the influence of scenic delusion" (*Last Man*, 203). Lionel's description of the performance indicates that, like the theater of Shelley's time, the presentational style of acting has given way to the representational one.[11] At this point, the strength of this play's powerfully realistic production enables the audience to forget the external world and draws them into its own. However, that bridge between life and art collapses two scenes later when the nobleman Rosse prepares Macduff for the news of his family's murders beginning with the following lines:

> Alas, poor country; / Almost afraid to know itself! It cannot
> Be called our mother, but our grave: where nothing,
> But who knows nothing, is once seen to smile;
> Where sighs, and groans, and shrieks that rent the air,
> Are made, not marked; where violent sorrow seems
> A modern extasy: the dead man's knell
> Is there scarce asked, for who; and good men's lives
> Expire before the flowers in their caps,
> Dying, or ere they sicken. (*Last Man*, 204, from *Macbeth* IV.iii.164-73)

The body politic image expressed in Shakespeare's tragedy reminds Lionel of the very real horror outside the play's reality, a horror he had witnessed first-hand just prior to entering the theater. What happens next in the theater represents the artistic ideal for Lionel: one of the actors no longer "acts," and the audience ceases to be enthralled observers of a Shakespearean play and become actors as well in the real life drama unfolding off the stage and outside the theater:

> Each word struck the sense, as our life's passing bell; we feared to look at each other, but bent our gaze on the stage, as if our eyes could fall innocuous on that alone. The person who played the part of Rosse, suddenly became aware of the dangerous ground he trod. He was an inferior actor, but truth now made him excellent; as he went on to announce to Macduff the slaughter of his family, he was afraid to speak, trembling from apprehension of a burst of grief from the audience, not from his fellow-mime. Each word was drawn out with difficulty; real anguish painted his features; his eyes were now lifted in sudden horror, now fixed in dread upon the ground. his shew of terror encreased ours, we gasped with him, each neck was stretched out, each face changed with the actor's changes — at length while Macduff, who, attending to his part, was unobservant of the high wrought sympathy of the house, cried with well acted passion: "All my pretty ones. . ." A pang of tameless grief wrenched every heart, a burst of despair was echoed from every lip.–I had entered into the universal feeling — I had been absorbed by the terror of Rosse — I re-echoed the cry of Macduff, and then rushed out as from an hell of torture, to find calm in the free air and silent street. (*Last Man*, 204)

What occurs is the complete identification of art and life, of actor and observer — the face of each onlooker changes with that of the actor; the lines epitomize the grief and terror caused by the plague rather than the artificial tragedy for Macduff; and a "universal feeling" descends on nearly everyone present. Lionel is frightened by the power of art's ability to imitate life. He runs out of the theater, seeking the "dear soothings of maternal Nature," the powerful emotion too much for him to bear. He is also unnerved by the reality of the performance. He finds he has identified with Macduff, re-echoing aloud the actor's cry. Shelley effectively contrasts Shakespeare's hero and Lionel. Macduff is able to exact revenge (as he is fighting against an individual, not a plague) and is able to restore order by securing the crown for Malcolm, Duncan's son. Lionel, however, is rendered powerless by the plague.

Lionel's autobiography demonstrates his uncertainty regarding his role in the drama of life. He is torn between two parts as exemplified by his closest friends: Adrian, the man of contemplation, and Lord Raymond, the man of action. Adrian loves books, learning, nature, and solitude; Raymond yearns for conquests, projects, society, and politics. Initially what Lionel would most like is to play the role of hero as Raymond does. He repeatedly tries to catch the spotlight, but each time he is thwarted in his attempt.

When he was a youth, the world was a stage for the young and rebellious Verney. After a day of poaching on neighbors' estates, Lionel and his friends pretended to be gypsies, structuring their escapades into exciting narratives of "hair-breadth escapes, combats with dogs, ambush and flight" (*Last Man*, 11). He admits "appetite for admiration," requiring companionship and "applause": "I panted for enterprises beyond my childish exploits, and formed distempered dreams of future action. . . . I was born for something greater than I was — and greater I would become" (*Last Man*, 12). The tendency to perceive reality as a drama continues as Lionel engages the public spotlight in Vienna as an ambassador for Adrian, employing the world-as-stage metaphor for his entrance into Vienna's social life: "All was strange and admirable to the shepherd of Cumberland. With breathless amaze I entered on the gay scene, whose actors were — the lilies glorious as Solomon, / Who toil not, neither do they spin" (*Last Man*, 26). Despite his admiration for Adrian and his life of contemplation, Lionel nevertheless yearns for the public spotlight: "Methought the time was now arrived, when, childish occupations laid aside, I should enter into life. . . . Life is before me, and I rush into possession. Hope, glory, love, and blameless ambition are my guides, and my soul knows no dread" (*Last Man*, 25). Caught up in social life, Lionel finds only an "intoxicating delusion," as he loses his sense of self, "devoured by a restless wish to be something to others" (*Last Man*, 26). He compares himself to a rustic, pastoral shepherd amidst the glamorous public figures of Viennese society, revealing the contrast he perceives between himself as observer and others as actors. Desiring "to be something to others" demonstrates his awareness that masks and playing roles are often essential to social approbation and acceptance.

Adrian wisely deters Lionel from his youthful rebellious acts by introducing him to literature and philosophy. As a result of Adrian's friendship, Lionel feels "born anew," his "plastic soul . . . remoulded by a masterhand" (*Last Man*, 19-20). Admiring Adrian to the point of idolatry, Lionel willingly exchanges his life of action for one of contemplation. Despite his title as second Earl of Windsor, Adrian shuns the spotlight, preferring to "seek his reward, not in the applause or gratitude of his fellow creatures . . . but in the approbation of his own heart" (*Last Man*, 30). Lionel depicts Adrian as the ideal man of sensibility and reason, the man who truly knows himself and who does not need "applause" from an audience to establish a sense of self-worth. For Adrian, the world was "a dwelling, to inhabit with his chosen one; and not either a scheme of society or an enchainment of events, that could impact [sic] to him either happiness or misery" (*Last Man*, 23). Even in his despair resulting from unrequited love for Evadne, Adrian recognizes the link with humanity: "Life is not the thing romance writers describe it; going through the measures of a dance, and after various evolutions arriving at a conclusion, when the dancers may sit down and repose. While there is life there is action and change. We go on, each thought linked to the one which was its parent, each act to a previous act" (*Last Man*, 32). Lionel admires Adrian's ability to remain true to himself. When he refuses to challenge Ryland for the Protectorship and nominates Raymond instead, Adrian indicates that reality must supplant dreams: "the visions of my boyhood have long since faded in the light of reality; I know now that I am not a man fitted to govern nations; sufficient for me, if I keep in wholesome rule the little kingdom of my own mortality" (*Last Man*, 68). No grand designs for Adrian; keeping home rule is enough to satisfy him.

Although Lionel respects and admires Adrian, he is intrigued with playing the heroic role. However, whenever Lionel has the opportunity to enact his dream for public greatness, he is unable to achieve it. In Vienna, he encounters rejection upon his official entrance into the world and retreats from society, unable to play the socialite or dandy with any success. Another example occurs in his early relationship with Idris. He first imagines himself a hero, fantasizing how he will rescue her, then rejects that role for fear of failure: "Methought that probably to her mother's ambitious schemes, I ought to come forward to protect her from undue influence, guard her from unhappiness, and secure to her freedom of choice, the right of every human being. Yet how was I to do this? She herself would disdain my interference. Since then I must be an object of indifference or contempt to her, better, far better avoid her, nor expose myself before her and the scornful world to the chance of playing the mad game of a fond, foolish Icarus" (*Last Man*, 35). Evoking the mythological daredevil, Lionel realizes he is afraid to take the action required for such an heroic role; "how was I to do this," he wonders, echoing the question he had asked himself earlier when Idris had asked him to find Adrian. Better to sit back and watch, he decides, than to "expose myself before her and the scornful world." In fact, Idris enables him to play the role of hero. She escapes before her mother was able to take her back to Austria, and, making her way through snow and darkness to Lionel's cottage, she pleads with him to take her to Adrian in London before she is discovered missing. The hero is slow to react: "the idea shot across me—is she also mad? . . . I was frightened by her vehemence, and imagined some mistake in her incoherent tale" (*Last Man*, 61). Such doubt and delay seem odd for one who had earlier expressed such concern about Idris's safety. Though Lionel wants to be the hero, he is frightened by the role. However, he reluctantly helps Idris to London and as they proceed, assumes the behavior associated with fictional and dramatic heroes rescuing the fair lady in distress: "I lifted her up in my arms; her light form rested on my breast. — I felt no burthen, except the internal one of contrary and contending emotions. Brimming delight now invested me. . . . Her head lay on my shoulder, her breath waved my hair, her heart beat near mine, transport made me tremble, blinded me, annihilated me–" (*Last Man*, 61). Lionel does succeed in "saving" Idris this time, more through her exertions than his. With the Queen's return to Austria, he finally realizes his dream of marrying her.

For several years, Lionel, Idris, Raymond, Perdita, and Adrian live a contented and quiet life in Windsor. Satisfied with family life and influenced by Adrian, Lionel willingly forgets his desire for fame and heroics. In spite of Adrian's influence, he nevertheless finds himself intrigued with the adventurer-leader-hero, Lord Raymond, whose "name and exploits . . . filled the world with admiration" (*Last Man*, 27). Lionel has carefully studied Raymond, who, as the man of action, gradually replaces Adrian as hero-type: "I became intimate with him, and each day afforded me occasion to admire more and more his powerful and versatile talents" (*Last Man*, 34). Raymond represents perhaps Mary Shelley's most vehement indictment of the egocentric actor in the novel. His desire for fame and greatness disrupts the Edenic life at Windsor and destroys his marriage. It also accounts, in part, for the spread of the plague by his insistence on storming the city despite reports of the danger. Lionel recognizes that, to accomplish fame and glory, Raymond must participate in a public arena — a stage on which Raymond enacts the role of hero and leader so completely that he finds he cannot separate the acting from life itself.

Lionel's description of Raymond reveals that his subject is everything that Lionel is not. From a "noble but impoverished family," Raymond is ambitious and proud, so proud that he leaves England (which does not appreciate him) to fight in the Greek wars. He returns home as a wealthy hero desirous of achieving his goal — the Protectorship. In contrast to Adrian, who believed he was but a cog in the wheel, "that he made a part of a great whole," the self-centered Raymond "looked on the structure of society as but a part of the machinery which supported the web on which his life was traced. The earth was spread out as an highway for him; the heavens built up as a canopy for him" (*Last Man*, 31).

Like Lionel, Raymond has always desired greatness and fame. Although he abandons his first bid for the Protectorship and chooses marriage to Perdita instead, he does succeed in his second attempt. Granted, Raymond initiates the group's interest by nominating Adrian for the position; however, when Adrian presents a convincing case for his friend, Lionel notes that Raymond is quick "to confess his secret wishes for dignity and fame" (*Last Man*, 69) and to realize his life-long dream. Later, Raymond demonstrates the depth of his desire for fame by risking exposure to the plague in Constantinople for the possibility of future glory. His honor and effort, not the justness of the situation, determine his decision: "By my past labours, by torture and imprisonment [I] suffered for them, by my victories, by my sword, I swear — by my hopes of fame, by my former deserts now awaiting their reward, I deeply vow, with these hands to plant the cross on yonder mosque" (*Last Man*, 140). Note the frequency of "my"; Raymond's ego has turned the Greek-Turkish war into his own personal battle for fame and glory. With words that echo those of Victor Frankenstein and Castruccio, he admits, "The prayer of my youth was to be one among those who render the pages of earth's history splendid; who exalt the race of man, and make this little globe a dwelling of the mighty" (*Last Man*, 141).

Raymond, Lionel writes, "entered upon life," commanding the spotlight's attention so that he can play his chosen role to its full advantage. Indeed, Raymond excels on the public stage, casting himself in the part of hero, leader, warrior; he plans for a better England by improving public works, the arts, and medicine. He is aware that public life puts one in the spotlight, and when nominated by Adrian to be the next Protector, he fears that "absence from the busy stage had caused him to be forgotten by the people" (*Last Man*, 69). Despite his fear, Raymond quickly masters his role, and one of his strengths that Lionel greatly admires is his control of the audience through language. His demeanor and responses to the speech of his rival, Ryland, during his first attempt at the Protectorship amazes the observing Lionel: "I can ill record the flow of language and graceful turns of expression, the wit and easy raillery that gave vigour and influence to his speech. . . . his changeful face was lit up to superhuman brilliancy; his voice, various as music, was like that enchanting" (*Last Man*, 43). Just before his ride into Constantinople as conqueror, Raymond gives an impassioned speech that is replete with melodramatic language and gesture, as these excerpted lines indicate: "But I am about to die!–nay, interrupt me not — soon I shall die"; "Alas, for Raymond! the prayer of his youth is wasted — the hopes of his manhood are null"; "From my dungeon in yonder city I cried, soon I will be thy lord" (*Last Man*, 141). These lines are as intense and dramatic as any delivered on stage; they are uttered by an actor who plays his role so well that he cannot separate from it. Furthermore, the

self-referential third-person voice demonstrates that Raymond's subjectivity enables him to objectify himself. As Lionel duly notes, "reason came
unavailing to such high-wrought feelings" (*Last Man*, 141).

Raymond is adept at portraying a determined, decisive figure who can
manipulate a crowd, plan enterprising projects for the country, and lead the
Greeks against the invading Turks. A man of action, Raymond criticizes
those merely observing on the sidelines. He is contemptuous of Lionel's
determination to help the stricken Adrian, mad with unrequited love for
Evadne: "Every man . . . dreams about something, love, honour, and pleasure; you dream of friendship, and devote yourself to a maniac. . . . Happy
are dreamers . . . so that they not be awakened!" (*Last Man*, 34).[12]
However Raymond's contempt is but an act itself, a mask to conceal his
love for Perdita. In his first bid for the Protectorship, Raymond must keep
the support of the ex-Queen and her contacts, which means relinquishing
Perdita and marrying Idris, whom Raymond respects but does not love.

So caught up in his part, Raymond cannot act beyond the dictates of the
role. He abandons will to fate, suggesting that he is no longer capable of
making decisions or accepting responsibility. Interpreting Evadne's dying
words as a prophecy of his own death, he believes that his action is neces-
sitated by fate. He tells Lionel that he has no choice, that he is the "sport
of fortune" for "such is the will of fate" (*Last Man*, 141). Raymond abandons will to fate just as Victor Frankenstein did, particularly in the 1831
edition. He sees himself as a "heaven-climber" victimized by the "crawling
reptiles of his species" (*Last Man*, 141). In both novels, Shelley criticizes
such a response to the results of one's own action: because Raymond chose
to play the role of the hero and leader whose drama would be recorded in
history books for all posterity, he should accept even the undesirable consequences of that role.

Lord Raymond is generally effective when he dons a public mask to play
the hero's role, an ability of which Lionel is very envious. Lionel cannot
conceal his desire to play a hero, a fact he recognizes when riding back to
Paris, imagining the worst about Adrian's delay in meeting him. Upon
hearing Adrian's voice, he nearly hugs him with joy: "I rushed into the Hall
of Hercules, where he stood surrounded by a crowd, whose eyes, turned in
wonder on me, reminded me that on the stage of the world, a man must
repress such girlish extacies" (*Last Man*, 294-295). Although Lionel recognizes that public roles require a decorum and a mask to cover the vulnera-
ble self, he has difficulty playing the part. However, so does Raymond on
occasion. Once he is out of the spotlight, Raymond is rendered helpless
because he cannot control his passions. Lionel observes that his friend is
able "to govern the whole earth in his grasping imagination, and . . . only
quailed when he attempted to rule himself" (*Last Man*, 40). Raymond himself recognizes that the private sphere demands the public mask be stripped
away to reveal the inner self, which he does when he finally decides to relin-

quish the Protectorship (his first bid) and marry Perdita: "I will not act a part with you, dear girl, or appear other than what I am, weak and unworthy, more fit to excite your disdain than your love" (*Last Man*, 48).

However, Raymond can indeed "act a part" and "appear other than [he is]." He conceals his affair with Evadne, deceiving both himself and Perdita. Guilt-ridden about his secret liaison, he attempts to elicit sympathy by playing the innocent husband and accusing Perdita of playing "the part of the injured wife to admiration" (*Last Man*, 89). Witness to the scene, Lionel recognizes that Raymond begins to accept as truth the role he chooses to play: "He forgot that each word he spoke was false. He personated his assumption of innocence even to self-deception. Have not actors wept, as they pourtrayed imagined passion? A more intense feeling of the reality of fiction possessed Raymond" (*Last Man*, 89). For a time, Perdita's pain touches her husband, and Lionel suspects that Raymond "felt perhaps somewhat ashamed of the part he acted of the injured man, he who was in truth the injurer" (*Last Man*, 90). But never having achieved mastery of his passions, Raymond slips out one more time to Evadne. Finding her nearly lifeless, he spends the evening there instead of at the ball arranged by Perdita in his honor.

His domestic life in shambles, Raymond's public role becomes ineffectual. Adrian and Lionel plead with him to master his passions and to know himself, but Raymond argues that he cannot. At one point in this exchange, Raymond seems to have recognized the difference between the mask and the self, between "acting" and living. He does perceive both his and Perdita's weaknesses, yet, like Victor Frankenstein, he is reluctant to take responsibility, blaming others rather than himself:

> Perdita, wedded to an imagination, careless of what is behind the veil, whose character is in truth faulty and vile, Perdita has renounced me. With her it was pretty enough to play a sovereign's part; and, as in the recesses of your beloved forest we acted masques, and imagined ourselves Arcadian shepherds, to please the fancy of the moment — so was I content, more for Perdita's sake than my own, to take on me the character of one of the great ones of the earth; to lead her behind the scenes of grandeur, to vary her life with a short act of magnificence and power. This was to be the colour; love and confidence the substance of our existence. But we must live, and not act our lives; pursuing the shadow, I lost the reality — now I renounce both. (*Last Man*, 110)

To live one's life, not act it. There is a distinction between living and acting; one is "real"; the other is an imitation of life, an illusion. Although Raymond recognizes that distinction, he attributes his failure to Perdita's ambition, rather than his own. Furthermore, he has not fully comprehended the devastation his role playing has caused, nor can he abandon the theater of the world. He merely recasts himself into another role — that of the solitary, a "wanderer, a soldier of fortune." His goal in returning to

Greece is to discover "new scenes" and perhaps play again the role of leader.

Admittedly, the novel's first-person point of view makes it difficult to determine if Raymond himself perceives the world as a stage on which to play his hero's role or if Lionel simply invests him with that image and language as he records the events years later in Rome. We can probably assume both possibilities; what is significant is that Lionel sees himself as an observer of life's drama in contrast to Raymond as an actor in it. Lionel is also quick to parallel himself with Raymond whenever possible. He uncannily echoes Raymond's line, "we must live and not act our lives," following his return to England after Raymond's and Perdita's deaths in Greece:

> How unwise had the wanderers been, who had deserted its shelter, entangled themselves in the web of society, and entered on what men of the world call 'life,'– that labyrinth of evil, that scheme of mutual torture. To live, according to this sense of the word, we must not only observe and learn, we must also feel; we must not be mere spectators of action, we must act; we must not describe, but be subjects of description. . . . Who that knows what 'life' is, would pine for this feverish species of existence? I have lived, I have spent days and nights of festivity; I have joined in ambitious hopes, and exulted in victory: now,–shut the door on the world, and build high the wall that is to separate me from the troubled scene enacted within its precincts. Let us live for each other and for happiness; let us seek peace in our dear home, near the inland murmur of streams, and the gracious waving of trees, the beauteous vesture of earth, and sublime pageantry of the skies. Let us leave 'life,' that we may live. (*Last Man*, 158)

This passage reveals Lionel's disillusionment with the public stage. He would rather "shut the door" or have the curtain fall so that the private is contained and protected from the "troubled scene" of the outside world. The public world may privilege the actor and marginalize the spectator; however, Lionel finds the actor's role too difficult, too demanding, too sorrowful. Maybe some people, as he once did, can define life as acting rather than observing, but "real" life is the life beyond the stage, in the domestic sphere.

Lionel seems to adjust to his role as observer and author. However, when Adrian answers the call to lead the country at the height of the plague, Lionel feels those heroic urges once again. He sees that Adrian, once the quintessential man of contemplation, becomes the man of action, playing the role of hero. When the plague reaches England and Ryland can no longer govern, Adrian fulfills what was once his destiny by virtue of his birth — assumption of the Protectorship. Lionel's fears for his friend's previous weak health seem needless: "the energy of his purpose informed his body with strength, the solemn joy of enthusiasm and self-devotion illuminated his countenance; and the weakness of his physical nature seemed to pass from him, as the cloud of humanity did, in the ancient fable, from the divine lover of Semele" (*Last Man*, 178). Lionel reveals his envy of Adrian's new role, not only by likening him to Zeus, whose powerful presence destroyed his earthly mate, but also with glowing terms befitting a hero: "Here was a youth, royally sprung, bred in luxury, by nature averse to the usual struggles of a public life, and now, in time of danger, at a period when to live was the utmost scope of the ambitious, he, the beloved and heroic Adrian, made, in sweet simplicity, an offer to sacrifice himself for the public good. The very idea was generous and noble,–but, beyond this, his unpretending manner, his entire want of the assumption of a virtue, rendered his act ten times more touching" (*Last Man*, 182). Adrian is like one brought back from the dead. "O, I shall be something now," he exclaims once he accepts the duty from Ryland.

Lionel agrees to nominate his friend, but when the time comes, he recommends himself instead. When queried by the amazed Adrian, Lionel excuses his action by attributing it to his desire to protect Adrian. Yet as Adrian tells Lionel, the plague is the great leveler and "ten years hence the cold stars may shine on the graves of all of us" (*Last Man*, 185). What Lionel does not tell us, or perhaps does not even realize, is that he is once again seduced by that starring role in the spotlight. Note in his description of what occurred that, despite a shaky beginning, he gets into his role quite quickly, making an appealing case:

> I had risen mechanically — my knees trembled; irresolution hung on my voice, as I uttered a few words on the necessity of choosing a person adequate to the dangerous task in hand. But, when the idea of presenting myself in the room of my friend intruded, the load of doubt and pain was taken from off me. My words flowed spontaneously — my utterance was firm and quick. I adverted to what Adrian had already done — I promised the same vigilance in furthering all his views. I drew a touching picture of his vacillating health; I boasted of my own strength. I prayed them to save even from himself this scion of the noblest family in England. My alliance with him was the pledge of my sincerity, my union with his sister, my children, his presumptive heirs, were the hostages of my truth. (*Last Man*, 183)

The self-presentation with the emphasis on "I" demonstrates how completely Lionel is immersed in this part. Humility cast aside, he boasts of his physical health and questions Adrian's. Nevertheless, he fails in this attempt and must settle for a supporting role to Adrian's starring one.

Lionel also endeavors to play the hero's role in his attempt to rescue Juliet and Adrian from the false prophet in Paris. Although Lionel's admitted motive for helping Juliet is to repay the debt incurred when she helped Idris in the storm, such dangerous and drastic action is usually not undertaken by him. To save her from the Calvinist sect, when he cannot save anyone from the plague, would benefit Lionel's frail ego."I presented myself to her" (*Last Man*, 283), he writes, declining to divulge how he invaded the enemy camp. When captured by guards, Lionel plays the part of the brave hero well, warning the false prophet that Adrian knows of this plan (he does not) and that the prophet "will long lament the tragedy [he is] about to act" (*Last Man*, 284). In the prison, Lionel regrets his actions; they neither effect Juliet's freedom, nor demonstrate that he can meet the role's demands. In a decidedly non-heroic soliloquy, he ponders his fate: "My imagination was busied in shaping forth the kind of death he would inflict. Would he allow me to wear out life with famine; or was the food administered to me to be medicined with death? Would he steal on me in my sleep; or should I contend to the last with my murderers, knowing, even while I struggled, that I must be overcome?" (*Last Man*, 285). Such thoughts reflect a frightened person regretting his rash actions rather than a stoic figure waiting for an heroic death.

If Lionel cannot enact the role of hero in life's drama, then perhaps he can do so in his autobiographical chronicle as the last man. Under Adrian's tutelage, Lionel discovered a love for literature. In his sister's cottage after the marriage of Raymond and Perdita, he immersed himself in literature and histories: "my sole companions were my books and my loving thoughts" (*Last Man*, 55). Those thoughts directed toward Idris encourage Lionel's tendency to merge art and life. Ever the observer, Lionel recounts his daily habits at that time: "I watched the movements of the lady of my heart. At night I could see her shadow on the walls of her apartment; by day I viewed her in her flower-garden, or riding in the park with her usual companions. Methought the charm would be broken if I were seen, but I heard the music of her voice and was happy. I gave to each heroine of whom I read, her beauty and matchless excellences" (*Last Man*, 55). This passage demonstrates that Lionel has already indulged in play acting and playwriting. It also reveals how readily he can construct a fiction from reality. From an early age, he has had practice for what will be his ultimate role.

In the aftermath of Raymond's downfall as Lord Protector, Lionel is disillusioned with his role as a hero and turns back to literature, discovering empowerment through writing:

> I had been wedded to literature. I felt convinced that however it might have been in former times, in the present stage of the world, no man's faculties could be developed, no man's moral principle be enlarged and liberal, without an extensive acquaintance with books. To me they stood in the place of an active career, of ambition, and those palpable excitements necessary to the multitude. The collation of philosophical opinions, the study of historical facts, the acquirement of languages, were at once my recreation, and the serious aim of my life. I turned author myself. My productions however were sufficiently unpretend-

ing; they were confined to the biography of favourite historical characters, especially those whom I believed to have been traduced, or
about whom clung obscurity and doubt.

As my authorship increased, I acquired new sympathies and pleas-
ures. I found another and a valuable link to enchain me to my fellow-
creatures; my point of sight was extended, and the inclinations and
capacities of all human beings became deeply interesting to me. Kings
have been called the fathers of their people. Suddenly I became as it
were the father of all mankind. Posterity became my heirs. My
thoughts were gems to enrich the treasure house of man's intellectual
possession; each sentiment was a precious gift I bestowed on them. Let
not these aspirations be attributed to vanity. They were not expressed
in words, nor even reduced to form in my own mind; but they filled my
soul, exalting my thoughts, raising a glow of enthusiasm, and led me
out of the obscure path in which I before walked, into the bright noon-
enlightened highway of mankind, making me, citizen of the world, a
candidate for immortal honors, an eager aspirant to the praise and
sympathy of my fellow men. . . . But this account, which might as prop-
erly belong to a former period of my life as to the present moment,
leads me far afield. (*Last Man,* 112-13)

Despite his desire to be a man of action, Lionel is relegated to be an
observer of life. However, he finds a substitute — literature. Books, he
admits, "stood in the place of an active career." Although he cannot be the
heroic figure Raymond is, he will have his vocation. Literature empowers
Lionel, who shares a dangerous affinity with Victor Frankenstein:
"Suddenly I became as it were the father of all mankind," he writes. He discovers a sympathy to link him with others. As an author, he chooses biographies of those "about whom clung obscurity." Lionel realizes that he will
never go down in history as Raymond will — as a public hero. However,
he can achieve fame as author, becoming "a candidate for immortal honors."

His newly found vocation is useful in Greece as Lionel plays a pioneer-
ing journalist-historian. The events he observes become a "living drama"
as he dissects them to shape them into form:

I was inquisitive as to the internal principles of action of those around
me: anxious to read their thoughts justly, and for ever occupied in
devining [sic] their inmost mind. All events, at the same time that they
deeply interested me, arranged themselves in pictures before me. I gave
the right place to every personage in the groupe, the just balance to
every sentiment. This undercurrent of thought, often soothed me
amidst distress, and even agony. It gave ideality to that, from which,
taken in naked truth, the soul would have revolted: it bestowed picto-
rial colours on misery and disease, and not unfrequently relieved me
from despair in deplorable changes. This faculty, or instinct, was now

> rouzed. . . . Attentively perusing this animated volume, I was the less surprised at the tale I read on the new-turned page. (*Last Man*, 126)

Lionel is very confident of his skill in depicting his characters, placing them appropriately and revealing their emotions. He offers a variation of the *theatrum mundi* metaphor by describing life as an "animated volume" that he creates through the act of writing.

Lionel admits that his writing effort is cathartic: "I had used this history as an opiate; while it described my beloved friends, fresh with life and glowing with hope; active assistants on the scene, I was soothed" (*Last Man*, 192).[13] But writing also provides Lionel with a role in the public arena. Regretting having to relay the horrors of the plague, Lionel nevertheless finds himself ready for the task: "Time and experience have placed me on an height from which I can comprehend the past as a whole" (*Last Man*, 192). In his estimation, he is fully capable of taking on the role of historian, biographer, and autobiographer to shape and develop the work into a thing of art: "in this way I must describe it, bringing forward the leading incidents, and disposing light and shade so as to form a picture in whose very darkness there will be harmony" (*Last Man*, 192).

Lionel relies on melodramatic language to increase the theatricality of his history. Considering the plague's devastating ability and the imminent doom for humanity, he indulges in elevated rhetoric that could grace the stage with ease as he says his farewells to civilization: "to the patriotic scene, to the love of liberty and well earned meed of virtuous aspiration"; "to knowledge that could pilot the deep-drawing bark through the opposing waters of shoreless ocean"; "to the arts,–to eloquence, which is the human mind as the winds to the sea"; "to poetry and deep philosophy, for man's imagination is cold, and his mind can no longer expatiate on the wonders of life" (*Last Man*, 233-34). Believing he is truly the last man and fully aware of his mortality, Lionel also says goodby to life, as a theatrical experience and as an actual existence: "Farewell to the well-trod stage; a truer tragedy is enacted on the world's ample scene, that puts to shame mimic grief: to high-bred comedy, and the low buffoon, farewell!–Man may laugh no more" (*Last Man*, 234). Such melodramatic language, with its theatrical allusions and elevated style, reflects Mary Shelley's own style when indulging her emotions and the style of many novels of writers such as Godwin, Hays, and Dacre. Nevertheless, it also reinforces Lionel's view of life as a literary construct and intensifies the melodramatic quality of his narrative.

Furthermore, Lionel relies on various elements of theatrical tradition as he constructs his history. Certainly one source for the well-read Lionel was the Gothic drama, which was noted for real or imagined specters whose appearance often signaled a disturbance in the social balance or in the psychological makeup of a character. Lionel evokes familiar Gothic images and figures to enhance the terror and horror that accompany the plague.

As the survivors make their way from Paris to Switzerland, he writes that each "evening brought its fresh creation of spectres; a ghost was depicted by every blighted tree; and appalling shapes were manufactured from each shaggy bush" (*Last Man*, 298). It was difficult to separate the illusion from the reality, and Lionel admits that he had trouble keeping himself "free from the belief in supernatural events" (*Last Man*, 298). The perils of the eighteenth-century Gothic heroine take on another dimension of reality in Shelley's contribution to the genre: a plague becomes the villain stalking the innocents whose senses are painfully heightened by "realities [that] took ghostly shapes." Lionel recalls two particular incidents that unnerved the survivors. One was a white specter who appeared to perform for the group, leaping into the air wildly. When it saw its audience, the "goblin" bowed, evoking laughter from the watchers, before it capered off into the night. The ghost was none other than an opera-dancer, Lionel discovers, who, "in an access [sic] of delirium . . . had fancied himself on the stage, and, poor fellow, his dying sense eagerly accepted the last human applause that could ever be bestowed on his grace and agility" (*Last Man*, 299). The ghostly figure's presence adds to the eeriness of this scene, and Lionel's interpretation of its purpose reflects his own desire for "human applause." The other apparition is the "Black Spectre," a French nobleman, who having lost all family and friends, sought human companionship. As symbolic manifestations of the very real horror of the plague, these Gothic-like figures represent the mental anguish and terror the survivors feel, recalling dramas such as Joanna Baillie's *Orra* and novels such as Charles Robert Maturin's *Melmoth the Wanderer* or Charles Brockden Brown's *Wieland*.

Another theatrical convention that Lionel finds effective is the soliloquy. In depicting himself and other characters, Lionel uses spoken thoughts for dramatic effect. Perdita's soliloquy following Raymond's failure to attend the ball reveals as much of Lionel's dramatic skill as it does of her personal turmoil. As if he were in the room observing her, Lionel creates a dramatic scene by describing her actions and recording her thoughts: "At length she rose, more composed, not less miserable. She stood before a large mirror — she gazed on her reflected image; . . . 'Vase am I,' she thought, 'vase brimful of despair's direst essence'" (*Last Man*, 97). Perdita continues, describing herself as on a "barren desart" or as chained to a "solitary rock" Prometheus-like. Such elaborate language and metaphors are not characteristic of the uneducated and free-spirited Perdita, but they are consistent with Lionel's manner. No doubt true to the feelings that Perdita then felt, the passage exudes a stage-like quality that Lionel, not necessarily Perdita, has imagined.

Lionel superimposes his dramatic sensibility onto the other characters as well, frequently describing their action in theatrical terms. Raymond's bid for the Protectorship is a mini-drama in Lionel's eyes. According to Lionel, Perdita's "part of the drama" was difficult "since it had to be performed alone" (*Last Man*, 72). Following Raymond's successful election, Lionel describes Perdita's duties as those of a "first lady," a role she now must play: "It was pretty enough to see my sister enter as it were into the spirit of the drama, and endeavour to fill her station with becoming dignity" (*Last Man*, 75). When the ex-Queen returns to England during the plague's worst years, she protests to Idris that the "young are impatient to push the old off the scene"; Lionel remarks wryly that it "was a strange speech, now that, on the empty stage, each might play his part without impediment from the other" (*Last Man*, 241). The false prophet, who tries to kill Adrian in Paris, was "resolved to keep up the drama to the last act" (*Last Man*, 296), which he did until Juliet exposed his intentions.

As the devastation of the plague threatens every corner of his world, Lionel's powers as author seem to fade. Escaping to the glorious past of Greek mythology, he mourns the bleak present: "The utter inutility that had attended all my exertions took from them their usual effects of exhilaration, and despair rendered abortive the balm of self applause — I longed to return to my old occupations, but of what use were they? To read were futile — to write, vanity indeed. The earth, late wide circus for the display of dignified exploits, vast theatre for a magnificent drama, now presented a vacant space, an empty stage — for actor or spectator there was no longer aught to say or hear" (*Last Man*, 223). In Rome, Lionel is inspired by the history displayed there, as the "Diorama of the ages passed across my subdued fancy" (*Last Man*, 336). He claims to have fallen into "self-knowledge." He determines that fate has destined him to survive, that he should not be "playing the school-boy's part of obedience without submission" (*Last Man*, 337). Nevertheless, Lionel tries to escape reality through art: "I endeavoured to read. . . . I endeavoured to conceal me from myself, and immerse myself in the subject traced on the pages before me" (*Last Man*, 338). He gazes at art in galleries, losing himself "in a reverie before many a fair Madonna or beauteous nymph" (*Last Man*, 336). Recalling Radcliffe's *The Italian* and Madame de Staël's *Corrine*, Lionel "reflected how the Enchantress Spirit of Rome held sovereign sway over the minds of the imaginative, until it rested on me — sole remaining spectator of its wonders" (*Last Man*, 336). He mourns the tragedy that he has experienced and all the roles that he has played in it: "Ah! while I streak this paper with the tale of what my so named occupations were — while I shape the skeleton of my days — my hand trembles — my heart pants, and my brain refuses to lend expression, or phrase, or idea, by which to image forth the veil of unutterable woe that clothed these bare realities" (*Last Man*, 339). Despite the devastating grief and loneliness, Lionel recognizes that the handiwork of these artists has remained long after their death, and he is reminded that authorship is a path to fame as well as political or military vocations are.

Finding writing materials in an author's study, Lionel decides to write a book, dedicating it with "silly flourish" to "the Illustrious Dead," who, after all, will be the audience for his last great effort. Despite the dedication, Lionel entertains thoughts of a living audience: "Yet, will not this world be re-peopled, and the children of a saved pair of lovers, in some to me unknown and unattainable seclusion, wandering to these prodigious relics of the ante-pestilential race, seek to learn how being so woundrous [sic] in their achievements, with imaginations infinite, and powers godlike, had departed from their home to an unknown country" (*Last Man*, 339). Although a chronicle of the last years of humanity's existence, the work is also Lionel's monument to himself: "I will write and leave in this most ancient city, this 'world's sole monument,' a record of these things. I will leave a monument of the existence of Verney, the Last Man" (*Last Man*, 339). The work takes a year to write, and upon its completion, Lionel lays down the pen to take up the role of the solitary, the wanderer. However, literature will remain an important part of what future he has: he visits libraries to take Homer's epic poetry and Shakespeare's tragic dramas with him.

With Homer and Shakespeare as models, Lionel Verney hopes to make his mark in literary history. It is a cruel irony that, having found a role to which he is suited, he has no readers or audience to applaud his accomplishment. Nor does Lionel quite have the "last word." His chronicle is edited by the author of the introduction, who found it written on the Sibylline leaves. The unnamed discoverer of the manuscript edits and arranges it for publication: "I present the public with my latest discoveries in the slight Sibylline pages. Scattered and unconnected as they were, I have been obliged to add links, and model the work into a consistent form. But the main substance rests on the truths contained in these poetic rhapsodies, and the divine intuition which the Cumaean damsel obtained from heaven" (*Last Man*, 3-4). As editor, this character initially takes credit for the work: "Sometimes I have thought, that, obscure and chaotic as they are, they owe their present form to me, their decipherer" (*Last Man*, 4). However, she quickly recants and admits that her editing was strictly to make the leaves' contents understood by the public. The editor finds comfort in reading and editing Lionel's text, identifying with him as she works: "My labours have cheered long hours of solitude, and taken me out of a world which has averted its once benignant face from me, to one glowing with imagination and power" (*Last Man*, 4). The allure of imaginary existences extends well beyond the borders of Lionel's text, as the editor's words reveal.

The editor finds these leaves in the Sibyl's cave in 1818.[14] Once again, Shelley has presented a frame tale, one that transcends temporal constraints. Generally in a frame structure, the character-editor lives in the present time and finds the ancient manuscript, which then comprises the central tale. Shelley's "author" also lives in the present but has found ancient pages which tell a story set in the future by over two hundred years. Why the frame, and why the time disjunction? Lynn Wells reads the frame as a disturbance of Lionel's text and "its illusion of representative stability."[15] Perhaps the future setting lends a germ of truth to the story. In 1818, there is obviously no such plague and no such last man, but as a prophecy, the potential remains viable. However, another reason may be that the frame raises the question of Lionel's authorship, suggesting that perhaps the spotlight is only an illusion after all. The events as described are actually a prophecy by the Sibyl; they have not yet occurred. Lionel is but a fictional character within a tale authored not by him, but by the Sibyl herself. In both *Frankenstein* and *The Last Man*, Shelley challenges authorial control. Victor Frankenstein's dreams of fame and glory may have ended with the destruction of both his creations, and it is possible that there will be no trace of his accomplishments or even of his existence. Lionel Verney's oblivion may result from his never having existed except in a Sibyl's prophecy.

In all three of her first-person novels, Mary Shelley refigures the *theatrum mundi* motif to critique a self-centered dramatic sensibility that intensifies confusion between illusion and actual life and that endangers the domestic sphere so crucial to linking a person to others. Victor Frankenstein, Robert Walton, Mathilda, Lord Raymond, and Lionel Verney experience the devastating effects from playing the heroic or tragic figure on the stage of life, and they may well identify with the conclusion of an eighteenth-century character, Emma Courtney, who closed her autobiography with this lament: "And is this all of human life — this, that passes like a tale that is told? Alas! it is a tragical tale! . . . The dawn of my life glowed with the promise of a fair and bright day; before its noon, thick clouds gathered; its mid-day was gloomy and tempestuous. —It remains with thee, my friend, to gild with a mild radiance the closing evening; before the scene shuts, and veils the prospect in impenetrable darkness" (Hays, 198-99).

Chapter 5 Notes

1. See Shelley's undated letter to Charles Ollier in which she requests a book on Constantinople (*Letters*, 1: 431) and that of 27 September 1825 to John Howard Payne in which she notes her trip to Windsor and Eton (*Letters*, 1: 502).
2. See 29 July 1826 letter to Payne (*Letters*, 1: 525).
3. See 28 January/7 February 1826 letter to Payne, (*Letters*, 1: 510).
4. Sir Timothy Shelley had warned his daughter-in-law to keep the Shelley name out of print, threatening to terminate her allowance should she not agree, and he was recently upset with the publication of *Posthumous Poems*, a collection of Percy Shelley's poetry. Mary Shelley was sensitive to her father-in-law's threat and therefore did not "sign" her novel. However, as Feldman and Scott-Kilvert have pointed out, the public knew by then that Shelley had written *Frankenstein* (*Journals*, 2: 498 n.2), so reviewers did not hesitate to refer to her. As a result, Sir Timothy temporarily withheld support until his solicitor, William Whitton, and Thomas Love Peacock intervened on Shelley's behalf. See also Sunstein, 260-272.
5. For an answer to the *Gazette*'s question, "why not the last woman," see Barbara Johnson's essay, "The Last Man," in *The Other Mary Shelley: Beyond Frankenstein*, ed. Audrey A. Fisch, Anne K. Mellor, and Esther H. Schor (New York: Oxford University Press, 1993), 258-266.
6. See Hugh Luke's Introduction to *The Last Man* and Audrey Fisch's "Plaguing Politics: AIDS, Deconstruction, and *The Last Man*," in *The Other Mary Shelley: Beyond Frankenstein*.
7. In an letter to John Bowring, written a month after the novel's publication, Mary Shelley refers to the parallel: "I have endeavoured, but how inadequately to give some idea of him in my last published book — the sketch has pleased some of those who best loved him — I might have made more of it but there are feelings which one recoils from unveiling to the public eye" (*Letters*, 1: 512). A year later, she also comments on the parallels in a letter to Teresa Guiccioli: "Have you read my <u>Last Man</u> — You will find in Lord Raymond and Count Adrian faint portraits but <u>I hope</u> not displeasing to you of B. and S. — but this is a secret" (*Letters*, 1: 566).
8. Previous efforts included Thomas Campbell's poem, "The Last Man," and Byron's "Darkness"; also Thomas Lovell Beddoes began a draft of the theme for a play. The French novel *Le dernier homme* (1805) had been translated into English by 1806 under the title *Omegarus and Syderia, A Romance on Futurity in 1806*. The idea of a plague's dangers had been addressed in *Journal of the Plague Year* (1772), Daniel Defoe's journalistic account of the 1664-65 London plague, and in *Arthur Mervyn* (1799), Charles Brockden Brown's novel of pestilence-stricken Philadelphia. Shelley had read both Defoe's *Plague Year* and Brown's *Arthur Mervyn* in the spring and summer of 1817. For details on the last man theme, see

Morton D. Paley's "Mary Shelley's *The Last Man*: Apocalypse Without Millennium," *Keats-Shelley Review* 4 (1989), 1-25.

9. Lionel does speculate about the possibility of some survivors, however; see pages 318 and 339 in the text.

10. Mary Shelley more than likely had Edmund Kean in mind. She greatly admired him, and he was regarded as one of the finest tragic actors of the period.

11. See Joseph Donahue, *Theatre in the Age of Kean*, 180-181.

12. The parallels between Shelley's characters in this novel and Percy Shelley's in "Julian and Maddalo" (written 1818; published 1824) are striking: Raymond — Maddalo; Lionel — Julian; and Adrian — the maniac. The similarities suggest that Mary Shelley may have written this section of the novel in response to the issues her husband had raised.

13. After her husband's death, Mary Shelley used her journal to indulge her despair, loneliness, and bitterness. However, she seemed to have intended such writings to remain a private record, as her entry on 2 October 1822 suggests: "White paper — wilt thou be my confident? I will trust thee fully, for none shall see what I write" (*Journals,* 2: 429).

14. The author of the introduction provides this date for her expedition into the Sibyll's cave (1).

15. "The Triumph of Death: Reading and Narrative in Mary Shelley's *The Last Man*," in *Iconoclastic Departures: Mary Shelley after "Frankenstein,"* ed. Syndy M. Conger, Frederick S. Frank, and Gregory O'Dea (Madison: Fairleigh Dickinson University Press, 1997), 215.

Valperga: Theatrical Plots and Dramatic Intrigue

When we are born, we cry that we are come
To this great stage of fools.
— Shakespeare, *King Lear*

With both *Valperga; or, the Life and Adventures of Castruccio, Prince of Lucca* (1823) and *The Fortunes of Perkin Warbeck* (1830), Mary Shelley demonstrates her skill with the historical novel. Popularized by Sir Walter Scott and Jane Porter, this narrative type is characterized by an authentic past setting, usually in a time of conflict and change for dramatic effect, and by a storyline in which fictional characters interact with historical figures. By the time Shelley was writing *Valperga* in 1820, Scott had published several of his most successful romances: *Waverley* (1814), *Rob Roy* (1817), *The Heart of Midlothian* (1818), and *Ivanhoe* (1819). Although his works are perhaps the most recognized examples of historical fiction, Sophia Lee's *The Recess* (1783-85), Maria Edgeworth's *Castle Rackrent* (1800), Jane Porter's *The Scottish Chiefs* (1810), and William Godwin's *Mandeville* (1817) were other notable novels familiar to the early nineteenth-century reading public.[1]

Valperga and *Perkin Warbeck* are not the only examples of Mary Shelley's venture into this genre.[2] *The Last Man*, written between these two novels, incorporates conventions of the historical romance as well, despite its futuristic rather than past setting. Especially significant is her depiction of Lord Raymond, a public figure whose obsession with power and political ambition ultimately destroys him and his family. From 1823 to 1832, Shelley also wrote several short tales that are set during politically chaotic past times. "A Tale of the Passions" (1823), like *Valperga*, takes place in late thirteenth-century Italy during the Guelph and Ghibelline conflicts; "Ferdinado Eboli" (1828) is set during the Napoleonic wars; "The Swiss Peasant" (1830) features characters who struggle to find love during the French Revolution; and "The Brother and Sister: An Italian Story" (1832) returns us once again to political friction in northern Italy during the middle ages.

Lisa Hopkins observes that both Valperga and Perkin Warbeck depart from the historical narrative tradition of Scott and Porter: rather, Shelley "steers the historical novel toward historiography proper as she uses her text to challenge rather than reinforce the version of events that we think we know"[3] In both *Valperga* and *Perkin Warbeck*, Shelley indeed directs her readers to reconsider the idea — and the facts — of history as so often presented in chronicles. While working within the traditional historical romance conventions as well, Shelley finds a new way to focus the *theatrum mundi* metaphor. Rather than dwell exclusively on private individuals in fictitious events as she did in *Frankenstein* and *Mathilda*, Shelley chose to depict how a dramatic sensibility can affect national heroes and leaders in the public spotlight and how it affects their domestic life. She uses theatrical metaphors to denounce the self-serving roles the public figures perform and the false masks they don to achieve ambitious goals. They appropriate the world's stage to enact these roles, oblivious or unsympathetic to the self-deception and disintegration of private life that result.

In *Valperga*, Castruccio Castracani dei Antelminelli and Beatrice of Ferrara are victims of such ambition. They become so obsessed with one role that they will not or cannot function in any other capacity. Castruccio desires to be ruler, first of Lucca and eventually of Italy. Although entitled by birthright to such aspirations, he sacrifices his private life to his political goals, with great cost to himself and others. For him, the role of great leader is everything; life off the public stage is not worth living. The passionate, eloquent Beatrice defines herself solely through her roles as a prophet and as Castruccio's lover. When she can no longer play those parts, life becomes an empty stage for her. Like Lear, she ultimately rues that she ever came to "this great stage of fools." These characters' conscious theatrics also victimize others, especially ones who love them. The novel's central figure, Euthanasia dei Adimari, Countess of Valperga, resists adopting masks and roles until her people and principles become threatened. Unlike Castruccio, she does not see herself as the principal player in a self-created drama that she scripts herself, nor will she compromise her integrity or others' well-being for personal glory. Refusing to let the spotlight of the political stage blind her, Euthanasia does not succumb to self-deception.

Perhaps because this historical romance is written in the third person, the dramatic motif is less explicit than in Shelley's first-person narratives that feature characters constructing their life histories as tragic dramas. Nevertheless, *Valperga* employs the *theatrum mundi* metaphor through the language and perceptions of its characters who frequently refer to themselves as actors on the world's stage. Also, the novel's narrator, who functions as a chorus to address the audience/reader and to reflect philosophically on the events, often employs the metaphor herself.[4] Aware that the power of good story-telling lies in the story's dramatic potential, the narrator often presents the characters as actors and the action as scenes, a technique that enhances the theatricality of the narrative.

Mary Shelley first conceived of the idea of *Valperga* at Marlow, in the summer of 1817. Although Percy Shelley had encouraged her to write a drama, she decided to try an historical romance similar to ones by Porter and Scott (Sunstein, 138). After much reading and research, she began her novel in the spring of 1820, working on it for more than a year. "I get on with my occupation & hope to finish the rough transcript this month," Shelley wrote in a letter of 30 June 1821 to Maria Gisborne; "it has indeed been a child of mighty slow growth, since I first thought of it in our library at Marlow. . . . [It is] a work of some labour since I have read & consulted a great many books" (*Letters*, 1: 203). Initially, Shelley intended to title her work *Castruccio*, but Godwin suggested *Valperga*, after the name of Euthanasia's castle (Sunstein, 162). The revised title is more apt since Euthanasia, like many female protagonists of historical novels, quickly becomes the central figure. By November 1821, Shelley was correcting the novel and gave the fair copy to her father to arrange its publication (*Journals*, 1: 384, n. 1). Although Godwin edited out portions of "historical detail" that he felt hampered the action, he commented that the novel was more brilliant than *Frankenstein* (Sunstein, 235). The Shelleys had hoped that Ollier would buy *Valperga*; however, the publisher, about to go bankrupt, refused to pay the £400 requested, and in February 1823 G. and W. B. Whittaker published the novel.[5]

Recent critics often focus on the political issues in *Valperga*, and the novel does indeed reflect Mary Shelley's disdain for tyrannical governments and for oppressive social strictures that threaten individual freedom and happiness. For example, Jane Blumberg, who regards the novel as one of Shelley's best works, draws parallels between the turbulent fourteenth-century Italy and the nineteenth-century English Castlereagh government, which Shelley despised.[6] Anne Mellor examines how women, powerless in a patriarchal world, are unable "to influence political events or to translate an ethic of care . . . into historical reality" (*Mary Shelley*, 210). James P. Carson and Betty T. Bennett read *Valperga* as a liberal view to social reform.[7] So does Stuart Curran. Euthanasia, he writes, "represents conciliation rather than antagonism, peace instead of conflict. She thus stands for a liberal democratic alternative not just to Casturccio Castracani . . . but also to the war-weary Europe of the early nineteenth century and particularly to England."[8] However, Joseph Lew questions placing Mary Shelley in a liberal context; he suggests the novel reflects "rationality, domesticity, and selfless sympathy for others."[9]

Contemporary critics were also divided on the merits of the novel. Although the *La Belle Assemblée, or Court and Fashionable Magazine* and *The Examiner* highly recommended the work to their readers, *Blackwood's Edinburgh Magazine* regretted that Shelley did not focus solely on

Castruccio's character and was sidetracked by other incidents: "we cannot spare four days of the life of Castruccio Castracani to singers and tale-tellers, and so forth, with whom he and his story have nothing to do" (Review of *Valperga*, 284). *Blackwood's* critic missed the point: Shelley's novel suggests that recorded history often overlooks many significant events and human interest perspectives.[10] There is more to the story than Castruccio's political career, for not all history takes place in the public spotlight. Reviewers who praised the novel were generally more interested in its historic detail and depiction of characters and their passions. In *Valperga*, wrote *The London Literary Gazette's* critic in 1823, "it is not the events that interest us so much as the actors" (Review of *Valperga*, 132). The characters are indeed more memorable than the political and histori-cal details, significant and intriguing as these details are; their struggle with internal conflicts caused or exacerbated by the perception of the world as a stage and they as actors upon it is what lingers in the reader's mind long after the plot's particulars blur.

Valperga's third-person narrator reinforces the message the characters dramatize. In one sense, the narrator diminishes the dramatic effect of the novel by her obtrusive presence, redundant comments, and moral plati-tudes. On the other hand, she strengthens the *theatrum mundi* metaphor by her very reliance on it to depict the characters' perceptions of life and the conflict between public and private life. She reveals that she too sees life as a stage on which one plays out one's dreams, hopes, and aspirations. In describing Euthanasia's emotions following Beatrice's death, the narrator remarks: "By degrees however the feelings of actual life returned to her; and she longed to quit a town, which had been for her the theatre of tremendous misfortune."[11] Frequently she refers to the characters as actors: Castruccio is "about to act on the great theatre" (*Valperga*,1: 59); Tripalda is "an actor" in the crimes against Beatrice (*Valperga*, 3: 120); Euthanasia is fearful of "acting such a part" (*Valperga*, 3: 203). The night before the last rebellion against Castruccio by the Guelph Florentines, the narrator notes that the insurgent group met one last time to "determine the conduct of this last act of the tragedy" (*Valperga*, 3: 214). She often uses the word "scene" to emphasize the theatrical power of both the narrative's descrip-tion and the setting for the action: there are the "last scenes" of Pepi's life as he is slain and his castle ransacked by those in debt to him; the "scenes" that Beatrice witnesses during her dream-like imprisonment; the "scene" of Castruccio's last triumph (the siege of Florence) that entices Euthanasia to play a part in the Florentine plot against him; and the "scene" in Lucca (now a prison for all Guelphs) from which Euthanasia wishes to flee (*Valperga*, 2: 117; 3: 121; 3: 191; 3: 215, respectively). In each of these examples and many others, the narrator's vivid description and use of dia-logue shows rather than merely tells the characters' experiences.

Just as the narrator dramatizes her story, so too the characters dramatize their lives, perceiving themselves as actors on the world's stage. Castruccio Castracani dei Antelminelli was born into a Ghibelline[12] family and quickly rose to power during Italy's turbulent fourteenth century. Shelley researched his history in many sources, including Sismondi's *Histoire des républiques italiennes du Moyen-Âge* and Tegrino's *Life of Castruccio*. Despite altering the dates and the few personal facts then known, Shelley is faithful to most of the events of the actual Castruccio's life.[13] However, true to the form of historical novels, Shelley's work accurately reflects the time period while focusing on domestic events that are typically excluded from factual chronicles.

In his early childhood Castruccio experienced first-hand the devastating effects of the power struggle between the Guelphs and Ghibellines. The once powerful Antelminelli family, Luccan Ghibellines, were exiled when Castruccio was a child, and the proud young Castruccio resents the poverty and obscurity they endure. This experience, coupled with his undisciplined sensibility, encourages the youth to pursue his dreams of vindicating his family's name and of achieving glory as a Ghibelline leader. For the embittered young Castruccio, the world is indeed a stage, and he intends to be a major player on it. After the deaths of his father and mother, he journeys to visit his father's friend, Guinigi, formerly a noted general, who is now quite content to farm and enjoy the tranquillity of private life. Castruccio is astounded that Guinigi has no desire for fame and political power. A youth of seventeen who remembers too well the events that had destroyed his family's fortune, Castruccio exhibits the pride and ambition that will be his eventual downfall: "Imagination, ever at work, pictured his future life, brilliant with glowing love, transcendant with glory and success. Thus, in solitude, while no censuring eye could check the exuberant vanity, he would throw his arms to the north, the south, the east, and the west, crying, — "There — there — there, and there, shall my fame reach!" — and then, in gay defiance, casting his eager glance towards heaven: — "and even there, if man may climb the slippery sides of the arched palace of eternal fame, there also will I be recorded" (*Valperga*,1: 42-43). This vivid scene depicts Castruccio's view of the world (and possibly heaven as well) as a stage for his life's performance. With such passionate ambition, Castruccio not surprisingly considers life with the unassuming Guinigi in the rural countryside tedious; he had expected to find an active knight, not a "contented farmer, a peasant whose narrow views soared not beyond the wine-vat and the ox's stall" (*Valperga*,1: 48). Unlike the eager boy who imagines only the greatness of war, Guinigi deplores the endless battles that plague Italy and recognizes the "false halo of glory" (*Valperga*,1: 49). Realizing Castruccio's disappointment, he tries to reassure the young boy: "You come to the dwelling of a peasant who eats the bread of [sic] his own hands have sown; this is a new scene for you, but you will not find it unin-structive" (*Valperga*, 1: 47).

However, still desiring fame and glory, Castruccio cannot appreciate the humanistic teachings of Guinigi, and he rejects living unknown as an "ignoble youth." As he tells his father's friend, "You have passed through life, and know what it is; but I would rather, while alive, enter my tomb, than live unknown and unheard of. Is it not fame that makes men gods? Do not urge me to pass my days in indolence; I must act, to be happy,–to be anything" (*Valperga*, 1: 54). Note again the echo of Victor Frankenstein, who rhetorically asks, "Is it not fame that makes men gods?" In the above passage from *Valperga*, "act" denotes taking action, being active rather than still; however, it also implies a theatrical context, especially when one examines Castruccio's choice of words in other passages. Riding with Guinigi to Venice, Castruccio "dreamed of futurity; and the uncertainty of his destiny only gave more scope to his imagination, as he figured the glo-rious part which he flattered himself he was about to act on the great the-atre" (*Valperga*, 1: 59). His pride, ambition, and desire for revenge require that he perform his life on the public stage; a quiet private existence, like that of Guinigi, who "thought only of the duty of man to man" (*Valperga*, 1: 48), is not for one such as Castruccio, who imagines himself to be the future prince of Lucca. To Castruccio, the public history of one's life is what essentially defines one's existence; the private history of those like Guinigi matters little in the chronicles of human achievement.

The narrator, however, questions Castruccio's goals: "would he not have been happier, if they had failed, and he, in blameless obscurity, had sunk with the millions that compose the nations of the earth, into the vast ocean of oblivion?" (*Valperga*, 1: 43).[14] The narrator is not so naive as to suppose that one should never strive for political leadership, but she does question the motive. Castruccio's reasons are not grounded in justice, but in revenge and desire for fame and power. The young Luccan shows no inclination toward compromise for the good of Italy, as Euthanasia does; his ideology, and no other, must prevail. He and those around him would have been hap-pier had he moderated his ambition with sympathy and recognized that life can be as fully lived off the public stage as well as on it.

Through Guinigi's connections in Venice, Castruccio finds that he has a relative in England and journeys there. He is amazed with Edward I's court: "the animated picture which Atawel [Guinigi's friend] drew of the discontent and turbulence of the English barons, although it would have excited terror in these quiet times, delighted Castruccio, as affording a hope of having now found a fitting stage on which he might commence his active career" (*Valperga*,1: 70). England, however, would not be the stage for his initiation. Losing his temper, Castruccio kills an insulting English nobleman with his stiletto and is forced to flee. Back on the continent, he meets Alberto Scoto, a notorious commander of mercenary Italian troops for the French king, Philip le Bel. Scoto sows "the seeds of craft," instructing Castruccio "to understand and meditate the part he should act, when he returned to [Italy]" (*Valperga,* 1: 94). The narrator, however, warns that "Scoto's was an evil school," known for its artifice and hypocrisy. As such, it only fuels Castruccio's ambitious plans, directing him to a path that his father and Guinigi had rejected.

By the time Castruccio is a young adult, he is decidedly adept as a versatile performer on life's stage and is able to change direction with the political wind in order to accomplish his goals. The narrator assures us that, although not an evil person, Castruccio does not let people or ethics stand in his way: "Castruccio was fond of power; yet he was neither arrogant nor tyrannical; words of kindness and winning smiles he bestowed at will on all around. He appeared to fit himself for each scene in which he was to take a part" (*Valperga,* 1: 162). He has clearly learned much from his experiences in London, with Scoto, and in Henry's army,[15] and he is able to adopt a dramatic mask at will: "His face expressed extreme frankness, a frankness that did not exist in his mind" (*Valperga,*1: 163). Even before attaining his powerful position as prince of Lucca, Castruccio has become a skilled actor so obsessed with his role that he can no longer separate the drama that he has envisioned from the much larger and greater action of life itself.

Castruccio views other characters as performers as well. After telling Beatrice, his one-time lover, that he must go back to Euthanasia, he rationalizes his actions: "we part for a while;–this is necessary. Does not your character require it? the part you act in the world?" (*Valperga,* 2: 95). To Castruccio, the public roles that they each play, he as a Ghibelline leader and she as a prophet, take precedence over their personal relationship. Also, Castruccio finds this public duty a convenient excuse to extricate himself from an uncomfortable predicament with Beatrice, who views their relationship as one established by God. Another character, the evil, self-serving Benedetto Pepi, whom even Castruccio despises, sees himself as an actor in life's drama. Meeting him at his home to learn what Pepi has long wished to show him, Castruccio "wondered what new scene a being, whom he considered as half a buffoon, and half a madman, intended to act" (*Valperga,* 2: 104). Before he shows Castruccio the trunk full of bonds and titles that he had cheated out of his neighbors, even Pepi reveals his own theatrical perception, pleading with Castruccio to "not disdain to act a friendly part" (*Valperga,* 2: 106).

Castruccio continues to play the ambitious leader. He plots the murder of the King of Naples and vengefully exiles Guelph families from Lucca. As the narrator remarks with Machiavellian echoes, "He became all in all to himself; his creed seemed to contain no article but the end and aim of his ambition" (*Valperga,* 2: 171). He cannot restrain his desires to maintain his relationship with Euthanasia, and he expects her to renounce her hope for a peaceful, unified Italy in order to further his glory. By the time Castruccio decides to destroy Valperga and deny Euthanasia her heritage, his metamorphosis into a Prince worthy of Machiavelli's description is complete.[16] True, he cannot bring himself to put Euthanasia to death with the other conspirators; however, Castruccio renounces the last of any humanity that may have existed within him by exiling her to Sicily. He has become a one-dimensional representation of ambition, an actor who can only play one role in life's drama.

Mary Shelley had visited the gravesite of the actual Castruccio, probably in the fall of 1820, a trip she recommended to the Hunts in an 1823 letter: "If you have time you can go to the Church of San Franceno . . . half way up the aisle on the right hand side you will see on the wall a slab to the memory of Castruccio & underneath this newer one the little old one which contains the inscription I have quoted" (*Letters,* 1: 364). Shelley quotes the inscription in Italian at the very end of her novel: "Behold I live and will live, the fame of Italian history, the splendor of war, the glory of Lucca, the ornament of Etruria, Castruccio from the line of Gerius and Antelminelli. I have lived, I have sinned, I have grieved. I have yielded to demanding nature. You who wish well, come to the aid of a pious soul. You who are about to die, for a brief moment remember me" (*Letters,* 1: 365, n. 1, trans. Betty T. Bennett). Shelley's re-creation of the Luccan prince accurately depicts his primary concern for being remembered as a great leader, the "fame of Italian history," and an "ornament" of his family and country. Even those about to die should, in their last moments, remember him.

Shelley's Castruccio (and quite likely the historical one as well) so desires a public role to gain entrance into the history books that he cannot fathom why those such as Guinigi and Euthanasia do not share his ambition. He does not recognize that such fame often denies one a complete history — that which includes the private as well as the public. Shelley offered her version of that complete history with *Valperga.* For that reason, she disappointed the *Blackwood's* critic who bemoaned her focus on the private lives of both the novel's historical and fictional characters. The action off the stage and behind the scenes of public life furnishes that complete history. Perhaps that is why the narrator concludes with these lines: "The private chronicles, from which the foregoing relation has been collected, end with the death of Euthanasia. It is therefore in public histories alone that we find an account of the last years of the life of Castruccio" (*Valperga,* 3: 263). Yet those public records are inadequate for knowing a complete history, which the narrator makes a point of telling us: "We can know nothing of his grief, when he found that she whom he had once tenderly loved, and whom he had ever revered as the best and wisest friends, had died" (*Valperga,* 3: 263). To emphasize her argument, the narrator refrains from supplying those details and concludes Castruccio's last years in a few pages.

She recognizes what Castruccio cannot: that the real story or drama of one's life is off the public stage; that life requires we play many roles; and that obsession with one role can result in a sterile, flat existence that ultimately has little significance in the scheme of things. And so, to this "great stage of fools," Castruccio came to perform his self-assigned part.

Another powerful political character who adopts roles to accommodate his selfish desires is Battista Tripalda, a pivotal player in Castruccio's ensemble. Like Alberto Scoto, Benedetto Pepi, and ultimately Castruccio, Tripalda represents a trait of human nature that Mary Shelley found deplorable: willful deception of trusting people. In *Frankenstein*, *Mathilda*, and *The Last Man*, Shelley portrays a self-delusion that occurred through good, albeit misdirected, intentions. In *Valperga* and later in *Perkin Warbeck*, she denounces those who willfully assume a mask that deceives in order to accomplish selfish and usually immoral goals. Such artifice, dangerous enough for Victor or Mathilda, becomes villainous in the likes of a Scoto and Tripalda.

Once a canon of a church in Perugia, Tripalda now seeks a living among Luccan nobility, although no one likes or trusts him. A master actor, Tripalda is adept at masking his motives and character from others. Like a chameleon, he changes appearance to suit the surroundings: "when he became familiar with his new friends, he cast off his modest disguise, and appeared vain, presumptuous and insolent" (*Valperga*, 2: 240). Like an actor, Tripalda is skillful in performing various characters, slipping easily into one persona after another. The narrator compares him to a fairy-tale dwarf, who may appear to be "small and impotent" but can take the "form of tremendous giants" (*Valperga*, 2: 240). Even Euthanasia is at first taken in by him, but the narrator excuses her misjudgment: Tripalda "had not yet thrown off his mask of humility and virtue, which he ever wore on his first appearance on a new scene" (*Valperga*, 2: 241).

Tripalda's past has been a mystery, and part of that past seems to have been associated with the bizarre experience the prophet Beatrice once had as a prisoner in the strange house outside of Rome. Recovering in Lucca, Beatrice experienced a setback after seeing Tripalda: "from what she said in her delirium, it might be gathered, that he had been an actor in the frightful wrongs she had endured during her strange imprisonment in the Compagne di Roma" (*Valperga*,3: 120). Although we can only speculate about the role Tripalda played, there is little doubt that it was one of deception. His influence notwithstanding, Tripalda's trickery wins him few friends in Lucca. Mordecastelli, a close aid of Castruccio, is repulsed by the ex-priest's double dealings even though Tripalda has provided vital information to the Ghibellines. When Tripalda approaches Mordecastelli to reveal the Guelph plot in which Euthanasia has played a role,[17] Mordecastelli recalls a similar occasion: "I remember well the detestable part that you then played, and it had been well that your head had been struck off instead of Leodino's" (*Valperga*, 3: 220).[18] Tripalda, Scoto, and Castruccio sharply contrast with other Ghibellines such as Arrigo (Guinigi's son) and Mordecastelli who, though politically aligned with Castruccio, do not succumb to hypocritical artifice and masks; they are honest and forthright, the exterior façade no different from the person within.

Another prominent actor in this drama is Beatrice of Ferrara, who may be Mary Shelley's most disturbing and intriguing character next to Frankenstein's monster. She falls victim not only to self-delusion but also to the expectations and whims of others. Born to the heretic Wilhelmina of Bohemia[19] and raised by the Bishop of Ferrara and his sister, Beatrice is regarded by many in the city as a prophet. An eloquent speaker, she is able to command a crowd's attention through her delivery and presence and is often consulted by Ghibelline leaders in planning strategy. Castruccio becomes acquainted with her while in Ferrara to gain support for his struggle against the Guelph stronghold in Florence. Meeting with the Bishop, he sees Beatrice and is taken by her beauty and mysticism. At Castruccio's request, the Bishop relates Beatrice's history and admits how much he loves her as a daughter. Awed by her abilities, he tells Castruccio that he is nevertheless skeptical of her professing to be God's chosen one, attributing her prophetic faculty to imagination rather than to divine revelation: "Beatrice herself is wrapt up in the belief of her own exalted nature, and really thinks herself the *Ancilla Dei*, the chosen vessel into which God has poured a portion of his spirit: she preaches, she prophesies, she sings extempore hymns, and entirely fullfilling the part of *Donna Estatica*, she passes many hours of each day in solitary meditation, or rather in dreams, to which her active imagination gives a reality and life which confirm her in her mistakes" (*Valperga*, 2: 43).[20] Although Castruccio and the Bishop doubt Beatrice's divine powers, she herself does not. When challenged by the Inquisition and forced to undergo the *Judgement of God*, a bizarre spectacle that forced one to walk through burning ploughshares, Beatrice exhibits no trepidation. Castruccio had begged the Bishop to take her away the evening before the public display, but the Bishop knows she will not leave: "willingly she will never consent to desert the high character she has chosen to assume," he warns Castruccio (*Valperga*, 2: 52). His choice of words is significant, implying that Beatrice is complicit with regard to her self-delusion and interprets her actions as a role she must play. She has chosen this "high character" — of prophet — and her imagination has constructed a dream-world, a personal drama, that will inevitably clash with the actual world. Beatrice becomes even more sure of her power when she "passes" the test that, unknown to her, has been rigged by the Bishop and others so that she would not be burned.

Fed by her imagination and by the well-intentioned but misguided machinations of others, Beatrice presumes that her love for Castruccio is blessed and directed by God: "She prayed to the Virgin to inspire her; and, again giving herself up to reverie, she wove a subtle web, whose materials she believed heavenly, but which were indeed stolen from the glowing wings of love. . . . These were her dreams,–alas! to her they were realities" (*Valperga*, 2: 80). The narrator stresses several times that Beatrice cannot distinguish dream from reality; regarding herself to be a "divine vessel," the young woman assumes that her desires must also be God's. Despite this powerful delusion, or perhaps because of it, Beatrice is conscious of her theatrical experience and knows how to use it to achieve her wishes. Like an actress, she rehearses how she will confess and offer her love to Castruccio: "She had framed the mode of her address, conned and reconned the words she should say" (*Valperga*, 2: 81). Her skill as a performer before eager crowds has been honed for years, and, although she appears to believe in the divine inspiration, her rehearsal of the scene suggests an artificial behavior that supersedes any supernatural directive. Castruccio's ultimate rejection of her as a lover nearly destroys Beatrice, who is then forced to question not only her power but also her part in life's drama. No longer able to play the role of prophet, Beatrice finds herself at a loss without a self-identity. As she later tells Euthanasia, "unsupported by my supernatural powers, I now shrunk from all display; no veil, no wall could conceal me sufficiently; for it could not hide me from myself" (*Valperga*, 3: 72). A self-created drama fed by vivid imagination can be as disastrous as one fueled by ambition, and an obsessive egocentricity too often leads to self-delusion rather than self-knowledge. Once stripped of her role, Beatrice is forced to see herself for what she is: a mortal woman with no divine powers.[21] Mary Shelley may very well have recalled her husband's description of Beatrice Cenci for her character: "The crimes and miseries in which she was an actor and a sufferer are as the mask and the mantle in which circumstances clothed her for her impersonation on the scene of the world" (Preface, "The Cenci," *Shelley's Poetry and Prose*, 242).

We do not hear about Beatrice's fate after the fiasco at Ferrara until the third volume. Although she visited Euthanasia at Valperga disguised as a pilgrim, her history since Ferrara is not revealed until she is discovered nearly dead, imprisoned as a Paterin in a Luccan jail.[22] Released into Euthanasia's care, Beatrice relates her story; "for five years," she tells her new friend, "my life has been one scene of despair: you cannot tell what a fall mine was" (*Valperga*, 3: 42). The "fall" refers to more than the theatrical staging at Ferrara, and the word "scene" understates the ordeals she has since encountered. A wanderer and outcast, Beatrice encounters horrific experiences that, more real than any of her prophetic powers, seem a dream or "scene of despair" that turns into reality as she is drugged and enslaved in a place she describes as a "dreary, large, ruinous house, half like a castle, yet without a tower, dilapidated, and overgrown with moss" (*Valperga*, 3: 82).

Although historically accurate for such places during this period of Italian history, this description recalls settings in Gothic novels as well. Beatrice's reaction is not unlike that of Emily St. Aubert upon seeing Udolpho for the first time: "Emily gazed with melancholy awe upon the castle . . for, though it was now lighted up by the setting sun, the gothic greatness of its features, and its mouldering walls of dark grey stone, rendered it a gloomy and sublime object. . . . Silent, lonely and sublime, it seemed to stand the sovereign of the scene, and to frown defiance on all, who dared to invade its solitary reign. As the twilight deepened, its features became more awful in obscurity" (Radcliffe, *Mysteries of Udolpho*, 226-27).[23] Like Emily, Beatrice is shaken by the recalled vision of her prison, seeing her dream come alive before her eyes: "I came to that scene; if I live, I did! I saw it all as I had before seen it in the slumbers of the night. Great God, what am I?" (*Valperga*, 3: 83). She reveals enough particulars about her three-year experience imprisoned in "the carnival of devils" to make Euthanasia shudder. Freed when the Church destroyed the house and its satanic leader, Beatrice became a wanderer again until rescued by a kindly old Paterin man who "restored" her reason. Peacefulness, however, is short-lived as the heretical man is burned at the stake and Beatrice is imprisoned.

Like Victor Frankenstein, Beatrice perceives her life as a literary construct. As she narrates her history since leaving Ferrara, she refers to her life as a tale several times. She apologizes to Euthanasia for "dwelling on the particulars of my tale" and confesses that her experience is "a tale for the unhallowed ears of infidels" (*Valperga*, 3: 85). Beatrice not only displays an effective narrative skill to elicit audience sympathy and to justify her actions, but she also dramatizes the telling with theatrical analogies. Events are "scenes," microcosms of actions within the drama of her life. She objectifies herself, using the third person as if she were merely a character. For example, she tells Euthanasia that "the vain, self-sufficing, cloud-inhabiting Beatrice was in truth a poor dependent creature" (*Valperga*, 3: 78). To the witch, Fior di Mandragola, Beatrice suggests that she herself becomes as a character in her dreams: "when this dream comes over me, as it now does, I am no longer myself" (*Valperga*, 3: 131).

Beatrice also characterizes others as actors. When she recuperates enough to walk about Lucca, she recognizes Battista Tripalda, who "had been an actor in the frightful wrongs she had endured during her strange imprisonment in the Compagne di Roma" (*Valperga*, 3: 120). Furthermore, Beatrice is destined to live her life as an actor. Unable to manage her powerful imagination without a public role to play, she becomes an easy target for Mandragola, who is determined to end Castruccio's power. The setting for the witch's revenge, a "woody amphitheatre, an open space in the midst of the trees" (*Valperga,* 3: 149), highlights the enacting of the dramatic scene. However, the theatrical plan backfires on Mandragola, as Beatrice, near madness, is caught up in the action. Like a tragic heroine, she places herself in Castruccio's way: "Beatrice threw herself on her knees, in the midst of the path by which they must pass; with flashing eyes and out-stretched arms, she gazed eagerly forwards: the dark wood covered her; the moon beams fell on her; and there she, once the loveliest, now the most lost, the most utterly undone of women, kneeled in frantic expectation" (*Valperga,* 3: 154). Note the narrator's theatrical description: the "dark wood," "the moon," the "flashing eyes and outstretched arms"–such images recall scenes from a Gothic melodrama. Rendered insensible by the sight of Castruccio and Tripalda, Beatrice never regains sense and dies a few days later. Perhaps the elaborate public funeral Castruccio gives Beatrice is a fitting end for one who believed her life had meaning only when defined in the role as a divinely ordained prophet and consort.

Euthanasia, however, feels that Beatrice's funeral should have been "private and unnoticed" (*Valperga,* 3: 163). Her views regarding the public ritual reflect the Countess's ambivalence toward the public limelight. Euthanasia rejects playing roles that compromise integrity and that demand a mask to disguise the self to the public. She disdains performances and artifice. As a Guelph leader and as the Countess of Valperga, she is aware that duty and responsibility to her subjects may conflict with personal desires. Although a prominent figure, she values everyone on her estate. She also recognizes the difficulties in maintaining her Guelph political affiliation when she is the fiancee of a Ghibelline. If the world is a stage, Euthanasia would argue that "man in his time plays many parts," some of which are indeed enacted for a public audience. However, the danger is obsession with a role that privileges fame and denies the drama played out in the private sphere.

Unlike Castruccio, who is adept at masks and concealment, Euthanasia is open and honest; her image projects her character. Despite her public position as a Guelph and a Countess, Euthanasia disdains the spotlight and is sincerely interested in the unheroic acts of everyday life. She would agree with Guinigi that living life is more fulfilling than playing it on stage and that often a self-centered drama creates an illusion with no basis in reality. In her personal narrative to Castruccio, Euthanasia demonstrates her out-wardly-directed sensibility and sincere concern for peace and the well-being of the Italian peoples. Like Elizabeth Lavenza, she focuses on others rather than herself. Her "history" is actually a philosophical treatise on liberty and freedom rather than a self-centered autobiography. Recounting the education in Roman and Greek classics that her father gave her, Euthanasia explains to Castruccio how important liberty and freedom are to her, and she credits her father with teaching her to blend wisdom and compassion: "But he, whether he taught me to consider the world and the community of man, or to study the little universe of my own mind, was wisdom's self, pouring out accents that commanded attention and obedience" (*Valperga*, 1: 198). Castruccio's and Euthanasia's views of history are markedly different. She sees history as a continuum, with each individual's actions contributing to the drama of human existence: "She did not acquire that narrow idea of the present times, as if they and the world were the same, which characterizes the unlearned; she saw and marked the revolutions that had been, and the present seemed to her only a point of rest, from which time was to renew his flight, scattering change as he went; and, if her voice or act could mingle aught of good in these changes, this it was to which her imagination most ardently aspired" (*Valperga*, 1: 28-29). For Castruccio, however, history is a series of disparate, discrete acts defined by the accomplishments of great figures who achieve a place in the "arched palace of eternal fame" (*Valperga*, 1: 42-43).

Euthanasia's father warned her about letting passions rule her, a maxim she prided herself on following. Forthright and open, Euthanasia assumes that Castruccio behaves the same way towards her. She trusts his veiled promise not to attack or invade Florence, the stronghold of Guelphs. Because she herself cannot practice deception, she assumes he is unable to either, at least until the crafty Galeazzo plants doubt in her mind. Pretending to think that Euthanasia is privy to Castruccio's plans, Galeazzo reveals just enough to make her question her future husband's former promise. Yet, like Mary Hays' Emma Courtney and Mary Wollstonecraft's Maria, she has created an image of the man whom she desperately wants to exist. During their re-acquaintance as adults and then their courtship, Euthanasia forgets her father's words and allows passion to rule: "she was penetrated with love; and, admiration and esteem forming but a part of this, she made a god of him she loved, believing every virtue and every talent to live in his soul" (*Valperga*, 1: 189). The narrator further notes that Euthanasia "separated the object of her love from all other beings, and, investing him with a glory, he was no longer to her as one among the common herd" (*Valperga*, 2: 191-192). The love she has for Castruccio certainly has merit in its sincerity, but it compromises her objectivity to recognize that one such as he, with ambition for glory on the public stage, would unlikely abandon that goal for the quiet life of those who never appear as heroes in history. After Galeazzo's words, Euthanasia tries to justify Castruccio's plan — what Galeazzo referred to, she rationalizes, is a unified Italy in which Guelphs and Ghibellines are at peace. However, she is soon convinced that such is not the case.

When Euthanasia finds her principles threatened and her duty as a public figure challenged, she too must assume a role in the political intrigue, though she despises such subterfuge. She first considers what to do after Galeazzo's unfair trick: "her mind was too much disturbed to know immediately what part to take" (*Valperga*, 2: 130). After she breaks off their relationship, the Luccan prince unfairly accuses her of being in league with Florentine Guelphs who are trying to depose him. Although she abhors his actions, Euthanasia assures Castruccio that she is no traitor to him: "My lord, your mistake would be pardonable, had you not known me long enough to be assured that I am incapable of acting the part you attribute to me" (*Valperga*, 2: 211). Castruccio is so accustomed to masking his feelings and motives that he cannot fathom someone's inability or unwillingness to do the same, and he claims that Euthanasia has "acted a treasonable part" (*Valperga*, 2: 221). The role he expects her to play should be in his drama and for his ambitious desires; when she does not, he considers her a traitor.

Thoroughly disillusioned by Castruccio's latest attack on Florence, Euthanasia agrees to the Florentine Guelphs's plan to oust Castruccio from power. Although she is motivated by the promise that no harm will come to him if she aids the plotters, she also recognizes that his atrocities can no longer continue. The country is being ravaged, and the people are devastated. The narrator's choice of words reveals that Euthanasia is an unwilling actor in the political plot although she supports the goals: "With this matured judgement and depth of feeling, she was called upon to take an arduous part in a most doubtful and perilous undertaking" (*Valperga*, 3: 196). Despite reservations, Euthanasia goes to Lucca "to take the part allotted to her" (*Valperga*, 3: 202). A sense of theatricality pervades the plot itself, and the characters become caught up in the intrigue's drama, referring to themselves as actors. Yet Euthanasia is still unconvinced that she is doing the right thing: "it appeared to her that in acting such a part she would have merited the disapprobation of mankind" (*Valperga*, 3: 203). The narrator suggests that Euthanasia worries about the appearances of her actions and experiences a conflict regarding the mask she must assume, the role she must play, the deceit she must practice to accomplish a desired goal. To end what she despises — the horrible wars and destruction — she must do what her enemy, once her lover, does: adopt a role to deceive. Protesting Tripaldi's involvement with the plot, Euthanasia tells Bondelmonti: "I hope no false view, no veiled passion, misleads me now, when I most desire to act well, justly towards others, and towards myself" (*Valperga*, 3: 201). She recognizes that she too has become Machiavellian by hoping the end may justify the means.

In addition to characters perceiving themselves as actors, several very theatrical events reinforce the dramatic style of the novel. Castruccio witnesses one such exhibition as a young man. A traveller had told him in Ancona that "a strange and tremendous spectacle would be exhibited [in Florence] on the first of May of that year. . . . Preparations were made to exhibit Hell, such as it had been described in a poem now writing [sic] by Dante Alighieri, a part of which had been read, and had given rise to the undertaking" (*Valperga*, 1: 17). Perhaps responding to his own theatrical tendencies, Castruccio rides to Florence to observe the dramatization of Dante's *Inferno*. The spectators have positioned themselves on a quay and a bridge. The area around them, including the Arno river, is an eerie stage setting depicting Hell:

> [The Arno] was covered by boats, on which scaffoldings were erected, hung with black cloth, whose accumulated drapery lent life to the flames, which the glare of day would otherwise have eclipsed. In the midst of these flames moved legions of ghastly and distorted shapes, some with horns of fire, and hoofs, and horrible wings; others the naked representatives of the souls in torment; mimic shrieks burst on the air, screams and demoniac laughter. The infernal drama was acted to the life; and the terrible effect of such a scene was enhanced, by the circumstance of its being no more than an actual representation of what then existed in the imagination of the spectators, endued with the vivid colours of a faith inconceivable in these lethargic days. (*Valperga*, 1: 20)

The effect is so powerful, the narrator tells us, that Castruccio "felt a chill of horror run through his frame; the scene before him appeared for a moment as a reality, rather than a representation" (*Valperga*, 1: 20). Then suddenly, he experiences the same uncanny merging of life and art that Lionel Verney does watching *Macbeth*: the illusion becomes a reality of horror as the bridge collapses, killing many and causing an incredible commotion in the streets of Florence. At first, Castruccio tries to help, "seized with a superstitious dread, which rebuked [him] for having mimicked the dreadful mysteries of their religion" (*Valperga*, 1: 21). Then he runs, feeling as though he has escaped from hell to heaven. He cannot help but think–"what if I had been on that bridge?" The theatrical re-enactment warns us and an unheeding Castruccio that representation can all too often become a reality for which one is unprepared. The message is not unlike the one Victor Frankenstein learns: some things are not for us to know or perform.

Another theatrical event is Beatrice's *Judgement of God* trial initiated by the Inquisition that challenges her claim to be a divine prophet. Like the Inferno scene Castruccio witnessed in Florence, this spectacle demonstrates the hypocrisy and delusion associated with misguided theatrics: "The square presented a busy, but awful scene; the houses, the windows of the monastery, the walls of the convent, were covered by people; some clinging to the posts, and to the walls; fixing their feet upon small protuberances of stone, they hung there, as if they stood on air. A large part of the square had been railed off in a semicircle round the door of the monastery, and outside this the people were admitted, while it was guarded on the inside by Gascon soldiers, that with drawn swords kept in awe the eager spectators, whose fury of hope and fear approached madness" (*Valperga*, 2: 57-8). As she did in *Frankenstein* with the creature's observing the De Lacey family through the proscenium-like chink in his hovel, Mary Shelley again creates a theatrical setting. The town has essentially become a theater: the roped-off square is the stage, and the townspeople are the spectators who position themselves at various levels to observe the action. This spectacle, dramatic in its own right, reinforces the dangers of illusions that people willingly create or are unknowingly tricked by. Beatrice and the spectators believe in the test; after all, Beatrice has walked the burning path and proven herself divine. They are deluded through the machinations of the Bishop and monk who, to save face (and Beatrice), have rigged the display. Exuberant, Beatrice is set up for the inevitable downfall when Castruccio rejects her love and when she later learns the truth of the test.

There is yet another theatrical display worth noting: the court that Euthanasia holds following her engagement to Castruccio. Such an event was not uncommon for nobility, but why, as a contemporary critic asked,[24] did Mary Shelley devote two lengthy chapters to the court? Arguments can be made for a variety of reasons: to add realism regarding the nobility's way of life or to detail the scenery of the Tuscany region which Shelley so dearly loved. However, part of the court's activities also reinforces the theatrical motif. On the second day, the storytellers and actors direct the entertainment. An amphitheater had been built, and on it is acted the story of Troilus and Cressida, which ironically reverses the roles of Castruccio and Euthanasia.[25] Unlike Cressida, Euthanasia remains true to her lover, at least until his actions prove him unworthy of her.[26] Castruccio is the unfaithful one, indulging his physical passion for Beatrice and subordinating his love for Euthanasia to achieve his ambitions. Telling and enacting stories indeed were a common court custom during this time; however, Shelley's inclusion of this custom, detailed as it is, emphasizes the unsettling boundary between art and life, a boundary that her characters cannot always define to separate the representation and the reality.

Although Mary Shelley positioned *Valperga* in the historical romance tradition, she still used conventions associated with Romantic/Gothic drama and fiction, especially with regard to settings. The dramatic productions of works by writers such as Joanna Baillie, Matthew Gregory Lewis, and Charles Robert Maturin employed vivid and elaborate backdrops to reinforce the theme: the ominous Gothic house or castle with its labyrinthine passages represented evil and disorientation; the waterfall suggested mutability; and the dark woods signified the unknown. Such settings were, of course, the mainstay of the dark Romantic tradition with which Shelley was so familiar and which echoes throughout *Valperga*. Beatrice's ordeal in the house of evil recalls Radcliffe's *Udolpho*, and her imprisonment in Lucca invokes the horror experienced by Lewis's Agnes in the catacombs of Ambrosio's monastery. Valperga's beautiful waterfall and precipice indeed suggest the mutability of human relationships: they provide the background for Castruccio's proposal to Euthanasia and later the means for his men to secretly storm her castle. The novel's affinities with the more Gothic-like historical romances, such as Scott's *The Bride of Lammermoor*, cannot be overlooked either: both Valperga castle and the mysterious house recall Wolf's Crag Tower, and the raven and Kelpie maiden at the well reveal omens as dark as those of Mandragola. Although literary as well as stage devices, these settings and motifs are inherently dramatic, providing recognized conventions to enhance the novel's theatricality.

In *Valperga*, Shelley continues exploration of the *theatrum mundi* motif established in her first two novels. She alters her approach by focusing on the masks and conscious deception many of the novel's characters employ, a strategy that she would return to again in *Perkin Warbeck*. What remains consistent is her vehement assertion that playing roles is all too often destructive, fueling the Romantic ego to embrace an existence that privileges the public by reducing or denying the private. Shelley laments not only the poignant physical death of Euthanasia, but also the tragic symbolic one. Euthanasia, the narrator tells us, was later forgotten; only nature mourned for her loss as she "slept in the oozy cavern of the ocean" (*Valperga*, 3: 261). Shelley wanted to rectify this oversight of such characters. James P. Carson rightly observes that Valperga "delineates a type of history that while less public, may be more useful and more true than 'general' history" (173). Historian Diane Owen Hughes, writes Ann Frank Wake, "suggests that women's exclusion from public life became a function of the narrative constructions of the histories themselves."[27] We could add their exclusion from public record as well. That Shelley privileges her heroine's history over Castruccio's is evident by her decision to close the history with her death: Euthanasia's last days constitute the final chapter; Castruccio's comprise merely the brief epithetic conclusion. Like *Frankenstein*, *Valperga* is also a frame tale of sorts. Within Victor's narrative as told to Walton are the histories of the creature and the De Laceys, whose lives contrast sharply with Victor's and Walton's. Within the tale of the historical Castruccio's political deeds are embedded the fictional biographies of Beatrice and Euthanasia, representative of figures who quite likely were part of this drama but whose roles were cut from the history chronicles. Both Victor and Castruccio would have perceived the respective novels as texts about themselves; Mary Shelley, however, denies them the center stage. Their stories, she asserts, are merely decorative frames for the inner ones about characters whose lives will never appear in historical accounts of conquerors, leaders, and heroes; nevertheless, those lives are worth the telling.

Chapter 6 Notes

1. Shelley records having read these Scott novels, excepting *The Heart of Midlothian*, during the years of 1817 to 1820, and Edgeworth's *Castle Rackrent* in 1816. She was familiar with works by Sophia Lee and Jane Porter, although there is no conclusive evidence that she read either *The Recess* or *The Scottish Chiefs*.

2. Betty T. Bennett analyzes how Shelley used the historical genre to depict her belief that history is a conflict between freedom and tyranny in "The Political Philosophy of Mary Shelley's Historical Novels: *Valperga* and *Perkin Warbeck*," in *The Evidence of the Imagination: Studies of Interactions Between Life and Art in English Romantic Literature*, ed. Donald H. Reiman et al (New York: New York University Press, 1978), 354-71; hereafter cited in text.

3. "The Self and the Monstrous: *The Fortunes of Perkin Warbeck*," in *Iconoclastic Departures: Mary Shelley after "Frankenstein,"* ed. Syndy M. Conger, Frederick S. Frank, and Gregory O'Dea (Madison: Fairleigh Dickinson University Press, 1997), 261.

4. Although the narrator is not specifically gendered, I use the feminine pronoun for her since she is a persona of a woman writer

5. No record of the fee that Whittaker paid for *Valperga* has been yet discovered. Mary Shelley did give the proceeds from this novel to Godwin, who, as always, was in debt.

6. See Blumberg's study, *Mary Shelley's Early Novels*.

7. See James P. Carson, "'A Sigh of Many Hearts': History, Humanity, and Popular Culture in *Valperga*," in *Iconoclastic Departures: Mary Shelley after "Frankenstein,"* ed. Syndy M. Conger, Frederick S. Frank, and Gregory O'Dea (Madison: Fairleigh Dickinson University Press, 1997), 167-192; hereafter cited in text. See also Betty T. Bennett, "The Political Philosophy of Mary Shelley's Historical Novels: *Valperga* and *Perkin Warbeck*."

8. Introduction to *Valperga: or the Life and Adventures of Castruccio, Prince of Lucca*, by Mary Shelley, ed. Stuart Curran (New York: Oxford University Press, 1997), xxiii.

9. See "God's Sister: History and Ideology in *Valperga*," in *The Other Mary Shelley: Beyond "Frankenstein,"* ed. Audrey A. Fisch, Anne K. Mellor, and Esther H. Schor (New York: Oxford University Press, 1993), 163.

10. In "God's Sister: History and Ideology in *Valperga*," Joseph Lew examines Shelley's novel in the tradition of both the historical and political fiction of the late eighteenth and early nineteenth centuries, works that depict women lost in "the tapestry of male history" (165). Lew notes the influence of Sydney Owenson, better known as Lady Morgan, whose work Byron greatly respected and whose 1818 *Florence MacCarthy: An Irish Tale* Shelley read in March 1822. See Dale Spender, *Mothers of the Novel* (301-14), for background on Owenson.

11. Mary Shelley, *Valperga: or, the Life and Adventures of Castruccio, Prince of Lucca*, 3 Volumes (London: G. and W. B. Whittaker, 1823), 3:167; hereafter cited in text as *Valperga* with volume number noted.

12. Modern consensus is that "Ghibelline" (two l's) is the correct spelling; Mary Shelley spells the word "Ghibeline."

13. In the novel, Castruccio was born in 1290 and died in 1328; historical records give the dates as 1283-1330. No record indicates whether or not the actual Castruccio had been involved with women on whom Beatrice and Euthanasia may have been based. Emily Sunstein suggests that Madame de Staël's fictional Corinne and the historic figure Joanna Southcott were models for Beatrice and that Euthanasia's character was based on two eleventh-century Tuscan countesses, Beatrice and Mathilda (53n).

14. This motif of questioning the significance of one's existence has a long history in literature and is especially prominent in eighteenth-century works, such as Thomas Gray's "Elegy in a Country Churchyard," which pays tribute to "th' unhonored dead."

15. Henry VII, German emperor, wanted to restore control of Italy. From 1310 to 1313, he invaded northern Italian provinces, attempting to unify them against Papal authority. Although he was crowned Holy Roman emperor, support for Pope Clement V and the Italian states' fear of German dominance diffused his power.

16. To be fair to Machiavelli, we should recall that his descriptive rather than prescriptive ideas of leadership were often misrepresented. He wrote *The Prince* with genuine concern for the unity of Italy, not to advocate tyrannical rule for its own sake. For background on Machiavelli, see Silvia Ruffo-Fiore, *Niccolo Machiavelli* (Boston: Twayne Publishers, 1982) and Victor Anthony Rudowski, *The Prince: A Historical Critique* (New York: Twayne Publishers, 1992).

17. What Tripalda understandably does not reveal is that he has also been a member of this plot. At meetings, Euthanasia had voiced suspicions regarding his involvement, having revised her initial opinion of his character. Tripalda, whom the narrator overtly depicts as a misogynist, undermines Euthanasia's influence with the other group members.

18. Leodino was the husband of Euthanasia's cousin, Lauretta dei Adimari; he was beheaded by Castruccio for his part in an uprising protesting Castruccio's takeover of Lucca. Leodino was also a distant relative of Castruccio's old mentor, Guinigi.

19. In "Beatrice in *Valperga*: A New Cassandra," Barbara Jane O'Sullivan agrees with Emily Sunstein that Wilhelmina is based in part on the eighteenth-century Joanna Southcott, who was branded a heretic for believing herself to be a prophet; see O'Sullivan's essay in *The Other Mary Shelley: Beyond "Frankenstein,"* ed. Audrey A. Fisch, Anne K. Mellor, and Esther H. Schor (New York: Oxford University Press, 1993), 140-158. One may also draw parallels to Mary Wollstonecraft, considered a social "heretic" for her radicalism and feminism.

20. Mary Shelley provides a footnote on the *Donna Estatica*; they were women who, like Beatrice and Joanna Southcott, believed themselves to be God's prophets. She includes a comment by Ludovico Antonio Muratori, an early eighteenth-century Italian historian, who believed that these women's "ardent imagination" was the real source of their prophecies (3: 43). Shelley read Muratori's *Dissertazioni sopra le Antichità Italiane* (1751) in 1820.

21. In medieval society, women were highly respected if they were thought to possess divine powers. Reduced to ordinary status, not only is Beatrice personally devastated, but she is also denied a place in the chronicles of public history, an irony that reinforces Shelley's theme of private versus public

22. The Paterins (more commonly spelled today as Patarine) were reformists who challenged Papal power and exposed corrupt practices. The Roman Catholic church, not surprisingly, viewed them as dangerous heretics and made every effort to destroy them.

23. The passage exemplifies Radcliffe's skill with depicting the sublime in nature, an aesthetic of many Gothic and Romantic works. Its relevance to the dramatic sensibility in Shelley's novels lies in its power to provide a dramatic background and to evoke a powerful emotional response.

24. See the Review of *Valperga* in *Blackwood's Edinburgh Magazine* (248).

25. Shelley was certainly familiar with the Troilus and Cressida tale from Shakespeare's play, an obvious anachronism for *Valperga*'s setting. However, the story is generally credited to Benoît de Sainte-Maure, a twelfth-century French writer and the probable source for both Boccaccio and Chaucer in their renditions of these lovers' fates.

26. Betty T. Bennett notes that Euthanasia rejects Castruccio's love; he desires hers, but only at the expense of her political and moral views; see "Political Philosophy," 363.

27. "Women in the Active Voice: Recovering Female History in Mary Shelley's Valperga and Perkin Warbeck," in *Iconoclastic Departures: Mary Shelley after "Frankenstein,"* ed. Syndy M. Conger, Frederick S. Frank, and Gregory O'Dea (Madison: Fairleigh Dickinson University Press, 1997), 237.

Perkin Warbeck: Problematic Roles and Identities

Here has appeared, though in a several fashion,
The threats of majesty, the strength of passion,
Hopes of an empire, change of fortunes; all
What can to theatres of greatness fall,
Proving their weak foundations.
— John Ford, Epilogue to *Perkin Warbeck*

John Ford, perhaps better known for his tragedies *'Tis Pity She's a Whore* and *The Broken Heart*, also wrote the historic drama *Perkin Warbeck* (1634), based on a pretender to Henry VII's throne who claimed to be Richard IV. Warbeck professed to be the Duke of York, Edward VI's second son, who, with his elder brother, was imprisoned by his uncle, Richard III. The fate of the princes in the tower has never been completely resolved, although many historians presume they were murdered and discredit Perkin's assertion. However, Mary Shelley believed otherwise. In the preface to her novel, *The Fortunes of Perkin Warbeck* (1830), she wrote: "It is not singular that I should entertain a belief that Perkin was, in reality, the lost Duke of York. . . . no person who has at all studied the subject but arrives at the same conclusion. Records exist . . . which put the question almost beyond a doubt."[1] (*Perkin Warbeck*, v-vi).

While sympathetic toward the character of Perkin, John Ford does not examine him in depth in the play; in fact Perkin is merely one of many figures and is even secondary to Henry VII, James IV of Scotland, and Huntley (father of Katherine Gordon). In contrast to Ford, Shelley saw Richard as "a fitting object of interest — a hero to ennoble the pages of a humble tale" (*Perkin Warbeck*, preface, viii). Mary Shelley diligently and thoroughly researched a variety of sources to present a complete picture of Richard.[2] Reading through the various documents on the subject, she realized how many of these accounts slight Richard's history: "I became aware of the romance which his story contains, while, at the same time, I felt that it would be impossible for any narration, that should be confined to the incorporation of facts related by our old Chroniclers, to do it justice" (*Perkin Warbeck*, preface, v). The facts do not "do it justice" because they frequently omit the important facets of private life. Although careful to preserve accuracy, she recognized that the historical novelist, as James Kerr notes, "not only combines romance with 'reality,' but, viewing history as simply another way of seeing things that is at odds with the perspective of romance, writes history anew."[3] The historical novel is not merely a factual recording of public events, as noted in the prior chapter. It is also a revision of history as it explores the potential drama of daily existence: "In order to glean the dramatic from history, we must first realize that drama is fashioned out of the sadness and laughter in the happenings of everyday experience. All drama is hewn out of the basic materials of life: human personalities, their loves, their longings, their clashes. And so, we must train our powers of observation and our insights and apply them to the life around us."[4] So, like *Valperga*, Mary Shelley's fifth major work is an historical romance that explores the problematic roles and private lives of public figures, and also like one of her sources, Francis Bacon's *History of Henry VII*, it presents the life of an historical figure who had an existence off as well as on the public stage.[5]

In *Perkin Warbeck*, published four years after *The Last Man*, Mary Shelley uses the conventions of the historical romance to explore once again the dangers of an introspective sensibility that fosters one's perception of the world as a stage on which to enact selfish aspirations that threaten to destroy the domestic life beyond the stage's spotlight. As Betty T. Bennett has aptly observed, the novel clearly depicts "the inadequacy of personal love when linked to personal ambition" ("Political Philosophy," 363). The fictional character Monina de Faro and the historical Robin Clifford and Frion discover the limitations and perils of playing roles and adopting disguises. Shelley also dramatizes the ironic fate of Richard Plantagenet, who attempts to assert publically his actual identity as rightful heir to the throne after having assumed another identity as "Perkin Warbeck" in private life. In Shelley's interpretation, Richard is denied his claim and his identity and must accept the role of impostor (Perkin). In a decidedly deterministic tone, the third-person narrator questions any attempt to depart from the role fate has assigned one, remarking, "We can only resolve, or rather endeavour, to act our parts well, such as they are allotted to us. Little choice have we to seek or to eschew our several destinations" (*Perkin Warbeck*, 2: 266). Fate indeed limits Richard in his search for public affirmation of himself as Richard Plantagenet, the elder of the missing princes. The alias, created to protect him, casts him in a role that by birthright he was not meant to play. Only two characters "act well" the parts assigned them by fate: Lady Katherine Gordon and Edmund Plantagenet, Richard's cousin. Determined and strong-willed, they nevertheless agree with Hamlet that, "There's a divinity that shapes our ends," and they recognize that they cannot control their destiny or direct the drama of their lives by re-casting themselves into roles other than those "allotted" to them.

As early as the fall of 1826, Mary Shelley had decided to write about the pretender to Henry VII's crown. She approached the publisher Henry

Colburn with the idea, but he was then not receptive (Sunstein, 275). Her 13 July 1827 journal entry indicates that she was busy writing that summer (*Journals*, 2: 503), and the second half of the novel was completed two years later (Sunstein, 299). She first offered the novel to John Murray but ultimately sold the work to Colburn for £150, and on 13 May 1830, *Perkin Warbeck* was published. Although not the success she had hoped, the novel was generally well-received. In 1830, *The Athenæum*'s critic commented that the volumes of *Perkin Warbeck* "are the productions of no ordinary pen. . . . The characters are drawn with great vividness, and in some of them, especially, there is an originality which strikingly marks the powerfully-creative mind of the author of *Frankenstein*" (Review of *Perkin Warbeck*, 323). Though faulting Shelley for not combining "with sufficient skill what is fictitious and what is true," the *Edinburgh Literary Journal*'s critic regarded the novel as a "talented work" that "bears the stamp of a powerful mind" (Review of *Perkin Warbeck*, 351). Especially praised by this critic are the characters, who "are sketched with bold vigour and fine discrimination" (352). Many studies, however, treat lightly the strengths of *Perkin Warbeck*, dismissing it perhaps too readily[6] or briefly mentioning it in conjunction with *Frankenstein*, *Mathilda*, and *The Last Man*.[7] While certainly deserving attention if only as an example of historical romance, the novel also holds its own with the previous works of the Shelley canon.

Perkin Warbeck opens with loyal Yorkists — the Earl of Lincoln, Lord Lovel, Lady Brampton, and others — planning to challenge Henry VII's claim to the throne by presenting to the English public Edward VI's heir, Richard Plantagenet. Disguised as Perkin Warbeck, son of a Flemish moneylender, Richard has lived in hiding since his escape from the Tower. These principal players perceive their plan to restore Richard to the throne as analogous to a drama, as evidenced by the language they use. Even though the metaphor is often merely suggested by the words "act" or "spectator" or "participator," such subtle references become significant when contextualized with others and with the Shelleyean theme of the dangers of theatrics. The Earl of Lincoln had long ago conceived the dramatic plan that is now put into action, and the narrator's choice of words demonstrates Lincoln's penchant to describe his role with dramatic terms: "the design was originated on which he [Lincoln] was now called to act" (*Perkin Warbeck*, 1: 35-6). Upon hearing of Richard III's death, Lincoln remarks that now the former King is no longer an actor in the drama: "the past is his: with the present and future he has no participation" (*Perkin Warbeck*, 1: 39). Lord Lovel, who has risked life and title to protect Richard, advises the pretender's guardian Madeline not to address him as Duke of York before the young prince is ready for his entrance: "It is dangerous," he warns her, "to play at majesty, unaided by ten thousand armed assertors of our right" (*Perkin Warbeck*, 1: 96-7). Even Richard's mother, the former queen, Elizabeth Woodville, uses theatrical and literary terms in her speech.

Unaware that her son has survived the Tower, she demands that she see the boy "to end at once this silly masque" and accuses Lincoln as "a party to this tale" of Richard's existence (*Perkin Warbeck*, 1: 78). Henry VII, the narrator notes, wears a "mask of indifference" to conceal his fear about Richard's claim (*Perkin Warbeck*, 2: 14).

The dramatic analogy pervades the novel as even the minor characters reveal their desire to play on the stage. The Cornish army that Monina de Faro organizes for Richard's final battle with Henry is comprised of characters who perceive they are destined for better things:

> Such were the chiefs Monina found desirous, and in their own conceit capable, of placing England's diadem on Duke Richard's head. Heron, the bankrupt mercer, who fancied himself the base-born offspring of the late Earl of Devonshire, and whose first deed of arms would find him Heron no more, but Sir John Courteny; Skelton, a luckless wight, whose shears ever went astray, (the true cause why Walter of Hornbeck paid not for his misshapen suit,) and who, therefore, believed himself born for greater things; and Tereife, the younger prodigal son of a rural franklin, who, cast off and disinherited, had served in the wars in Flanders, gaining in that country no small reverence for the good Duchess Margaret, and ready therefore to right her nephew; besides like a true hero, he abhorred this silken time of peace, and hoped to gather spoil, if not laurels, in the meditated insurrection. (*Perkin Warbeck*, 3: 70)[8]

Well-meaning and sincere are these men, who recall Ford's dramatis personae; however, each is deluded about his capacity for greatness and heroics, rather than accepting himself as the common man he is. Another convert to Richard's cause is Robert Ratcliffe, Lord Fitzwater's cousin. Ratcliffe was also attracted to the allure of the stage: he "had lived in poor disguise since the battle of Stoke, and gladly threw off his peasant's attire to act the soldier again in a new war of the Roses" (*Perkin Warbeck*, 2: 23).

The third-person narrator herself frequently employs the metaphor, comparing the historical action to a drama and the characters to players or actors.[9] Describing the Yorkists' predicament in challenging Henry VII, the narrator remarks that with the end of civil war, "the chief obstacle that presented itself was the difficulty of exciting the English to any act of rebellion against the king, without bringing forward the young Prince as the principal actor on the scene" (*Perkin Warbeck*, 1: 109). After the frustrated Henry imprisons his mother-in-law, Elizabeth Woodville, the narrator sadly observes that "now all hope was at an end for the unhappy lady. The various acts of her tragic history were to close in obscurity and poverty of a convent-prison" (*Perkin Warbeck*, 1: 126-127). When Hernan de Faro requests that Lord Audley care for the ailing Monina, the narrator sums up the events leading to such a request as a "strange drama" (*Perkin Warbeck*, 2: 166). Perhaps the passage that most powerfully demonstrates the world-as-stage motif is the one in which the narrator reflects on these past events and the relationship of man with nature: "In those times also man was closer linked with nature than now; and the sublimity of her creations exalted his imagination, and elevated his enthusiasm — dark woods, wild mountains, and the ocean's vast expanse, form a stage on which, when we act our parts, we feel that mightier natures than our own witness the scenes we present, and our hearts are subdued by awe to resignation" (*Perkin Warbeck*, 1: 142). These few examples illustrate how frequently Shelley relied upon the *theatrum mundi* metaphor to reinforce the dangers of dramatic illusions. The motif consistently informs the speech and attitude of the novel's minor characters and its narrator.

The opening of the novel might be described today as cinematic, for the narrator deftly sets before us a panoramic scene:

> The day had been sunny and warm: as the evening closed in, a west wind rose, bringing along troops of fleecy clouds, golden at sunset, and then dun and grey, veiling with pervious network the many stars. Three horsemen at this hour passed through the open country between Hinckley and Welford in Leicestershire. It was broad day when they descended from the elevation on which the former stands . . . The good steeds of the knights, for such their golden spurs attested them to be, bore them fast and far along the Roman road, which still exists in those parts to shame our modern builders. It was dusk when, turning from the direct route to avoid entering Welford, they reached a ford of the Avon. (*Perkin Warbeck*, 1: 2-3)

This excerpt cannot do justice to Shelley's careful engineering of the scene, the description of which runs several pages. The allusion to the Roman roads reinforces the continuum of history, and the word "knights" call to mind the Medieval protectors of Britain. The geographical scope of the scene reinforces the historical scope of the dramatic events that will unfold, and the scene invites comparisons with what Richard Schechner "environmental" style.[10] As Richard Hornby describes, this style is "a return to medieval methods of staging in which the entire performance space (which need not be a traditional auditorium) is potentially the stage — in which, in fact, there is no distinction made between the audience's space and the performers' space, and sometimes none made between the theatre building and the outside world."[11] England is Richard's performance space as he returns to claim his rightful crown. Boundaries of the spaces occupied by spectators and actors will soon dissolve, for the audience of this drama cannot remain spectators for long. The events will force them to participate — either to join with Richard or to oppose him.

In addition to explicit dramatic references, Mary Shelley explores the dangers when characters mask and unmask themselves. In his study of theatrical effects on narratives, David Marshall argues that Daniel Defoe was ambivalent about the usefulness of theatricality: Although *Moll Flanders* celebrates theater's potential through masking the self, *Roxana* illustrates its danger in exposing the self and creating a spectacle for spectators (*The Figure of Theater*, 132). Like Defoe, Shelley viewed masks as potential obstacles to self-knowledge, and many of her characters assume disguises or assign roles so frequently that they can no longer distinguish the mask from the face beneath it or the role from actual life. One such example is Richard Simon, a priest who helps the Yorkist cause. Simon is described by the narrator as "a prier into secrets — one who conducted the drama of life by back-stairs and tell-tale valet" (*Perkin Warbeck*, 1: 73). He perceives events as vignettes, mini-dramas within a larger one in which he hopes to play a leading role. As Simon conceives a plan to present Richard to the English public, the narrator notes that "no man was better fitted than Simon to act a prominent part in a state-plot" (*Perkin Warbeck*, 1: 109). The plot itself is theatrical, featuring impersonations and masks to confuse identities.

Simon's plan ironically reflects the reality of Richard's situation. Simon determines to hire an actor to play Richard in public while the real Richard is instructed to mask himself once again as Perkin Warbeck: "He [Simon] looked round for a likely actor for his new part, and chance brought him in contact with Lambert Simnel, a baker's son at Oxford" (*Perkin Warbeck*, 1: 111). For security reasons, the Yorkists decide to have Simnel impersonate the imprisoned Earl of Warwick instead of Richard. The dramatic event is staged in Dublin for an audience more than eager to rid themselves of Henry's power: "a gay and brilliant scene was acted, which raised the enthusiasm of the Irish, and spread a glory round the impostor they supported" (*Perkin Warbeck*, 1: 132). The plan backfires, however, when Henry discovers the plot and displays the real Warwick in London during a procession to St. Paul's Cathedral for an elaborate service. Such identity confusion does little to further the Yorkists' cause, and they find insufficient public support to face Henry's army. As a result, the Yorkists lose, Lincoln and possibly Lovel die in the battle, and Simon is captured. Forced to a confession of sorts by Henry, Simon remains the actor: he "played a dastardly and a double part, half revealing, half disguising the truth" (*Perkin Warbeck*, 1: 139). The "truth," Shelley suggests, can never be revealed or discovered with theatrics; playing roles and donning masks not only conceal the self from others, but also prohibit self-knowledge.

Another adept actor is Frion, Henry VII's spy, who at times aligns himself with Richard's cause. The narrator comments that Frion "played the crafty artisan, fashioning [the role] to his will" (*Perkin Warbeck*, 1: 159). Frion enjoys enacting little vignettes which feature him both as an actor assuming guises and masks and as a director controlling the other actors in his drama. The narrator likens him to a puppet master who "believed that he held the strings, which commanded the movements of all the puppets about him" (*Perkin Warbeck*, 3: 1). Before becoming Richard's trusted secretary, Frion attempts to help Henry capture the elusive challenger to the Lancastrian's throne. He lures Richard to the Baron Fitzwater's French residence, where the young Duke of York finds himself an unwilling participant in a little drama. Frion, the narrator notes, "went forward conning his part" (*Perkin Warbeck*, 1: 163) as he convinces Richard that the Baron is none other than the Frenchman Sire de Beverem, who had been a friend to Edward IV. Frion realizes that he has "a difficult part to play" (*Perkin Warbeck*, 1: 164) in convincing Fitzwater to take a role in the deception because the Baron discovers that he cannot betray a young innocent lad and becomes "ill-pleased at the part he had consented to play" (*Perkin Warbeck*, 1: 17). Frion's deceptive scheme fails: Richard sees "through the flimsy disguise which [Fitzwater] threw over his native speech" (*Perkin Warbeck*, 1: 170) and Robin Clifford comes to his aid. As if in anticipation of his future acts, Clifford willingly participates in Frion's drama, although not as the crafty double-dealer would have liked. He usurps Frion's role as director by revising the "drama" in order to free his childhood friend, whom he helps to escape with a female disguise. Again, a theatrical scheme to change the roles that fate has decreed fails. In addition to criticizing a deviation from the part fate has assigned one, Mary Shelley denounces the crafty intrigue of such schemers as Frion. Not only is the deception self-serving, but it also disorders lives and distorts one's ability to see things as they are. The layers of lies and masks are like packaged nesting boxes that conceal the contents, forcing one to unwrap one box after another to discover what is hidden inside the smallest box.

Frion proves that he is a skilled actor as well as a director. Once he joins Richard's cause, he disguises himself as an astrologer in order to discover any plans the king may have regarding Richard and to find more sympathizers for the prince. "The part he had played of astrologer" (*Perkin Warbeck*, 2: 151), the narrator tells us, enables him to enlist the aid of Lord Audley, whose wealth the Yorkists desperately need. Frion continues to control Richard's dramatic appearances in Ireland, France, and Scotland. He recognizes that theatrical direction is as effective for political image-making as it is for a dramatic production, and he carefully stages events to convince the English public of Richard's identity and legitimate claim to the throne. His rationale is that if Charles VIII of France and James IV of Scotland recognize Richard's birthright, then so should England. Frion exults in the director's role until first James and then Katherine replace his influence. Jealousy and pride override loyalty as Frion devises a plan to curtail Katherine's influence, a plan which demonstrates Frion's penchant for deceptive schemes that imitate a drama with multiple plots and machinations: "it was neither comprehensible, nor to be endured, that this banished Prince and his friends should walk straight forward in their allotted route, unaided by plot or manoeuvre" (*Perkin Warbeck*, 2: 259).

Frion's scheming nearly causes Richard's death and finally results in his own capture. Huntley, Katherine's father, exposes Frion's treacherous plan to ambush and kill Richard. At first receptive to the idea of preventing Richard's escape to Ireland, Huntley cannot bring himself to play the villain's part. On the surface, he "acted the part designed for him by the conspirators" (*Perkin Warbeck*, 3: 5), only to disclose later Frion's role to Richard and the others. Enjoying the turnabout plot he effects, Huntley tells the amazed spectators and the captured Frion, "Lo, the scene shifts again! Never be cast down, Master Frion; you are as subtle as any of your race — only to be outwitted by a niggard Scotchman, who can ill read, and worse write" (*Perkin Warbeck*, 3: 11). These and other examples illustrate how readily the characters in this novel perceive life as a series of scenes within a larger drama and how many of them try to rewrite that drama for their own ambitious purposes. At one point in Ford's play, Henry VII, in reference to Perkin Warbeck, remarks, "O, let him range: / The player's on the stage still, 'tis his part; / He does but act" (416). Shelley echoes the double layer of theatrical metaphor in Ford's work by depicting characters who consciously perceive themselves as actors in a dramatic production involving masks, disguises, and plots within plots.

Another such character is Sir Robert "Robin" Clifford, Richard's childhood playmate, who delights in the intrigues associated with the drama of Richard's challenge to Henry's crown. Although initially he plays the heroic role in helping extricate Richard from the clutches of Frion at Fitzwater's Lisle estate, Robin soon plays a chameleon to further his personal desires. As the Yorkists discuss strategy while Richard is entertained in France by Charles VIII, Clifford ponders "the part he was to act. He thought of what he might gain or lose by siding with the Duke" (*Perkin Warbeck*, 2: 7). Ultimately he decides to "act a wise man's part" and seek advice from Fitzwater, who, though reluctant to harm Richard, is "dissatisfied at the part of rebel he was forced he thought to play" (*Perkin Warbeck*, 2: 22). Clifford's progression to villainy begins when he can control neither his desire for Monina nor his resentment toward Richard, whom Monina loves. When Monina gently rejects his advances, Clifford becomes "a bold-faced villain" (*Perkin Warbeck*, 2: 82) and tries to undermine Richard at every opportunity. In one such incident, he captures Monina in hopes of gaining leverage with Henry, telling her "Let us not act a silly mime before [the troops]" (*Perkin Warbeck*, 2: 78). A consummate actor himself, he readily employs dramatic metaphors to describe nearly any action.

Clifford, like so many characters in this novel, assumes various identities for personal gain. Calling himself Wiatt, he joins a few insurgent Scots who resent Richard's presence in Scotland. While the Yorkists make a last attempt to challenge Henry's power, Clifford ambushes Richard; he "played a dastardly and villain's part," felling him from behind with "a coward's blow" (*Perkin Warbeck*, 3: 137). However, like the Gothic villains Schedoni and Manfred,[12] Clifford experiences sincere guilt for his deeds: "Never had crime visited with such torment ill-fated man; he looked a Cain after the murder; the Abel he had killed was his own fair fame — the ancestral honour of his race" (*Perkin Warbeck*, 3: 141). His excessive sensibility feeds his passions and ambitions. As the narrator remarks, "how often in the world do we see sensibility attributed to individuals, whose show of feeling arises from excessive susceptibility to their own sorrows and injuries" (*Perkin Warbeck*, 3: 143). His final act of treason toward his old friend accomplishes his goal as Richard is captured. It also results in a watery grave for the once vibrant and warm-hearted knight.

Such theatrical schemes and posturings by those around Richard predispose the Duke to regard himself as a player in this drama as well. After all, he is the catalyst for the action. Through the efforts of loyal Yorkists, Richard's existence has been concealed as he is groomed for his royal role and as armies and monies can be amassed to overthrow Henry. Since his rescue from the Tower, Richard has lived with Mynheer Jahn Warbeck, whose dead son's name, Perkin, Richard assumes. Thus, at an early age, masks and "pretending" have been a necessity for the pretender as he has been forced either to conceal his identity or to assume another. Richard's entrance onto the stage is carefully orchestrated by those who have risked much to protect the young prince: the Earl of Lincoln, Lord Lovel, Lady Brampton, and others. These characters, who themselves perceive the world as a stage, foster Richard's similar perception. Seizing the opportunity to activate their plan with Richard III's death, they direct Richard's initial performance in the drama. Unlike Castruccio, who initiates his own dramatic entrance, Richard finds himself cast by others *in media res*. He elicits our sympathy because he must take the stage if he is to assert his true identity as rightful heir to the throne. With the *theatrum mundi* motif, Mary Shelley can dramatically portray the tragic irony of Richard's situation: he must play the "pretender" to assert his authentic identity. Furthermore, he discovers that a fulfilling domestic life is possible only if he also enacts the role of the impostor, Perkin; he sacrifices that life if he "plays" himself on the public stage.

As Richard begins to understand the role in which he is cast, his use of the theatrical metaphor quickly develops. Suspecting that Frion may not be what he seems, Richard becomes "ill-satisfied with the part he played" in Frion's scheme to hold him at Fitzwater's French residence (*Perkin Warbeck*, 1: 165). While his Yorkist friends engage in strategies to challenge Henry's right to the throne, Richard is frustrated with his inactive part as he is hidden at Madeline's cottage in Tournay: "Mewed up here with women, the very heart of a Plantagenet will fail, and I shall play the girl at the sight of blood" (*Perkin Warbeck*, 1: 159). He is much happier grooming his battle skills under Edmund's tutelage in the war between the

Moors and the Christians in Spain, for both he and Edmund do not "feel inclined to lower the national character by keeping away from the scene of glory" (*Perkin Warbeck*, 1: 211). Although the war causes the death of his surrogate mother, Madeline, Richard is infused with its false romanticism, like the young Spanish knights who "painted war with pomp, and adorned it by their virtues" (*Perkin Warbeck*, 1: 211). Therefore, as he begins the first step to staking his claim to the throne, he justifies the war and death that result from his actions because the cause is just.

Dramatic references occur again and again as the plots evolve. Although some Yorkists wish "to make England itself the scene" of Richard's first onslaught (*Perkin Warbeck*, 1: 243), Lord Barry and others determine Ireland to be a safer place. Accordingly, Richard prepares to set sail from Spain to Ireland on a ship chartered by Meiler Trangmar, a spy employed by Henry to discover the Duke's whereabouts and to bring him back to England. Trangmar, however, has other plans. Hating all Yorkists, he devises a scheme to drown Richard at sea. Using forged letters as proof, he convinces Monina, her father (Fernan de Faro), Lady Brampton, and Edmund that he is acting on authority of the Duchess of Burgundy and Elizabeth Woodville. Although Monina experiences misgivings, it is the narrator who foreshadows the events to come: "Little knew they the strange and tragic drama that was acting on board the skiff that bore afar the idol of their hopes" (*Perkin Warbeck*, 1: 254). Dramatic, indeed melo-dramatic, are the events: an encounter with a nearly fatal storm and a for-tunate escape from Trangmar's midnight attempt to push Richard into the dark waters. During this "strange and tragic drama," Richard demon-strates his growing penchant for theatrical metaphors. Following the storm, the crew rests on French shores to give thanks. When Trangmar sug-gests they continue on land rather than sea, Richard asks him why: "Father Meiler, I watched you during the storm; you acted no coward's part then; why do you now?" (*Perkin Warbeck*, 1: 263). Later, his arrival in Ireland demonstrates his developing flair for grand entrances onto the political stage as he decides upon a strategic time to announce himself during the town meeting. As the narrator remarks, "Had Richard planned this scene . . . he could not have projected a better arrangement" (*Perkin Warbeck*, 1: 284). Richard may not have preplanned the scene as Frion would have done, but he is able to assess the situation and act accordingly.

From the Irish strongholds of Lord Barry and Dublin mayor O'Water to the French court of Charles VIII to the Scottish realm of James IV, Richard experiences and observes the various roles and mini-dramas enacted by those around him, all of which contribute to his unquestioning acceptance that the world is indeed a stage and that life is a drama. As he prepares to tell James his history, he says, "be pleased to hear the tragedy of one, who, born a prince, comes even as a beggar to your court" (*Perkin Warbeck*, 2: 199). Riding through the Scottish countryside, he likens the landscape to a "vast theatre whose shifting scenes and splendid decorations were the clouds, the mountain, the forest and the wave, where man stood, not as one of the links of society . . . but as a human being, animated only by such emotions as were the growth of his own nature" (*Perkin Warbeck*, 2: 243). As he and James ride to Huntley's estate to arrange the marriage to Katherine, Richard agrees with the Scottish king that they should "bear such gear as we may need, not to play too humble a part in Huntley's eyes" (*Perkin Warbeck*, 2: 239).

However, Richard soon recognizes the destruction his ambition causes: beholding the war-torn English countryside that has been ravaged by the Scots, he asks himself: "What had he done? . . . He was an invader; not arming one division of her sons against the other, but girt with foreigners, aided by the ancient ravagers of her smiling villages and plenteous harvests" (*Perkin Warbeck*, 2: 296). He surveys the damage to the land and people he has vowed to protect and sees the landscape for what it is, "a tragic corpse-strewn stage" (*Perkin Warbeck*, 2: 294). Hearing the cries of the people condemning the destruction, he realizes that he has been the cause of their suffering. Although duped by the Scots, Richard recognizes that he bears the ultimate responsibility. The Yorkists' glorious dream has become a brutal nightmare for the English people and for the Duke. Richard had witnessed the devastation of civil war in Spain; now he sees similar effects on England and realizes that he has caused the civil strife. Reacting against the Scottish invasion, he fights James' army, eliciting a Scottish soldier's rhetorical question: "is the fable ended, and you turned friend of Tudor?" (*Perkin Warbeck*, 2: 305). The narrator describes Richard's anguish: "During the whole day Richard had striven against his own emotions, trying to dispel by pride, and indignation, and enforced fortitude, the softness that invaded his heart and rose to his eyes, blinding them; but the sight of these miserable beings, victims of his right, grew into a tragedy too sad to endure" (*Perkin Warbeck*, 2: 307, emphasis added). In a letter to Katherine, Richard bemoans the role in which he has willingly been cast: "Oh, my mother, my too kind friends, why did ye not conceal me from myself?" (*Perkin Warbeck*, 2: 316). Like *Valperga*'s narrator, who questions Castruccio's early dreams of fame, Richard believes that perhaps the end does not justify the means. Meanwhile, James is slowly writing him out of the drama in Scotland: "Councils were held by James, in which York had no part" (*Perkin Warbeck*, 2: 298). Furthermore, he loses what little credibility he has established with the English: a dying monk who had had hopes for a Yorkist rule following the battle of Bosworth now refers to the pretender, not as Richard, but as "the ill-nurtured Perkin"; the monk adds "Once I thought — but no son of York would ally himself to these cruel border-robbers. God of my country, oh curse, curse him and his cause!" (*Perkin Warbeck*, 2: 303). Once again, Richard becomes Perkin to the monk, whose burial the narrator describes as "the opening scene to worse wretchedness" (*Perkin Warbeck*, 2: 304). Richard is now ready to give up England for Katherine and a life of peace. By the time he leaves Scotland to set sail for Ireland, the young duke feels he is a "dear sport of fortune, a tale to chronicle how faithless friends may be" (*Perkin Warbeck*, 3: 14).

Despite this newly-discovered awareness, Richard finds it difficult to disappoint his loyal friends, and his pride urges him to proceed for honor's sake. He tells Edmund, "I must have some part of my inheritance" (*Perkin Warbeck*, 3: 39). The opportunities to claim that inheritance quickly fade as the attack on Waterford fails, and the Yorkists barely escape to Cornwall. Upon seeing the ragged troops that Monina has gathered, Richard recognizes what Edmund already knows: these men are no soldiers, and the White Rose's cause is lost. For this ragged band of men, playing the role of soldier and hero is all well and good in the drills orchestrated by Monina: "It were fine mumming," Richard reflects, "under a hedge with the green sward for a stage" (*Perkin Warbeck*, 3: 78). However, the reality is different from such idealistic rehearsals: these eager but unskilled "soldiers" will be slaughtered on a very different stage than that of the "green sward"–the battlefield against Henry's trained army.

Although Richard regrets any more deaths, he admits that "it must be so; some few lives, each as dear to him that spends it, as is the life-blood to our own hearts. I can say no more. I have a secret purpose, I confess, in all I do" (*Perkin Warbeck*, 3: 83). That purpose is to redeem his honor. He will take one stronghold to make a stand against Henry, forcing the King to recognize him for who he is — Duke of York and heir to the throne. Richard does not see his "secret purpose" realized. Captured and imprisoned, he becomes a symbol of Henry's secure hold of the crown as he is displayed to the London public as Perkin Warbeck, not Richard Plantagenet, Duke of York: "The vulgar rabble, fond of any sort of show, were greedy of this new one. In all parts the name of the Duke of York, of the counterfeit Perkin, drew a concourse of gazers. The appetite was keenest in London; and many a tawdry masque and mime was put in motion, to deck the streets through which the defeated youth was to pass" (*Perkin Warbeck*, 3: 197). The public, the "vulgar rabble," is nothing more than spectators of a cruel display, and Mary Shelley's disdain for the "tawdry masque and mime" is evident. Shelley wittily demonstrates Richard's ironic situation with her play on words: to the public, Richard is the "counterfeit Perkin," the man who would be king; yet, the identity of Perkin is indeed counterfeit, for Richard is the Duke of York.

In prison, Richard bemoans his fate as a sport of fortune, wondering what had happened to those who were so determined to see him attain the throne and if they had forgotten him. They had not of course, and the narrator tells us, "Winter crept on into spring, and spring ripened into summer, and still the various actors in this tragic drama were spending their lives, their every thought and heart's pulsation, on one object" (*Perkin Warbeck*, 3: 213). Having lost his dream and his honor, Richard finally rejects the role he has played as Duke of York, a role that required no acting, since he was indeed the fated prince. He determines to play once more the impostor, to "become Perkin Warbeck in all men's eyes" if he could be reunited with Katherine. His decision is too late, however; Henry's patience has worn thin, and 25 November is set as the "destined termination of his fatal tragedy" (*Perkin Warbeck*, 3: 330).

Throughout this dramatic history, numerous actor-characters pose as Richard's friends. Most of them prove to be faithless. One who is not is another skilled actor, Monina de Faro. Monina assumes multiple identities and disguises, her earnest pledge to Richard governing all her actions. Nevertheless, obsession with the roles she plays contributes to Richard's downfall and to her own self-delusion. Raised with Richard since a young child, Monina embraces his cause with fervor and dedication. Unlike Frion and Clifford, who wear masks to conceal their intentions and inner selves, Monina's "countenance was the mirror of her mind" (*Perkin Warbeck*, 1: 215). However, that mind becomes shaped by war and subterfuge at an early age. "The slave of her own sensations" (*Perkin Warbeck*, 1: 215), Monina eagerly casts herself into any role that can serve Richard's cause and can elevate her own self-importance.

When the de Faro family moves back to Spain, Monina witnesses the atrocities of war despite Hernan de Faro's efforts to shelter them in Alcala during the war between the Moors and Christians. Thinking Madeline and Monina safe with Richard and Edmund, de Faro embarks on another voyage, leaving "his family spectators of the war" (*Perkin Warbeck*, 1: 210). De Faro does not foresee Richard's and Edmund's inability to remain "spectators" with Madeline and Monina. The Plantagenets participate in the war as an exercise to prepare for the battles that lay ahead in their efforts to claim the throne. Left unprotected, Madeline de Faro is killed while saving her young daughter from marauding soldiers. Alone, Monina views the events from a distance: she "had been left in Alcala-la-Real, a prey to fear, to gaze from the steep summit on the plain, whereon, beyond her sight, was acted the real drama of her life" (*Perkin Warbeck*, 1: 228). The "real drama" involves Richard, and longing to take a part in the action with him, she resents the passive role as onlooker and determines that becoming an actor in this drama is far better than being a spectator of it. Mary Shelley does not condemn Monina's decision to be an active participant and to exert some control over the future. However, she does question Monina's obsession with her role in the Yorkists' grand design, a role that enslaves her rather than emancipates her and that renders her unable to see life as anything but a drama of Richard's struggle for the throne.

Adept at disguise and subterfuge, Monina masks herself as a pilgrim in London and as Lord Stanley's daughter in the Tower. She infiltrates Henry's palace posing as one of Elizabeth's ladies. She plays the spy at every turn, discovering Henry's latest schemes for dealing with Richard. She acts the part of a general, attempting to ready the ragged band of eager Cornishmen who align themselves with Richard in his final attempt to the throne. So active and assertive is she that Edmund refers to her as "the chief mover of the rebellion" (*Perkin Warbeck*, 3: 63). In fact, Monina is so obsessed with the drama they are enacting that she cannot see the troops for what they are: an inept group of tailors, tradesmen, and farmers who "fancied themselves heroes at the mere sight of [a near fortress]"–from which they steal arms and take as a base (*Perkin Warbeck*, 3: 81). Her skill in masks and acting is such that the narrator comments at the story's end that Monina had had "a thousand disguises" and had been "used to penetrate everywhere" (*Perkin Warbeck*, 3: 266-267).

In sharp contrast to Katherine, who sees "the bare reality" (*Perkin Warbeck*, 3: 85), Monina seeks an unattainable ideal. According to the narrator, Monina's intentions are admirable; however, her obsession with accomplishing them are not: "There was no evil in Monina; if too much self-devotion, too passionate an attachment to one dear idea, too enthusiastic an adoration of one exalted being, could be called aught but virtue. . . . Yet while the Princess wept that Richard should encounter fruitless danger for a mistaken aim, gladness sat on Monina's brow: 'He goes to conquer; God will give victory to the right'" (*Perkin Warbeck*, 3: 94). Monina is unable to distinguish the bleak reality from her hope-filled illusion. As the group prepares for the final attack on Henry's army, Richard elicits from her a promise to protect Katherine aboard the Adalid (de Faro's ship); she willingly agrees but criticizes his lack of faith: "But why speak these ill-omened words? You will succeed; you will hasten the lagging hand of Fate, and dethrone one never born to reign, to bestow on England its rightful king" (*Perkin Warbeck*, 3: 95). Monina cannot accept what Katherine and ultimately even Richard can: the drama is nearly concluded, and their dreams of playing the victorious heroes and heroines will not be realized. They can neither "hasten" nor alter fate. Still, "the temerity of their designs . . . animated them to loftier hopes. When the thickening shadows of 'coming events' clouded their spirits, they took refuge in the sun-bright imaginations which pointed to each the accomplishment of their several hopes. Monina felt assured that the hour of victory was at hand" (*Perkin Warbeck*, 3: 96). There is, of course, no victory. Later we learn of Monina's fate from Edmund's meeting with Katherine: "Her gentle soul . . . has flown to join him for whom she lived and died. . . . She could not have survived our Prince many months; probably she died before him" (*Perkin Warbeck*, 3: 344-345).

In this meeting, years after "the last act of the sad tragedy" (*Perkin Warbeck*, 3: 340), Edmund becomes aware of the contrast between Monina and Katherine, a contrast that the reader has known for some time. Initially Edmund accuses Katherine of a duplicity that is foreign to her nature. Regarding her present circumstances as a lady of the court, Edmund bitterly remarks that "Yours is another existence, Lady; you need the adulation of the crowd — the luxury of palaces; you purchase these, even by communing with the murderer of him who deserved a dearer recompense at your hands" (*Perkin Warbeck*, 3: 347). As Katherine gently asks that Edmund listen to her story, Edmund realizes that "Katherine *is* Truth," to use the words of James of Scotland. What James once told Richard is now demonstrated to the weary Plantagenet: "The better part of yourself will, when she speaks, appear to leap out, as if, for the first time, it found its other half" (*Perkin Warbeck*, 2: 211). Like Mary Shelley herself, Katherine is a realist. She is loyal and faithful to Richard; nevertheless, she accepts what Monina cannot: life goes on after the public spotlight has dimmed and the curtain falls. She is also content to be true to herself (and to Richard's last request) rather than worry about appearances.

Both Katherine Gordon and Edmund Plantagenet are distinguished from Richard, Monina, and the other actors in this "sad tragedy." Edmund resists the allure of center stage, always focusing on Richard's claim to the throne, although Edmund, as the bastard son of Richard III, had a claim as well. Perhaps his mother had profoundly influenced him: she wanted him far from court and "in the scenes of private life" (*Perkin Warbeck*, 1: 20). Despite indulging "dreamy illusions" from time to time, Edmund cannot be what he is not: "Other men perform the various parts allotted to them, and yet are something else the while; as is the actor, even while he struts in the garb of royalty: but Edmund yielded himself wholly up, and was the mere creature of the thought within" (*Perkin Warbeck*, 3: 276).

Although both Edmund and Katherine emerge as survivors, Katherine is the character whom Mary Shelley holds as the exemplar to the rest. Unlike the Frions and Robin Cliffords, Katherine possesses a sensibility that is directed outwardly and that is balanced by reason. James recognizes the young woman's sympathy: "She is gay, more eager to create pleasure than to please; for to please, we must think of ourselves, and be ourselves the hero of the story, and Katherine is ever forgetful of self" (*Perkin Warbeck*, 2: 212). Indeed Katherine's words and actions demonstrate just how fully she rejects the hero's role for herself and recognizes the dangers it holds for her husband. Supporting his goal to take his place as king, she nevertheless sees the futility of it and suggests that life can be lived off the public stage: "what is there in the name or state of king, that should so take captive our thoughts, that we can imagine no life but on a throne?" (*Perkin Warbeck*, 3: 88). "Our best kingdom," she continues, "is each other's hearts" (*Perkin Warbeck*, 3: 89).

Knowing full well the risks in marrying Richard, Katherine accepts the offer by James and her father because she truly loves the prince. Although describing this decision in dramatic terms, the narrator makes it clear that such an analogy is misleading: "The Princess assumed her new character among the exiles with facility; yet the phrase is bad, for Katherine could assume nothing, not even a virtue, if she had it not" (*Perkin Warbeck*, 2: 254-55). Whatever role she plays is in character — as daughter, wife, would-be queen, and widowed woman with a last charge from her husband. When her father and James suggest that she abandon her husband following his unsuccessful "invasion" with the Scottish troops, she rejects the option, pleading with James to "permit your kinswoman to perform a wife's part unopposed" (*Perkin Warbeck*, 3: 3). She has married Richard freely and willingly, and so she will remain by his side, not simply for duty's sake, but because she loves him. Like Monina, Katherine possesses great loyalty and love, and what she has committed herself to, she will honor. However, she recognizes that Richard needs her not for strategic advising or maneuvering, but for the stability and reality checks that only she can offer him. As the narrator says, she is "a magic mirror, which gave [Richard] back himself" (*Perkin Warbeck*, 2: 236).

Recognizing both the futility of Richard's dream and the superficiality of public life, Katherine tries to inject realism into Richard: "It was strange that a girl of royal birth, bred in a palace, accustomed to a queen-like sovereignty over her father's numerous vassals in the Highlands, should aim at restricting the ambitious York to mere privacy" (*Perkin Warbeck*, 3: 59). The narrator contrasts her with Monina, for whom the public image or role is privileged over private life. Katherine does not hold that principle:

> The Lady Katherine saw a vain mask in all the common-place pomp of palaces; she perceived that power failed most, when its end was good; she saw that in accomplishing its purpose in the cottage, or in halls of state, felicity resulted from the affections only. It was but being an actor in different scenes, to be a potentate or a peasant; the outward garb is not the livery of the mind; the refinement of taste, which enables us to gather pleasure from simple objects; the warmth of heart which necessitates the exercise of our affections, but which is content when they are satisfied; these, to her mind, were the only, but they were the complete ingredients of happiness; and it was rarer to find, and more difficult to retain them, among false-hearted, ambitious courtiers, and the luxury of palaces, than among simple-minded peasantry, and a plain natural style of living. There was some romance in this idea; Katherine felt that there was, and subdued herself not to lay too much store by any change or guise of outward circumstance. (*Perkin Warbeck*, 3: 60-61)

The role Katherine privileges is the one off the public stage: "by devoting herself to the happiness of him to whom she was united . . . she was performing the part assigned to her" (*Perkin Warbeck*, 3: 61). Yet as the narrator has told us earlier, she does not play roles for public posturing or deception, or presume to be what is not in her character. When Richard loses the battle at Exeter, Monina refuses to believe all is lost: "her busy thoughts fashioned a thousand plans for his escape" (*Perkin Warbeck*, 3: 178). Katherine, however, "struggle[s] with necessity," mourning the loss of "we" (she and Richard) as much as the failure to win the last battle.

Mary Shelley uses the Cornwall scene of Richard's final attempt to gain the crown to contrast the different personalities of Monina, Richard, and Katherine. Monina sees the untrained Cornishmen who comprise Richard's troops as a ready army; Richard and Katherine see "the bare reality: some three thousand poor peasants and mechanics, whose swords were more apt to cut themselves than strike the enemy, were arrayed against the whole power and majesty of England" (*Perkin Warbeck*, 3: 86). However, Richard proceeds with battle in hopes that Henry will acknowledge his royal identity. Katherine tries to dissuade him: "You have not so far deceived yourself as to imagine, that with these unfortunate men, you can ride over the pride and power of this island; did I see on what else you founded the lofty hope, that has, since we came here, beamed in your eyes, I would resign myself to your better wisdom. But, wherever I turn my view, there is a blank" (*Perkin Warbeck*, 3: 87). She implores him to reject the public stage for the better love of "each other's hearts." Stationed in Henry's court after Richard's capture, Katherine is true to her husband; when Henry tries to play "the lover's part," she remains "artless" (*Perkin Warbeck*, 3: 208-209).

Mary Shelley was clearly intrigued with Katherine, and though the novel revolves around Richard, she makes it clear that Katherine, like Euthanasia of *Valperga*, is the hero who deserves our attention and our admiration. In a footnote to the concluding chapter of the novel, Shelley writes the following: "I do not know how far these concluding pages may be deemed superfluous: the character of the Lady Katherine Gordon is a favourite of mine, and yet many will be inclined to censure her abode in Henry the Seventh's court, and other acts of her after life. I desired therefore that she should speak for herself, and show how her conduct, subsequent to her husband's death, was in accordance with the devotion and fidelity with which she attended his fortunes during his life" (*Perkin Warbeck*, 3: 339). Perhaps at this point Shelley was considering writing about women in history as she later suggested to John Murray. With this note, Shelley also demonstrates how she refigures the play-within-the-play convention as a narrative-within-a-narrative. She gives her character a voice that previous historical accounts have silenced, a voice that literally has the last word. Speak Katherine does, and she reminds Edmund that she is in Henry's court because Richard had asked her to be with his sister, Elizabeth: "I am fulfilling, methinks, a task grateful in the eyes of Richard, thus doing my part to bestow on the England he loved, a sovereign [Prince Arthur, Elizabeth's son] who will repair the usurper's crimes, and bestow happiness on the realm" (*Perkin Warbeck*, 3: 351). She accepts fate's role for her, and Shelley may have had the Katherine of John Ford's play in mind. Several times Ford's Katherine advises Perkin Warbeck that "What our destinies / Have ruled-out in their books we must not search, / But kneel to" (*Perkin Warbeck*, 387); later she tells her attendant, "It is decreed; and we must yield to fate" (*Perkin Warbeck*, 410). Shelley's Katherine also sees life as a drama that encompasses much more than Richard's dream and recognizes that she is a part of it. At the end of Richard's tragedy, she does not succumb to death as Monina has done or deny her name as Edmund has his. She continues living, taking seriously her charge to Elizabeth and Prince Arthur and her duty to herself: "When my soul quits this 'bower of flesh' . . . I am content to be an imperfect creature, so that I never lose the ennobling attribute of my species, the constant endeavour to be more perfect" (*Perkin Warbeck*, 3: 353). Although both Katherine and Mary Shelley reject the ideal of perfectibility, they do suggest that we continue to improve ourselves, just not at the risk of losing our hold on reality.

Above all, Katherine remains a participant in the theater of life for herself: "When I have wandered out of myself in my endeavour to shed pleasure around, I must again return laden with the gathered sweets on which I feed and live" (*Perkin Warbeck*, 3: 353-354). Katherine's words suggest what Mary Shelley clearly felt and recorded many times in her journal — one's existence requires a sympathy for the human race and a connection to it, not alienation from it. Indeed Katherine's last words may well echo Shelley's sentiments: "Permit this to be, unblamed — permit a heart whose sufferings have been and are, so many and so bitter, to reap what joy it can from the strong necessity it feels to be sympathized with — to love" (*Perkin Warbeck*, 3: 354). So, Katherine, like Richard, is also a "mark to be pelted at by fortune,"[13] and she may very well agree with Antonio, Shakespeare's melancholy merchant of Venice, when he remarks to Gratiano: "I hold the world but as the world, Gratiano; / A stage, where every man must play a part, / And mine a sad one" (I.i.77-79).

Chapter 7 Notes

1. Mary Shelley, *The Fortunes of Perkin Warbeck*, with an introduction by Betty T. Bennett, 3 Volumes (Norwood Editions, 1976), v-vi; hereafter cited in text as *Perkin Warbeck*.

2. Since Shelley calls the character "Richard" rather than "Perkin," I will do the same when referring to her work.

3. James Kerr, *Fiction Against History: Scott as Storyteller* (Cambridge: Cambridge University Press, 1989), 2.

4. George McCalmon and Christian Moe, *Creating Historical Drama* (Carbondale: Southern Illinois University Press, 1965), 15.

5. According to Margaret Drabble, Bacon's history of Henry VII is significant as an early biography rather than as a mere chronicle of its subject's accomplishments as king of England.

6. For example, Jane Blumberg considers *Perkin Warbeck* vastly inferior to Shelley's earlier works

7. See, for example, Anne Mellor's *Mary Shelley*, 177-78.

8. Like their predecessors in Ford's play, these characters provide comic relief with their common speech and over-zealous enthusiasm.

9. As in *Valperga*, the third-person narrator reinforces the world-as-stage motif. Again, I refer to this persona as a female.

10. See Schechner, *Performance Theory* (New York: Routledge, 1988).

11. *Script into Performance; A Structuralist View of Play Production* (Austin: University of Texas Press, 1977), 61; hereafter cited in text.

12. Schedoni is the villainous priest in Ann Radcliffe's *The Italian*; Manfred, the guilt-ridden patriarch in Horace Walpole's *The Castle of Otranto*.

13. The phrase is from Mary Wollstonecraft's *Letters Written During a Short Residence in Sweden, Norway, and Sweden.*

Lodore: Public Spectacle and Private Lives

> Had I not wasted years in deliberating, after I ceased to doubt, how I ought to have acted — I might now be useful and happy. — For my sake, warned by my example, always appear what you are, and you will not pass through existence without enjoying its genuine blessings, love and respect.
>
> — Mary Wollstonecraft, *Maria, or the Wrongs of Woman*

In *Valperga*, *Perkin Warbeck*, and *The Last Man*, Mary Shelley examines how public figures fail to accommodate their quest or ambition with their own domestic lives or with the needs of those close to them. She reversed this perspective in her final two novels, *Lodore* (1835) and *Falkner* (1837), by focusing on how public theatrics of various types disrupt the lives of private individuals. Using the third-person point of view, Shelley emphasizes the results of the characters' dramatic sensibility rather than the process by which they view the world as a stage, a process that she stressed in *Frankenstein, Mathilda,* and *The Last Man*. Cornelia Lodore's and John Falkner's theatrical perceptions of life create an unwanted dramatic spectacle that draws their and others' private lives into the public spotlight. As with their predecessors, they often privilege audience reception over integrity of action. Furthermore, the results of enacting roles to justify their misguided acts extend beyond their own lives and interests. Like Elizabeth Inchbald's *A Simple Story,* Shelley's last two works are generational novels that illustrate how characters' actions affect not only their own fate, but also their children's.

Lodore does not adhere neatly to the conventions of any one narrative type; rather it is a blending, Shelleyean fashion — the novel of sentiment and sensibility and the novel of manners. It marks for Shelley a new approach to her craft, at least in longer fiction.[1] Sentimental novels were immensely popular from the 1740s to the 1780s. Samuel Richardson, Frances Brooke, Henry Mackenzie, Charlotte Smith, Frances Sheridan, and Laurence Sterne were but a few writers whose characters embody virtue, exhibit intense sensibility, and practice admirable benevolence despite struggles with adversity that often rivaled that of Job's. These three characteristics — virtue, sensibility, and benevolence — are the earmarks of most sentimental fiction. The impact of sentiment on the development of female characters was — and is yet — debated. On the positive side, it proved enabling by recognizing virtues associated with female propriety. As Janet Todd has noted, "female novelists in particular formed [passivity and virtue] into a fantasy of specifically female power, very different from the power of [Aphra] Behn's and [Mary Delariviere] Manley's knowing and manipulating women" (*Sign of Angellica*, 123.) On the negative, sentiment weakened arguments for women's reasoning faculties.[2] Women such as Mary Wollstonecraft challenged its association with unrealistic expectations; virtue, they insisted, was not always rewarded.[3] Sensibility is the earmark of the later eighteenth century and often perceived as one precursor to Romanticism. Although an outgrowth of sentimentality (and often indiscernible from it), sensibility broadened the aesthetic philosophy of feeling. It redirected the emotional experience to involve the reader more profoundly, thus its association with the Gothic genre. Furthermore, sensibility was not exclusively gendered, for it had become a desirable trait for both men and women. *Lodore* can also be described as a novel of manners that demonstrates how fully social customs and mores govern the behavior of characters who are making their entrance into the world. This narrative genre explored the accepted and challenged behavior of a defined society, be it a small, provincial village or cosmopolitan London. At times didactic in chronicling what one should or and should not to do for social approbation, these writers were nevertheless constructing realistic portrayals of characters striving for acceptance within a social circle.[4]

In *Lodore*, Shelley incorporates the characteristics of these narrative genres. She contrasts the idealized characters, Ethel Lodore and Horace Saville, both possessing an abundance of sensibility and benevolence, and the socially ambitious Cornelia Lodore. With Cornelia, Shelley subverts the typical pattern of the novel of manners. Rather than emphasizing how a character must learn proper and expected behavior, Shelley suggests that her heroine is too dependent upon social manners. Cornelia discovers that she cannot rely on "society's glass" as the barometer by which to play out the drama of her life and that the sympathetic role of the wronged wife she plays for society merely masks her desire for social approbation at the expense of familial love and personal integrity.

Mary Shelley first conceived the idea for *Lodore*, her fifth novel, in 1831, and she had completed it by July 1833.[5] The work was published on 7 April 1835 by Richard Bentley and Henry Colburn. On 16 January 1833, she wrote to Maria Gisborne that she was concerned about payment: "I am in all the tremor of fearing what I shall get for my novel, which is nearly finished" (*Letters*, 2: 183). Ollier promised her £100, with another £50 should at least 600 copies be sold. Getting *Lodore* published proved to be no easy task. First, Ollier questioned if the novel were long enough for the three-volume format.[6] Next, the printers lost two packets of manuscripts that Shelley had sent them. In letters to Ollier on 4 and 30 April 1833, Shelley revealed her frustration with the lost packets (*Letters*, 2: 200-2), and she had to rewrite the missing pages from memory as she had no copies. Finally, although the novel was printed as early as August 1834,[7] Shelley heard nothing about the publication date and made repeated inquiries about its status throughout the fall of that year. Despite the pre-publication problems, *Lodore*, when finally released in April 1835, was an unqualified success, second only to *Frankenstein*. Critics praised its treatment of believable, ordinary characters. Leigh Hunt reviewed it favorably, noting that its major weakness was simply that it lacked the power of *Frankenstein*, a novel, he admitted, which is a "thing to happen only once in many years."[8]

Focusing on two generations, *Lodore* is, in a sense, two stories linked together by one character, Cornelia Santerre Lodore. Although Cornelia and her daughter Ethel are the major protagonists, Lord Lodore's character warrants examination first since his actions largely determine those of his wife and daughter.[9] Although he envisions himself playing roles that correspond to his egocentric perception of life, Lodore also demonstrates, like Mathilda and Victor Frankenstein, that he is an adept dramatist, configuring others into actors who will, he hopes, enact parts that satisfy his drama's plot.

Like the Byronic hero, Lodore is a brooding, melancholy figure with a secret past that haunts him. He possesses a kind heart, but he has been raised by an indulgent family and, as a result, is spoiled and self-centered. He spends his early life wandering on the continent, where he falls in love with a woman, Theodora; when the relationship fails, he returned to England. Several years after his marriage to the young Cornelia Santerre, he and Theodora, now Countess Lyzinski, meet again. Her son, Casimir, is his child, although Casimir does not know this fact.[10] Cornelia, only a few years older than Casimir, is quite taken with the young man, playfully flirts with him, and plans to "school [him] on his entrance in the English world."[11] Lodore reacts with both husbandly jealousy and parental guilt; he is severe with Casimir, correcting and reprimanding him constantly. When he goes so far as to strike him, Casimir responds with a challenge to a duel. Refusing to fight his own son, Lodore flees to America with his daughter Ethel. He pleads with Cornelia to come with him, but she does not. After twelve years in Illinois, he decides to return to England in hope that he and his estranged wife can provide the fifteen-year old Ethel with appropriate social connections and education. His plans, however, are unexpectedly altered when he finds himself in a duel with a brash American and is killed.

The young and impetuous Lodore has literary antecedents in Charlotte Smith's Frederic Delamere, Eliza Fenwick's Arthur Murden, and William Godwin's brooding antagonist Ferdinando Falkland. Those characters' youthful sins, resulting from indulging passions and ambitions, perpetually haunt and ultimately destroy them. Had Lodore as a youth remained on his family estate in Longfield, Essex, he could have experienced comfort and ease, but he chose to gratify his desires and wanderlust. Upon Lodore's returning home to attend his father's funeral, his devoted sister, Elizabeth Fitzhenry, pleads with him to stay. She hopes that "he would, adorned by newly-inherited title, and endowed with the gifts of fortune, step upon the stage of the world, and shine forth the hero of his age and country" (*Lodore*, 24). However, Elizabeth's design for her brother's life is at odds with Lodore's melancholy personality. He "appeared to live rather in a dream than in the actual world" (*Lodore*, 24). Passionate by nature and undisciplined by habit, Lodore rejects "laudable ambition" for Theodora, who ultimately severs their relationship. As he later reveals, the experience left an indelible mark on his already darkened sensibility. Although he desires "to enter upon public life," enjoying "the life led at the seats of the great, and endeavoured to do his part in amusing those around him" (*Lodore*, 26), Lodore indulges his self-pity by playing the jilted lover as he half-heartedly attempts to redirect the drama of his life: "Youth wasted; affections sown on sand, barren of return; wealth and station flung as weeds upon the rocks; a name, whose "gold" was "o'er-dusted" by the inertness of its wearer;–such were the retrospections that haunted his troubled mind. He envied the plough-boy, who whistled as he went; and the laborious cottager, who each Saturday bestowed upon his family the hard-won and scanty earnings of the week. He pined for an aim in life — a bourne — a necessity, to give zest to his palled appetite, and excitement to his satiated soul" (*Lodore*, 26-27). Although Lodore does not directly utter the melodramatic language of the above passage, the narrator makes it clear that these "retrospections" were his thoughts. Unsuccessful in love and undirected in occupation, Lodore romanticizes the simple lives of others who find satisfaction with their work and families.

With marriage to Cornelia Santerre, Lodore believes that he will finally achieve happiness. However, he finds himself playing a secondary rather than leading role because of Lady Santerre, Cornelia's mother, who "was at hand to direct the machinery of the drama" and who "inspired him. . . to play a god-like part" while she simultaneously denied him the authority to do so (*Lodore*, 30). Resenting his supporting role, Lodore is unsympathetic to the needs and foibles of his young wife, whose reliance upon her mother displaces him as the center of her life. When the Casimir incident occurs, he again casts himself into the role of victim and begins to feel as though he were an actor in a dramatic tragedy. He writes the Countess the night he leaves: "Once before we parted for ever, Theodora; but that separation was as the pastime of children in comparison with the tragic scene we now enact" (*Lodore*, 46). He is denied love and domestic happiness a second time and blames Cornelia for "the part [she has] had in bringing on this catastrophe" (*Lodore*, 40). Like the reformed rake of sentimental fiction, Lodore reflects on his mistakes and misfortunes; however, he does not take responsibility for them or face the consequences of his actions. Instead, he constructs a scenario of what could have been if Casimir had loved him as a father; only "for a few seconds the fiction endured" (*Lodore*, 43). Circumstances and pride will not allow his "fiction" to become reality. Rather than brave a public spectacle that would tarnish the reputations of him, the Countess, and Casimir, he determines to establish a new identity as Mr. Fitzhenry in America where he will make a home which was "all his own creation" (*Lodore*, 8). So "with all the impetuosity of his fiery spirit, he resolved to quit at once the scene in which he had played his part so ill" (*Lodore*, 44).

Lodore's desire for life to imitate art further reveals itself as he educates Ethel. Borrowing from literary stock images and archetypes, he molded the plastic Ethel so that "she grew into the image on which his eye doted" (*Lodore*, 10). The parallels to *Frankenstein* are evident: Lodore is as intent on creating a perfect specimen as Victor was, a being that would not only bless him as a father, but also represent his ideal image of woman, an image that neither Theodora nor Cornelia could match. In an apparently heartening domestic scene by the hearth of their Illinois house, Lodore teaches Ethel, who sits at his feet on a stool as he instructs her: "Fitzhenry drew his chief ideas from Milton's Eve, and adding to this the romance of chivalry, he satisfied himself that his daughter would be the imbodied [sic] ideal of all that is adorable and estimable in her sex" (*Lodore*, 12). Lodore's curriculum for his daughter adhered to that advocated by many who believed men and women should have quite different educations given their polar natures, aptitudes, and social roles. Taking a cue from her mother's writings on women and education on *A Vindication of the Rights of Woman*, Shelley undercuts the sentimentality of this scene by suggesting that Lodore's educational philosophy serves his purpose rather than benefits his daughter's future. Not one of the three figures that he draws upon as roles for Ethel — Eve the helpmate, the fair damsel of romance, and *The Tempest*'s Miranda whose fate (at least initially) is completely dependent upon her benevolent father — teaches the young girl independence or selfhood. Rather all three shape her into the type of woman Lodore has imagined is the ideal: submissive, pliable, and dependent.

Lodore decides to return to England when he recognizes that his daughter has become a young woman in a country that cannot provide the society he feels she would need:

> [Lodore] had become aware that the village of the Illinois was not the scene fitted for the development of his daughter's first social feelings, and that he ought to take her among the educated and refined, to give her a chance for happiness. A Gertrude or an Haidèe, brought up in the wilds, innocent and free, and bestowing the treasure of their hearts on some accomplished stranger, brought on purpose to realize the ideal of

their dreamy existences, is a picture of beauty, that requires a miracle
to change in to an actual event in life" (*Lodore*, 54).

Lodore's desire to create Ethel into an obedient, ingenuous figure like
Haidèe or Gertrude, both of whom have been raised in isolated, natural
surroundings and were educated by their fathers, indicates what is his perception of the ideal woman.[12] Cornelia Santerre had been also been naive
and innocent, qualities that drew Lodore to her and that contrasted with
those of the strong-willed and dominating Theodora. Still bitter about his
first relationship, Lodore is determined that his wife and then his daughter
will be different; as the narrator observes, "white paper to be written upon
at will is a favourite metaphor among those men who have described the
ideal of a wife" (*Lodore*, 29). The "accomplished stranger" who is "to
realize the ideal" of Ethel's existence has questionable motives. Whitlock,
an English painter whom Lodore has hired to be an art teacher for Ethel,
sees an alliance with her as an opportunity to advance himself socially and
economically. Like Byron's Don Juan and Campbell's Henry Waldegrave,
Whitlock has "performed the part of the wandering stranger" in that he
stirs the emotions of the adolescent Ethel; however, Lodore determines that
he "was ill-fitted for [the role]," and he does not want Ethel to "be led on
the world's stage by one who was the object of its opprobrium" (*Lodore*,
55). He has worked too diligently in molding her to permit an alliance with
Whitlock whose reputation is dubious. He conveniently forgets that he
himself has not exactly been the object of society's admiration either.

Lodore again reveals his conscious role-playing at the New York City
coffee house to which he and several others go after Mrs. Greville's dinner.[13]
An American named Hatfield has been insulting England and English manners all night, infuriating Lodore, who struggles to keep calm and who
wonders if "he was acting a coward's part while he listened tamely"
(*Lodore*, 66). When Hatfield, who knows the Englishman as Fitzhenry,
refers to Lodore's refusal to accept Casimir's challenge as an example of
English cowardice, Lodore can take no more. He publicly identifies himself
as Lord Lodore. Faced once more with a duel, he sees an opportunity to
clear his tarnished reputation. The duel scene that takes place between
Lodore and the American is itself very theatrical: "The antagonists were
placed: they were both perfectly self-possessed — bent, with hardness and
cruelty of purpose, on fulfilling the tragic act" (*Lodore*, 69). For Lodore,
the staging of this event is critical to restoring his public image since he had
been branded a coward after the incident with Casimir. The dramatic event
profoundly affects the spectators as well. Edward Villiers, the Englishman
who offered to second Lodore, later reflects on the spectacle; the narrator
tells us, "Thus it was that a strange combination of circumstances brought
Villiers into contact with this unfortunate nobleman, and made [Edward]
a witness of and a participator in the closing scene of his disastrous and
wasted life" (*Lodore*, 88). So Lodore dies, and with him, his last chance to

avenge his honor. In a fitting epigraph, the narrator comments that Lodore was "departed from the busy stage, never to be forgotten" (*Lodore*, 88). Yet, he has left no epitaph for himself — no memoir or journal. Ethel is all that remains, and while very much dutiful and loving toward her father, she will become her own person, emerging quite successfully from his shadow and tutelage.

Another character who views life as a drama and people as actors is Lady Santerre. Trying to provide a fashionable life for herself and Cornelia on a limited budget, she recognizes a release from financial stress with her daughter's marriage to Lodore: "She was a clever though uneducated woman: perfectly selfish, soured with the world, yet clinging to it. To make good her second entrance on its stage, she believed it necessary to preserve unlimited sway over the plastic mind of her daughter" (*Lodore*, 31). "Unlimited sway" she does hold. Lady Santerre sets herself up as a barrier to an intimate relationship between Cornelia and Lodore. She has neither educated her daughter to be self-reliant or independent, nor relinquished authority of Cornelia to Lodore. Rather, as noted earlier in this chapter, she ensures that she will "direct the machinery of the drama" (*Lodore*, 30). Ironically, Lodore's dislike of his mother-in-law's control over her daughter does not prevent him from later exacting the same control over Ethel.

Several times Lady Santerre demonstrates her theatrical view of life by comparing people to actors on a stage. When Cornelia asks her mother for advice following Lodore's request that she accompany him to America, Lady Santerre instructs her daughter to ignore his plea, assuring her that Lodore will abandon his plans: "You are as lost as he, if you yield. A little patience, and all will be right again. He will soon grow tired of playing the tragic hero on a stage, surrounded by no spectators" (*Lodore*, 49). Because she herself cannot fathom playing a role without an audience to appreciate it or without personal gain, Lady Santerre assumes that Lodore cannot as well. In an attempt to reassure Cornelia, who is concerned about losing her daughter, she insists that Lodore will tire of being a father and will be "too glad to find that you will still be willing to act the mother towards his child" (*Lodore*, 49). Her choice of words–"act the mother"–indicates that Lady Santerre applies role-playing to the domestic sphere as well as the public one. The narrator's choice of words suggest Mary Shelley's indictment of Lady Santerre. While Shelley resisted many of the cultural norms expected of her gender, motherhood was a relationship that she took seriously. Although Lady Santerre is devoted to Cornelia's welfare, her language and actions reveal that prestige and wealth are the primary motivations for her decisions and that domestic happiness between Cornelia and Lodore is a low priority.

The narrator indicates just how completely dominant Lady Santerre's control is over her daughter. After Lodore and Ethel have sailed to America, she encourages Cornelia to play the role of the wronged wife to fashionable society, and she carefully stages their social activities: "Withering away in unhonoured age, still she appeared in the halls of the great, and played the part of Cerberus in her daughter's drawing-room" (*Lodore*, 54). The analogy to the three-headed dog guarding the entrance of Hades is hardly flattering; however, the comparison is an apt one. Lady Santerre is diligent in orchestrating and protecting her daughter's image that she has so carefully constructed for her own gain. As a woman who has taught her daughter "to view society's glass by which to set her feelings, and to which to adapt her conduct" (*Lodore*, 31), Lady Santerre is more concerned with appearance than with substance. Unfortunately, her lessons are well learned by her daughter.

Although the characters of Lodore and Lady Santerre illustrate the most detrimental effects of theatrical role-playing in the novel, Mary Shelley criticizes another as well. Edward Villiers, who essentially an admirable figure, is nevertheless dangerously close to becoming a victim of Romantic sensibility. Although Edward does not play the socialite that Cornelia does, he is unduly influenced by public opinion which credits appearance rather than substance. He severs his relationship with Ethel when he believes that his father has squandered the family's inheritance, thus leaving him penniless and ill-suited to court Ethel. Worried that society will perceive him as incapable of caring for her, he constantly urges her to stay with others as he attends to financial arrangements and begs her not to ask her aunt for money, both requests that Ethel ignores.

Edward is also inclined to dramatize events. Recalling the setting of the duel between Lodore and the American, Edward sees himself as an actor of a larger drama: "The moon-lit hill, and tragic scene, in which he had played his part, came vividly before his eyes" (*Lodore*, 93). He also tends to typecast others when he does not understand their circumstances and does not make the effort to look beyond the mask others wear to project an image or conceal their real character. Influenced by Elizabeth Fitzhenry's opinions of her brother's wife, he regards Cornelia as a cold woman and an unloving mother and is therefore surprised when she expresses sincere interest for her daughter during one of their early meetings. Despite his concern with a public image, he is no actor. He recognizes the foolishness of adopting roles to satisfy ambition or personal gain and agrees with his uncle's assessment of Colonel Villiers, his father, who is courting a young woman whose fortunes would alleviate his monetary difficulties. With dramatic language and allusions, Lord Maristow aptly describes his brother's actions: "'It is too ridiculous to see him playing a boy-lover's part at his time of life, trying to undermine a daughter's sense of duty — he, who may soon be a grandfather. . . . The whole thing is the farce of the day, and the stolen interviews of the lovers, and the loud, vulgarly-spoken denunciations of her father, vary the scene from a travestie of Romeo and Juliet to the comedies or Plautus or Moliere'" (*Lodore*, 132). Should Colonel Villiers' father succeed in his attempt to gain the young woman's inheritance, his son's troubles would be relieved. However, Edward's sense of propriety and manners prevents such wishful thinking, and his benevolent sensibility thwarts any thoughts of selfish, mean-spirited actions. Also, Edward benefits from the advice of a wise mentor, his uncle, and from the devotion of his wife, Ethel.

The dramatic perceptions of Lodore, Lady Santerre, and to some extent Edward Villiers set the stage, as it were, for those of Cornelia Lodore. Taking her cue from her mother, Cornelia Lodore is conditioned to view the world as a stage on which she can enact her role as a fashionable lady who attends the proper functions and associates with the proper people. Dominated by her mother and married at sixteen, Cornelia has had little chance for a variety of life experiences and to establish any sense of self-identity or esteem. As authority figures, neither Lady Santerre nor Lodore respect Cornelia as an individual; rather they see her as a means by which to further their own social or personal ambition. Lady Santerre realizes that, through her daughter's marriage to Lodore, she herself can achieve social prominence that will befit her title. Aware of Lady Santerre's financial problems, Lodore is entranced with playing the role of benefactor to Cornelia and thinks "how proud a part was his, to gift her with rank, fortune, and all earthly blessings, and to receive in return, gratitude, tenderness, and unquestioning submission" (*Lodore*, 29). Cornelia's inexperienced and impressionable nature does not, however, serve Lodore's purpose. She is inextricably bound to her mother, a tie that is even stronger than the one with her husband. Well-schooled by her mother, Cornelia regards her relationship as Lodore's wife merely as a role to play on the stage of English society.

Although inherently good-natured and kind, Cornelia is susceptible to the allures of high society and quickly learns to enjoy the benefits of Lodore's wealth and rank, which facilitate her entrance onto the public stage. Like Frances Burney's Evelina and Eliza Haywood's Betsy Thoughtless, she discovers the painful ramifications of misreading situations and characters. Her playful flirting with Casimir, harmless in intent, is instrumental in causing Lodore's and her downfall. As her husband reminds her following the fateful party where he struck Casimir, she is partly to blame, and he scolds her for "the part you have had in bringing on this catastrophe" (*Lodore*, 40). Cornelia continues the dramatic allusion to identify their situation, seeing, perhaps, an analogy between their lives and those of characters in a sentimental play by Kotzebue.[14] She remarks to Lodore that, "This sounds very like a German tragedy, being at once disagreeable and inexplicable" (41). "It is a tragedy," Lodore agrees, "a tragedy brought now to its last dark catastrophe. . . . [and] you have a part in this" (*Lodore*, 41). Although the dramatic metaphor may appropriately describe their predicament, Cornelia does not delve beneath its surface and try to resolve the conflict. Never having been taught to exercise common sense and self-will, she is quite willing to remain passive and adopt whatever role suits the events that carry her along. She would rather play the heroine-victim of a German tragedy than abandon theatrics and address the dilemma that she and her husband face.

After the death of her mother, Cornelia no longer has anyone to direct her life. Yet by this time, she has learned how to play to the conventions of society, and she has difficulty in abandoning the role with which she has defined herself. After hearing of Lodore's death, Cornelia is free to pursue a relationship with Horatio Saville, who has come to love her very much. A second son with scholarly rather than political or social ambitions, Horace seems an unlikely match for the more worldly Cornelia. Nevertheless, she is attracted to his sincerity and his genuine affection for her. As his sister Lucy says, "He is not of this world. Pure-minded as a woman, honourable as a knight of old, he is more like a being we read of, and his match is not to be found upon earth" (*Lodore*, 119). However, Cornelia once again plays the part of the coquette and allows the "artificial courtesies of society" to dictate her actions (*Lodore*, 89). As a result of her behavior, Horatio's sisters conclude that Cornelia cannot be serious about a second son with no title and tell their brother so. When Cornelia learns that Horatio has gone abroad, she is sure that he will return to her, just as she was convinced that Lodore would abandon his plan to go to America. Her actions suggest that, like Charlotte Lennox's Arabella, she has read too many romances. However, Horatio does not return; Sophia Saville tells Cornelia that Horatio has married a Neapolitan woman, Clorinda.[15] Once again Lady Lodore learns that role-playing does not accomplish her desire, and she "wondered at the part she had acted" (*Lodore*, 93). Realizing that their relationship is finished, she employs a theatrical description to describe her loss: "Yet wherefore ask these things? It was over; the scene was closed" (*Lodore*, 91).

Cornelia continues to view life as a drama in which she has determined to play a role that privileges appearance over substance. She reveals her theatrical perception of life to Edward Villiers, whom she has come to know by way of Horatio, who is Edward's cousin. When she learns from him that Ethel has returned to England and that Lodore's outdated will requires that she must forfeit her jointure should she assume the role of mother and guardian of her daughter,[16] Cornelia plans to spend the summer season in Paris to avoid a public spectacle should she and Ethel meet at a social function. She would not, she tells Edward, "present a domestic tragedy or farce to the Opera House — we must not meet in public" (*Lodore*, 95).[17] A domestic tragedy" played out in public is repugnant to Cornelia, who has so carefully performed the role of propriety and decorum, while in society's eyes her husband played the coward and deserter. At this point, the lonely young woman recognizes the emptiness of her life and begins to regret her past decisions. However, she cannot yet bring herself to give up the social amenities to which she is accustomed, nor does she have any motivation to do so, for she fears that the daughter whom she truly loves has been taught to despise her.

Although despondent over losing Horatio and resigned to keeping a distance from Ethel, Cornelia forces herself to "adopt as a mask, the smiling appearance which had been natural to her for many years" (*Lodore*, 176). When she hears of Ethel's and Edward's financial troubles, she decides that, despite social pretenses and legal dictates, she will intervene to help them and to convince her daughter, whom she imagines to be weak-willed, to come stay with her. Edward is serving a prison sentence, and he and Ethel share a shabby apartment in the prison section of London. Feeling that she should act the role of mother, she determines to visit her daughter, "making up her mind to perform her part with grace, and every show of kindness" (*Lodore*, 179). Meeting her daughter for the first time in nearly fifteen years, Cornelia realizes how wrongly she has cast Ethel into the role of a weak, insipid character. Impressed by Ethel's bravery and devotion to her husband, Cornelia promises to help her.

Edward, prejudiced against Cornelia for her behavior toward Horatio, does not believe she will ever want or be able to help them. However, Ethel does have faith in her mother's promise, and her assessment of her mother is accurate. Cornelia has finally decided that playing the part of the wronged wife for social appearances cannot supply the happiness that familial love and support can. As Katherine Hill-Miller notes, motherhood frees Cornelia: "Cornelia's new life of devotion to her daughter, for all its conventionality, allows her to escape some of the configurations of traditional marriage — in particular the patterns of dominance and dependence involved in her relationship to Lodore" (159). One might also add that she has cast off the dominance and dependence of Lady Santerre and social mores as well. Avoiding public spectacle, Cornelia permanently severs her connections with London's fashionable crowd with her plan to help Ethel. Visiting Gayland, the solicitor who is helping Edward, she arranges the sale of her jointure and turns her London house over to Ethel. In prior days, Cornelia would have continued to play the wronged wife and would have enjoyed her status among the well-connected; now, ridden with guilt and sadness, she quietly ensures her daughter's happiness without regard to her own welfare, and she swears Gayland to secrecy about her role in Ethel's and Edward's changed fortunes. Her plan to return to Wales where living is cheaper demonstrates her departure from the once-desired social circles. Unfortunately, it also represents escape, for there she can avoid contact with Ethel and the pain of reconciling with her daughter what she still has difficulty doing herself.

In the tradition of sentimental fiction, reward does come for Cornelia: she and her daughter reunite and Horatio Saville returns. His elder brother unexpected death leaves Horatio heir to Lord Maristow's title. Even more conveniently, Clorinda also dies suddenly, leaving him with a young daughter. Horatio and his child come back to England and joyfully reunite with the Saville family and with Edward and Ethel. Determined to find Cornelia, Horatio learns the details of Lady Lodore's generosity from Gayland, and Edward, regretting his hasty assessment of her character, joins in the search for her. However, through Elizabeth Fitzhenry, Ethel discovers Cornelia at the cottage of Elizabeth Fitzhenry's neighbor.[18] The homey, rural setting of their sentimental reunion is far removed from the artifices and theatrics of London society. For the epigraph of the novel's second chapter, Mary Shelley quotes a passage from Seneca that aptly sums up Cornelia's new-found happiness at the end: "Settle in some secret nest, / In calm leisure let me rest; / And far off the public stage, / Pass away my silent age" (*Lodore*, 6). This epigraph provides an effective contrast to the characters and fates of Lodore and Cornelia. Both of them seek "calm leisure" in rural homes: he to the wilds of Illinois; she to the outskirts of Longfield, Essex. However, Lodore escapes to evade his past; he simply casts off one mask for another. Not until just before his death, does he realize the futility of playing roles for social expectations. Cornelia, on the other hand, chooses the quiet, natural setting once she has discarded her mask and has attained self-knowledge and esteem. The setting is not an escape from herself, but from the public stage.

Throughout *Lodore*, Mary Shelley emphasizes Cornelia's dramatic tendencies by setting several London scenes against the backdrop of the theater and opera, which are favorite types of entertainment for Cornelia. Twice when Ethel and her mother meet, they are attending an opera or play. The occasional theatrical setting contrasts the artificial world of role-playing with the actual world of life itself. Cornelia, an accomplished actress for social appearances, feels at home in such a setting; Ethel, raised in the natural surroundings of Illinois, does not. Although Ethel enjoys the theater and opera, she is uncomfortable in formal society and "did not well know how to act" (*Lodore*, 129). Always herself, Ethel finds no need for adopting roles to accommodate any preconceived illusions of society.

Despite the parallels in education and upbringing, Ethel sharply contrasts her mother in many ways. Although observing social standards of propriety and decorum, she regards self-esteem and domestic happiness as truer measures of one's worth. When she and Edward experience the degradation of a debtor's imprisonment, she remains with him, refusing to live with either her mother or aunt. The narrator remarks that "Love in a cottage is the dream of many a high-born girl, who is not allowed to dance with a younger brother at Almack's; but a secluded, an obscure, an almost cottage life, was all that Ethel had ever known, and all that she coveted" (*Lodore*, 111). This passage reveals Mary Shelley's strong indictment of society's manners that often deny a young woman (or man) the chance for love with a partner who is compatible though not perhaps the most desirable for social advancement. Edward worries about appearance, but not Ethel: "A splendid dwelling, costly living, and many attendants, were with her the adjuncts, not the material, of life. If the stage on which she played her part was to be so decorated, it was well; if otherwise, the change did not merit her attention" (*Lodore*, 165). Unlike her mother, who reveres society's glass, Ethel's actions mirror her authentic character.

When Ethel was a child, Lodore had compared her to Miranda, probably for the purpose of elevating himself to the level of Prospero. Yet Ethel then bore resemblances to Miranda: there had been no one in her life but her father, and he controlled her and provided for her so that she saw no reason why she should break free of the passive role for which she had been formed by Lodore. Even in her relationship with Edward, Ethel seems quite willing to transfer the authority of father to husband without a thought for her own will. Nevertheless, although brought up to be dependent, Ethel, like the heroines of Ann Radcliffe and Charlotte Smith, quietly but deliberately challenges the boundaries imposed by marriage and a restrictive education. At first, she determines to play the dutiful wife and obey Edward's request that she stay with her aunt while he made arrangements in London: "The idea of an heroic sacrifice on his part, and submission to his will on hers, at first soothed her — but never to see him more was an alternative that tasked her fortitude too high" (*Lodore*, 111). In a delightfully comic scene, the narrator describes Ethel's journey, the only one she has ever taken alone and voluntarily. She learns how to ask for directions, how to use the transportation, and how to manage money, though her generous tipping reduces her pocketbook more than she planned.[19] She refuses to leave Edward alone in prison when he insists upon it, and although her decision results from her intense devotion to him, disobey she does.

Such daring actions by the sheltered Ethel are perhaps not surprising. The narrator has told us that Ethel could become a "heroine" if she were forced to (*Lodore*, 13). Her actions demonstrate that she can assert herself without adhering to the artificial constraints of social role-playing. She does employ a theatrical metaphor at one point, but in reference to her father, not herself. When she and Edward go to Eton, Ethel views the landscape and thinks that "every green field was a stage on which her father had played a part; each majestic tree, or humble streamlet, was hallowed by being associated with his image" (*Lodore*, 78). Nevertheless, unlike Lodore, Cornelia, and Lady Santerre, Ethel does not adopt dramatic roles; neither does she confuse life and art. At an inn in Brixton, where the couple spends their last few days before imprisonment, Ethel and Edward read Shakespeare's *Troilus and Cressida*.[20] When Edward expresses doubts about Fanny Derham's arrival with needed money, Ethel chides him: "Would Troilus and Cressida have repined at having been left darkling a few minutes? How much happier we are than all the heroes and heroines that ever lived or were imagined! they grasped at the mere shadow of the thing, whose substance we absolutely possess" (*Lodore*, 168). Like Mary Shelley herself, Ethel is quite aware of the distinction between reality and illusion and that domestic happiness is more important than self-interest and public masks, a lesson that fortunately Cornelia learns in time to enjoy the remainder of her life with her daughter.

In *Lodore*, Mary Shelley drew on the conventions of the novel of manners, sentiment, and sensibility to expose the artificiality and theatricality of social roles that often adversely affect one's ability to balance the public and domestic spheres. While she criticizes Lady Santerre's and Cornelia's playing to the dictates of society and its customs, she also, like Eliza Haywood and Frances Burney, condemns the emphasis on public rather than private virtue. "To thine own self be true," Polonius tells Laertes, for "Thou canst not then be false to any man" (*Hamlet* I.iii.82-4). In a world that privileges appearance over character and that encourages masked rather than sincere principles and morals, Polonius' advice is difficult to live by. Nevertheless, the "personages who formed the drama of this tale" (228), especially Cornelia Lodore, discover that roles played for the sole purpose of social acceptance, gain, or approbation result in unfilled and unhappy lives.

Chapter 8 Notes

1. In several of her tales and short stories, Shelley did focus on the everyday life of private figures whose actions are not set against a political or revolutionary landscape. See, for example, "The Mourner" (1823), "The Trial of Love" (1834), and "The Parvenue" (1836) in *Mary Shelley: Collected Tales and Stories*, ed. Charles E. Robinson.

2. See Katherine Rogers' study, *Feminism in Eighteenth-Century England* for an excellent overview of this subject.

3. See Janet Todd's discussion of sentiment and sensibility in *The Sign of Angellica*, especially pages 101 to194.

4. For a history of this narrative genre, see Charlotte E. Morgan, *The Rise of the Novel of Manners*, 1911, reprint (New York: Russell and Russell, Inc. 1963).

5. See Shelley's January-February 1831 letter to Charles Ollier (*Letters*, 2: 125). Although the writing progressed fairly smoothly, Shelley complained how slowly the proofs were sent to her; see also the letter of 15 and 18 March 1834 and that of 18 March 1834 to Ollier (*Letters*, 2: 199).

6. On 21 November 1833, Shelley told Ollier that she was mailing the conclusion of Volume One and most of Two and that she preferred sending the novel in parts so that she could double check as she completed the rest of it. She was very conscious of the constraints the three-volume form presented: "I want to see how much it will make before I decide as to the exact place where the second Vol. will end" (*Letters*, 2: 196). Five months later, Shelley voiced the same concern; she was firm on concluding Volume One as it was and preferred to add more to Volumes Two and Three if needed (*Letters*, 2: 199-200).

7. On 19 August 1834, Shelley wrote to Maria Gisborne and noted that Lodore was finally printed (*Letters*, 2: 213).

8. *London Journal* 58 (6 May 1835): 138-39.

9. Despite the novel's title, which leads one to expect Lord Lodore as the feature character, Mary Shelley wrote Ollier that Cornelia and Ethel are the focus: "A Mother & Daughter are the heroines — The Mother who after safrifising [sic] all to the world at first — afterwards makes sacrifises not less entire, for her child — finding all to be Vanity, except the genuine affections of the heart" (*Letters*, 2: 185).

10. There are few chronological details regarding Lodore's and Theodora's previous relationship. The narrator tells us that Casimir is nearly the same age as the nineteen-year-old Cornelia, and that, at the time of Theodora's visit to London, Lodore is about thirty-five. Casimir must have been conceived when Lodore first met Theodora in his early twenties. We do not know, for example, if Theodora was married to Count Lyzinski at the time of the affair or if Casimir was born out of wedlock. Also unknown is whether or not Casimir figured into the lovers' decision to separate.

11. Mary Shelley, *Lodore* (New York: Wallis & Wallis, 1835), 37; hereafter cited in text as *Lodore*.

12. Haidèe is the island maiden in the second and third cantos of Byron's *Don Juan* (1818-1824); Gertrude quite likely alludes to the heroine of Thomas Campbell's poem, *Gertrude of Wyoming* (1809).

13. Mrs. Greville is an Englishwoman who has asked if Lodore would escort her daughter's friend back to her parents in England. The young woman in question is none other than Fanny Derham, daughter of Francis Derham, Lodore's schoolboy friend.

14. Their circumstances somewhat parallel those of the husband and wife in Kotzebue's *Menschenhass und Reue*, which Richard Brinsley Sheridan brought to the English stage in 1798 as *The Stranger*. German tragedies notwithstanding, the bizarre and unforeseen situation resembles those in many English Gothic plays of the period as well.

15. Clorinda is quite likely modeled after Emilia Viviani, who was also in a convent (awaiting an unhappy marriage) and whose beauty and plight captured Percy Shelley's interest and sympathy in 1820. She is a variation of the character in Mary Shelley's 1824 short story, "The Bride of Modern Italy," also named Clorinda.

16. Lodore was in the process of revising his will when he was killed in the duel. The revision lifted all restrictions on interaction between mother and daughter. Although he had indicated to Edward Villiers that he hoped for reconciliation with Cornelia, Lodore had divulged the new will's contents to no one.

17. They had already met at the opera, although mother and daughter did not recognize each other.

18. Katherine Hill-Miller notes the significance of the natural and rural setting in her examination of Cornelia's character (159).

19. Mary Shelley may well have been drawing on her own experience of travelling alone when she returned to England in 1823, a year after her husband's death.

20. Recall that in *Valperga*, this Shakespearean play was a focal point of Euthanasia's court entertainment. In that novel as well as this one, Shelley may have chosen this play to dramatize a reversal of male-female loyalties. Unlike Cressida, Euthanasia and Ethel remain faithful to their lovers whose ambition and adherence to social appearance, respectively, threaten the relationships.

Falkner: The Illusion of Romance

And what's a life? — A weary pilgrimage,
Whose glory in one day doth fill the stage
With childhood, manhood, and decrepit age.
— Francis Quarles, "What is Life"

The domestic theme of *Lodore* continues in Mary Shelley's last novel, *Falkner* (1837). Relying once again on conventions of sentimental fiction and the novel of manners, Shelley at the same time subverts them with a decidedly Godwinian twist to explore the devastation that obsessive Romantic sensibility and dramatic role playing often effect on the order and happiness of private lives. Within the novel's framework of the protagonist's life with Elizabeth Raby, his adopted daughter, is the autobiographical history of John Falkner's youth and crime. This first-person narrative, like those autobiographies by Victor Frankenstein and especially Mathilda, reveals the egocentric and self-pitying perspective of a character whose dream of social recognition and marital happiness becomes a nightmare of public spectacle and domestic tragedy. This tale-within-a-tale section of the novel is also indebted to Richardson's *Clarissa*, although Shelley presents the point of view of the rakish hero-villain rather than the virtuous heroine. Like Lovelace, Falkner is indirectly responsible for the death of the woman he loves and respects, Alithea Neville. The novel follows the tradition of other narrative texts in which the private and public clash. William Ray, in a study of the 1678 French narrative, *La Princesse de Clèves*, describes this text as a "personal, emotion struggle of the protagonist . . . framed by an on-going semi-public drama of gossip and local reportage which mediates between the private realm of affect and personal experience, and the public domain of polities and history" (25). In *Falkner*, Mary Shelley also explores the effect of spectacle, the "drama of gossip and local reportage" when John Falkner must face the court and the public as a result of Sir Boyville's revengeful actions. Although the novel fits easily into the domestic genre, it also marks Shelley's return to narrative devices of her earlier fiction, particularly with the autobiographical — and quite dramatic — letter Falkner leaves for Elizabeth.

The success of *Lodore* prompted Charles Ollier, who acted as a literary advisor to publisher Richard Bentley, to ask Shelley for another novel, which she began in late 1835. In a letter to Ollier a few months later, Shelley admitted that she had not intended to write another: "but in consequence of what you said, I began to reflect on the subject — and a story presented itself so vividly to my mind that I began to write almost directly — and have finished one volume — the whole will be ready in the Autumn. It is in the style of Lodore, but the story more interesting & even, I should think, more popular" (*Letters,* 2: 263). However, Shelley sold her finished work to Saunders and Otley, who were more generous in advances and payment than Bentley (Sunstein, 334; *Letters,* 2:280).[1] *Falkner* was published in February 1837. Despite Shelley's hopes about the novel's popularity, *Falkner* did not receive the critical acclaim that *Lodore* did. Nevertheless, it sold well and generated several favorable reviews, including one by the *Monthly Review*, which called the novel her "finest work."[2]

Although Mary Shelley complained that poor health and time constraints (she nursed Godwin in the last days before his death in 1836) prevented her from remedying *Falkner*'s faults, she told Leigh Hunt in an 1837 letter that the novel "is a favourite of mine" (*Letters,* 2: 285-286). Remarking to Maria Gisborne that "the story writes itself," Shelley noted that its theme was "fidelity as the first of human virtues" (*Letters,* 2: 264; 260). The novel opens with sad story of the six-year-old orphan Elizabeth Raby; however, the central protagonist is John Falkner, whose dark mysterious past leads him to an attempted suicide at the grave site of Elizabeth's mother. Thinking he means to harm her mother's spirit, the child prevents the suicide. Falkner then accompanies her to the Baker home where she resides, and he learns from Mrs. Baker that Elizabeth's mother may have been a friend to Alithea, the woman he has accused himself of murdering. Out of sympathy and guilt, he "adopts" Elizabeth, who lovingly calls him her father. The entire first volume of this two-volume novel deals with Falkner's and Elizabeth's lives over approximately a ten-year period. Although we are given hints about Falkner's past, his narrative, which begins the second volume, reveals the secret that has haunted him for so long.

Like Mathilda, Falkner adheres to a dramatic structural pattern for his narrative and incorporates theatrical imagery and language to render it more dramatic than a confessional epistle might otherwise be. His introduction functions much like a prologue that explains the purpose or theme of the play about to be performed: "To palliate crime, and by investigating motive to render guilt less odious — such is not the feeling that rules my pen; to confer honour upon innocence, to vindicate virtue, and announce truth — though that offer my own name as a mark for deserved infamy — such are my motives."[3] (*Falkner,* 2: 1). His words echo those of another self-absorbed character, William Godwin's Mandeville, who insists in his autobiography that, "The purpose of these pages is, to be made the record of truth."[4] Falkner asserts that his narrative's intent is to exonerate Alithea: "I am not writing my life; and, but for the wish to appear less criminal in my dear child's eyes, I had not written a word of the foregone pages, but leaped at once to the mere facts that justify poor Alithea, and tell the tragic story of her death" (*Falkner*, 2: 39). True, his narrative does prove her innocence and refutes the rumor that she had willingly deserted her family. However, like the monster's, the De Lacy family's, and Safie's histories, which are enclosed within the frame structure of Victor's narrative and Walton's letters, so too is Alithea's story "buried at the work's emotional center" (Hill-Miller, 191). His protestations of authorial objectivity are suspect, for Falkner's narrative is not a straight-forward confession, whose primary purpose is to absolve Alithea's rumored infidelity. Rather it is a theatrical rendition of his life, a dramatic reconstruction that reinforces his perception of himself as both victim and villain. Thus he embarks on the story of his life and that is what takes center stage; Alithea's story becomes a more a device to elicit audience sympathy for Falkner.

In his confessional letter, Falkner carefully constructs biographical material to elicit sympathy, just as Victor Frankenstein, Mathilda, Lionel Verney, and Godwin's Caleb Williams and Mandeville do in theirs. The very act of recording his history suggests that, like these literary predecessors, Falkner is trying to present himself as both the hero that he has been unable to play in real life and the victim whose good intentions are thwarted at every twist of the plot. Indeed, from Falkner's perspective, he is as much a victim of circumstance as Alithea is. His childhood has been undeservedly unhappy; he is expelled from school for kindness to animals; he embarks on an admirable career only to have Mr. Rivers deride his station; and upon achieving wealth and title, he discovers that Alithea — his only connection to happiness and love — has married another. In most sentimental novels, such as *Clarissa* or *The Vicar of Wakefield*, the author presents the innocent and victimized protagonist's point of view, which, in *Falkner*, would be that of Alithea Rivers. Shelley, however, spotlights the character who is generally cast as the antagonist or villain. In giving Falkner the opportunity to voice his perspective through his dramatic narrative, she is able to emphasize his culpability, over-wrought sensibility, and inclination to view the world as a stage on which he can perform the role of his choice.

The narrative demonstrates Falkner's reliance on dramatic metaphors to enhance theatricality and to elicit the audience's sympathy. At one point, Falkner writes, "The drama of life . . . was unrolling before me" (*Falkner*, 2:29). He tells us that, as a child, he was physically and psychologically abused by his father. Unable to chart his own course, Falkner decides to enact the role in which others have cast him: "I declared war with my whole soul against the world; I became all I had been painted; I was sullen, vindictive, desperate. I resolved to run away; I cared not what would befall me — I was nearly fourteen — I was strong, and could work — I could join a gang of gipsies, I could act their life singly, and subsisting by nightly depredation, spend my days in liberty" (*Falkner,* 2: 12). He defines not only his actions as roles, but also events as scenes. When his indolent father reacts violently to the news of his elder brother's marriage, Falkner writes, "I let fall the curtain over the scene that ensued: you would have thought that a villainous fraud had been committed, in which I was implicated" (*Falkner,* 2: 9).

Falkner's selective inclusion of his life's events and his arrangement of them further encourage one to read his history as a drama that features him as the sympathetic villain-hero. Chapter One of Volume II provides the expository details of Falkner's unhappy childhood to invoke the sympathy and complicity of the audience/reader. Friendless at boarding school, Falkner receives an invitation from his dead mother's distant relative, Mrs. Rivers. At her home, he discovers love and kindness and forms a close bond with her daughter, Alithea. Chapters Two and Three provide the rising action, demonstrating Falkner's worthiness to claim Alithea by overcoming the obstacles preventing their union: his lack of a career and of an inheritance. However, when he returns from a ten-year appointment in India to assume title to his family's estate, Falkner learns of Alithea's unhappy marriage to a cold, insensitive man. Chapter Four is the turning point, beginning with Falkner's attempt to convince Alithea to run away with him and concluding with his abduction of her. Chapter Five concludes the drama with Alithea's tragic death and Falkner's eternal guilt for his culpable role.

Falkner has composed his history on the battlefield in Greece, where he has gone to expiate his guilt, just as Lord Raymond did. If he could die a hero in that respect, perhaps such action would redeem him for his role in causing Alithea's death: "Falkner played no false part with himself. He longed to die" (*Falkner,* 1: 105). Like Victor Frankenstein, he cannot take responsibility for his actions; he selfishly decides that death is his only answer. The horrors of war and the thought of death are minor compared to his haunted conscience: "my nerves, so firm amidst the din of battle, shrink and shudder at the tale I am about to narrate" (*Falkner,* 2: 2)

The tale as Falkner presents it reveals affinities not only to Victor Frankenstein, but also to the creature. Both are isolated and friendless; both are abandoned by their parents; and both seek relationships with a loving, caring family. The touching domestic scene at the Rivers' home recalls a similar one at the De Lacey family's cottage. Falkner is more fortunate than the creature, however, for he is accepted and loved. When he runs away from school after a serious altercation with a bully, he hides himself outside Mrs. Rivers' cottage. An outcast like the creature, he draws strength by his proximity to his adopted family: "I hid myself in the thicket near her house, sometimes I stole near it; then, as I heard voices, I retreated further into the wild part of the wood. Night came on at last, and that night I slept under a tree, but at a short distance from the cottage" (*Falkner,* 2: 25).

When Mrs. Rivers arranges for Falkner to attend a military school, he resolves to make good the faith she and Alithea have in him. The profession of soldier, he decides, is a role that will ensure their approbation: "My determination was to enlist as a soldier; I believed that I should so distinguish myself by my valour, as speedily to become a great man. I saw myself singled out by the generals, applauded, honoured, and rewarded. I fancied my return, and how proudly I should present myself before Alithea, having carved out my own fortune, and become all that her sweet mother entreated me to be — brave, generous, and true" (*Falkner*, 2: 26). Falkner clearly envisions a heroic future and easily imagines a dramatic scenario of his life. He will be "singled out" and honored, and his reward will be Alithea's hand and an idyllic life. With "generous ambition and ardent gratitude," Falkner departs for school, striving to assure himself of his motivation: "The drama of life, methought, was unrolling before me, the scene on which I was to act appeared resplendent in fairy and gorgeous colours; neither vanity, nor pride, swelled me up; but a desire to prove myself worthy of those adored beings who were all the world to me, who had saved me from myself, to restore me to the pure and happy shelter of their hearts" (*Falkner*, 2: 29). Like Victor Frankenstein and Perkin Warbeck, Falkner perceives the world as a stage and himself as a heroic figure upon it. Although he desires to achieve fame and glory, he is more desperate to demonstrate the worthiness of the only love he has known. Once he has done so, the drama will conclude with his union to Alithea, and, as with the sentimental hero, virtue will be rewarded.

Learning that his father and uncle have died and that he is heir to the family estate, Falkner returns to England, assuming that there is no longer a barrier to marrying Alithea. At last his dream will be realized. Again, he invents a scenario of events that have not yet happened: "my imagination had created home, and bride, and fair beings sprung from her side, who called me father" (*Falkner*, 2: 46). Unfortunately, his vivid imagination creates a world that can never exist for him, a vision with no basis in reality. As he ruefully notes later, "Living in a dream, I had not considered the chances and the storms, or even the mere changes, of the seasons of life. . . . I had lived in a fool's paradise" (*Falkner*, 2: 45). He returns to find Alithea married to Sir Boyville, a man unworthy of her. Subsequently, his dream becomes a nightmare: "one word defaced my whole future life and widowed me for ever" (*Falkner*, 2: 46). Falkner has so convinced himself of the domestic drama he has envisioned with Alithea and children that its failure to materialize has "widowed" him before he is even married. Desperate, he conceives a plan to reconstruct it: "Now began that chain of incidents that led to a deed I had not thought of. Incidents or accidents; acts, done I know not why; nothing in themselves; but meeting, and kindled by the fiery spirit that raged in my bosom, they gave such direction to its ruinous powers, as produced the tragedy for ever to be deplored" (*Falkner*, 2: 46). Falkner blames Sir Boyville for his despair, just as

Godwin's Mandeville blames the innocent Clifford for his. Mandeville writes that "[Clifford] had arrested me in my first step on the theatre of life. . . . He had thrown me down the ladder, just as I was stepping on the stage, and laid me prostrate, maimed, and unable to help myself, on the earth" (310). Falkner, too, has determined that he will play "on the theatre of life" as a successful man with Alithea at his side. When circumstances rewrite his plot, he chooses a far different role to play. No longer the sentimental or romance hero, Falkner plays the part of a rake, and like the creature, he aggressively performs the role that he believes will lead to the domestic happiness that he craves.

To implement his scheme, Falkner enlists the help of James Osborne, who later refers to Falkner as the "principal actor" of the tragedy that is about to unfold. Falkner impersonates Alithea's fictional sibling, adopting a "brother's part" to convince Osborne that his intentions are moral and legal (*Falkner,* 2: 54). He does not plan to abduct Alithea against her will; he merely wants her away from her house, on neutral ground, to convince her to take her children and run away with him: "I sought a solitary spot, for the scene of our last interview, or of the first hour of my lasting bliss. What more solitary than the wild and drear sea shore of the south of Cumberland?" (*Falkner,* 2: 66). So appropriate is the setting that years later, Alithea's son, Gerard Neville, surveys the landscape, contemplating "the scene in all its parts — the wild waste sea, dark and purple beneath the lowering clouds — the dreary extent of beach — the far stupendous mountains . . . it seemed as if actual vision could not bring it home more truly" (*Falkner,* 2: 127-28). Like Mathilda, Falkner carefully selects a setting that complements his mood and that provides an appropriate backdrop to his playing the role of the hero rescuing the distressed lady.

As Falkner and his beloved walk down the garden path with the young Gerard skipping along with his mother, the passionate, lovesick hero momentarily experiences doubts about his plan. Falkner realizes that "surely there is no greater enemy to virtue and good intentions, than the want of self-command" (*Falkner,* 2: 71). He decides not to execute his plan and recognizes that true heroism requires neither theatrics or egocentric play-acting: "For a moment I had become virtuous and heroic" (*Falkner,* 2: 71). But passions overtake him, and he forces Alithea into the carriage as Osborne in his excitement drives off before Gerard can get in with his mother. Alithea falls into a faint, partially from astonishment at Falkner's actions. What has most upset her, however, is leaving Gerard, who runs down the road after the carriage crying for his mother, a scene that replays itself for Gerard again and again. Falkner cannot fathom the extent of Alithea's love for her children despite her earlier informing him that the name "mother" is more dear to her than "wife" (*Falkner,* 2: 64). Despondent already that his long-held dream to marry her cannot become reality, he is again shocked that primal maternal instinct is greater than romantic love. However, he had never intended to separate Alithea from her child: "She had spoke of this child with such rapture that it would have been a barbarity beyond my acting to have separated her from him" (*Falkner*, 2: 70). Osborne's panic causes yet another unforeseen action in Falkner's drama.

Falkner bitterly experiences the illusion of romance with Alithea's accidental drowning: he was to have been her savior, not her executor. After her death, Falkner imagines the scene of Alithea awaking in the cottage and her futile effort to escape: "I saw it all; and how often, and for ever, do I go over in my thoughts what had passed during the interval of my absence" (*Falkner*, 2: 81). Re-living the scene, time and time again, reinforces his guilt, but it never prompts him to absolve Alithea even when he hears the slanderous version Sir Boyville has concocted. He acts well the part of the Byronic figure, yet he is unable to live up to real heroism. Instead he slips into an increasingly debilitating despondency that intensifies his self-victimization.

In her play *De Montfort*, Joanna Baillie warns against the danger of indulging one's passion, especially that of hatred. De Montfort confesses to his sister Jane that, "It is hate! black, lasting, deadly hate; / Which thus hath driv'n me forth from kindred peace, / From social pleasure, from my native home, / To be a sullen wand'rer on the earth, / Avoiding all men, cursing and accurs'd" (*Seven Gothic Dramas*, 261). Although Mary Shelley claimed that fidelity was her last novel's theme, she also warns, as she did in her prior novels, that a passion ungoverned by reason ultimately destroys one's hopes and dreams. For Falkner, the passion is, ironically, love. Early in the novel, the narrator remarks on Falkner's inability to control his emotions: "All his life he had cherished a secret and ardent passion, beyond whose bounds every thing was sterile — this had changed from the hopes of love to the gnawing pangs of remorse — but still his heart fed on itself — and unless that was interested, and by the force of affection he were called out of himself, he must be miserable" (*Falkner,* 1: 59). That passion, of course, is for Alithea. Falkner's love is not the self-sacrificing or disinterested love that Elizabeth Raby or Elizabeth Lavenza possess, but an obsessive emotion that causes the same tragic outcome that De Montfort's hatred does. Even Elizabeth's redemptive love cannot lift Falkner out of his despair. After the failed suicide attempt in the Cornwall cemetery, Falkner immerses himself in the care of Elizabeth, but he cannot forget the past or forgive himself. Watching Falkner, the narrator tells us, one notes "his piercing eyes fixed in vacancy, as if it beheld there a heart-moving tragedy" (*Falkner,* 1: 158).

When Falkner finally shows the letter to Elizabeth and Gerard, he assumes that Gerard will avenge his mother's death by challenging him to a duel. Caught up in a tradition associated with romances and tragedies, Falkner muses over the prospect. Continuing to indulge his melodramatic nature, he finds dying by Gerard's hand a fitting finale to his existence: "But as he confronted the injured son of a more injured mother, another

thought, dearer to his lawless yet heroic imagination, presented itself. . . .
His care must be to fall by the young man's hand. There was a sort of poetical justice in this idea, a noble and fitting ending to his disastrous story,
that solaced his pride, and filled him, as has been said, with triumph"
(*Falkner*, 2: 99-100). However, he does not anticipate Gerard's reaction.
Like Victor, Falkner has so carefully crafted his dramatic narrative, that its
readers, however horrified by the events, have difficulty perceiving him as
a villain. More significantly, both Gerard and Elizabeth demonstrate their
capacity for forgiveness, something Falkner has been unable to do for himself. They believe Falkner's assertion that he never meant Alithea to die,
and despite the tragic outcome, they recognize the just intentions that motivated the deed. Falkner has played so well the haunted victim that he convinces everyone else as well. With Gerard's refusal to consider a duel,
Falkner once again finds that his drama is unexpectedly altered. He is
forced to live with his guilt and to exonerate himself publicly when the bitter Sir Boyville decides to have him tried.

The trial is indeed a spectacle as the private lives of Alithea, Falkner, and
Sir Boyville take the public spotlight. "The gaze of thousands," writes the
narrator, is directed to Falkner (*Falkner*, 2: 272). The crowd is aware of
Falkner's crime, yet they are also aware of Sir Boyville's selfish interest in
playing the part of the wronged husband: "A breathless interest was awakened, not only in the spectators, but even in those hardened by habit to
scenes like this. Every customary act of the court was accompanied by a
solemnity unfelt before. . . . When once the trial had begun, and his pre-
liminary part had been played, Falkner sat down" (*Falkner*, 2:278). Like
Caleb Williams, who finds himself intensely uncomfortable in the position
of spectator of the dramatic courtroom spectacle following Falkland's
planting of evidence to implicate him, so Falkner sits back and views with
horror the public scene that displays the intimate details of Alithea's
unhappy marriage and his obsessed love for her. Granted, the courtroom
drama is a direct result of Sir Boyville who has earlier told Gerard "And
shall [Alithea's] exculpation be hushed up and private? I court publicity"
(*Falkner*, 2: 132). However, Falkner fully comprehends how those incidents
or accidents, well-intentioned though they may have been, lead to
unwanted spectacle: "He was, indeed, thinking of things more painful than
even the present scene; the screams and struggles of the agonized Alithea —
her last sad sleep in the hut upon the shore — the strangling, turbid waves
— her wet, lifeless form — her low, unnamed grave dug by him: had these
been atoned for by long years of remorse and misery, or was the present
ignominy, and worse that might ensue, fitting punishment?" (*Falkner*, 2:
278). Mary Shelley leaves the question to the reader. Although Falkner is
exonerated from the murder charge, he will carry his sentence until death.
After the trial he reflects that, although "the purity of his honour was tarnished — his heart told another tale" (*Falkner*, 2: 290). As Caroline

Ashburn in Eliza Fenwick's *Secresy* writes, "Fatal end of an ungoverned passion — virtuous in its object, but vicious in its excess."[5]

There are other subtle reminders in this novel that life is a drama and people are actors. Mrs. Raby, Elizabeth's aunt, "had something of the tragedy queen in her appearance" (*Falkner*, 2: 160). Like Cornelia Lodore and Edward Villiers, she is overly concerned with public appearance; she determines "to break at once the link between Elizabeth and her guardian, before the story gained publicity, and the name of Raby became mingled in a tale of horror and crime" (*Falkner*, 2: 163). Lady Cecil notes that Alithea felt that "we ought not to endeavour to form a destiny for ourselves, but to act well our part on the scene where Providence has placed us" (*Falkner*, 1: 198). Even Elizabeth, who possesses "no world fairy-like imagination" employs theatrical metaphors. She likens Falkner's narrative to a drama, and upon reading it, she remarks, "that the scene was closed, the curtain fallen. What more could arise?" (*Falkner*, 2: 145). She recalls her mother's words of a "better world, where all would meet again who fulfilled their part virtuously in this world" (*Falkner*, 1: 110). Caught up in the emotional language and plot, she replays the events in her mind, elevating Alithea's role to heroine status (for her motherly devotion) and absolving Falkner's crime.

Lady Cecil also demonstrates a dramatic flair. When she relates Gerard's version of Alithea's story to Elizabeth, she divides the narrative into two parts: one section for their pleasure as they ride through the country, the other for the evening entertainment after tea. She thoroughly enjoys her role as storyteller and views the telling of it as a performance. What she does not expect is Elizabeth's reaction. Lady Cecil refers to the narrative as a "frightful tragedy" (*Falkner*, 1: 278), and Elizabeth quickly picks up the dramatic reference. She draws analogies to Hamlet: just as the Danish prince attempts to exonerate his father, so Gerard tries to clear his mother's name. Such action, Elizabeth admires. However, Lady Cecil chides her, saying she had hoped that Elizabeth might aid in "weaning Gerard from his wild fancies, and in reconciling him to the world as it is; but you indulge in metaphysical sallies and sublime flights, which my common-place mind can only regard as a sort of intellectual will-of-the-wisp" (*Falkner*, 1: 279-280). Lady Cecil wants to "change him, from a wild sort of visionary, into a man of this world" (*Falkner*, 2: 280); Elizabeth appreciates his heroic convictions.

Elizabeth's apt comparison of Gerard to Hamlet is one that Gerard himself is quite conscious of. He acknowledges his familiarity with Shakespeare's play and quite willingly embraces parallels to Hamlet:

> "I have read that play," said Neville, "till each word seems instinct with a message direct to my heart — as if my own emotions gave a conscious soul to every line. Hamlet was called upon to avenge a father — in execution of his task he did not spare a dearer, a far more sacred

name — if he used no daggers with his mother, he spoke them; nor winced though she writhed beneath his hand. Mine is a lighter — yet holier duty. I would vindicate a mother — without judging my father — without any accusation against him, I would establish her innocence. Is this blameable? What would you do, Miss Falkner, if your father were accused of a crime?" (*Falkner,* 1: 181).

Two significant points in the above passage. One, as Gerard evokes the Hamlet dilemma of how to effect justice and retribution, he also reveals his predisposition to see himself as a revenging hero. Without a role model or mentor, he turns to a powerful dramatic figure from which to pattern emotion and action. Two, the last question–"What would you do, Miss Falkner, if your father were accused of a crime?"–eerily foreshadows what Elizabeth will soon face. What she does when she learns that Falkner is the "criminal" responsible for the death of Gerard's mother is to remain faithful to him, just as Gerard has been faithful in believing his mother's innocence. Despite his determination for revenge as revealed in the above passage, Gerard cannot avenge his mother's death in any bloody fashion once he reads Falkner's narrative. Initially, he plans to challenge Falkner to a duel: "He ended the tale, and he thought–'Yes, there is but one termination to this tragedy; I must avenge my sweet mother, and by the death of Falkner, proclaim her innocence'" (*Falkner,* 2: 121). However, he is moved by the story and is convinced of its truth. Furthermore, his love for Elizabeth prevents him from taking the life of the only man she has known as a father. Although he experiences some of Hamlet's famous indecisiveness, Gerard eventually asserts himself in opposition to his father's plan to create a public spectacle by making Falkner stand trial. He is indeed very much like Shakespeare's Danish prince: he is moody and introspective, and though wanting to take action, he is also inclined to wait and watch: "I am tied," he confesses when Sir Boyville implements his plan to publicize Falkner's crime, "forced to inaction — the privilege of free action taken from me" (*Falkner,* 2: 143). When his mother's body is exhumed, Gerard nearly throws himself into the grave as Hamlet did into Ophelia's. However, Gerard is able to emerge successfully from the throes of anger, extreme sensibility, and revenge. Unlike Hamlet, he works toward reconciliation. If we step out of the text for a moment, we might argue that his actions are possible as he is a character in a domestic novel of sensibility destined for a "happy" ending; he is not a tragic hero of Shakespearean tragedy. The conventions of these genres are quite different from one another: what is "realistic" for a character in one genre may not be "realistic" for a character in another genre. By motivating us to contemplate this notion, Shelley has again effectively emphasized the dangerous relationship between art and life and what happens when we — and her characters — too closely align ourselves with literary and/or dramatic archetypes as prescriptive models and substitute their imaginary world for the "reality" of our own.

Gerard also knows how to maximize a scene for theatrical effect. Well-aware that Lady Cecil, although sympathetic, does not approve of his obsessive search for the details of his mother's fate, he stages his entrances and delivers his lines as adeptly as any actor. After receiving a letter from a Gregory Hoskins, who had information regarding Alithea, Gerard enters the room where Elizabeth and Lady Cecil have been discussing the very same subject. He keeps the women in suspense for a few minutes so that the emotional effect of his announcement is fully appreciated. Not content merely to summarize the information he has learned, he sets up a *tableau*. Seating Elizabeth and Lady Cecil together, Gerard then sits at their feet. His audience in place, he announces to them, "You shall hear all by and by; I will relate all I have been told. It is a sad story if it be hers — if it be a true story at all" (*Falkner*, 1: 269). Gerard's reconstruction of his meeting with Hoskins and of the events that transpired on that lonely northern coast lends credence to his role as the avenging son determined to discover the truth and to bring the guilty to justice. It also reveals his ability to imagine the events as though he had been there himself: "To me it is as if I knew each act of the tragedy, and heard her last sigh beneath the waves breathed for me. She was dragged out by these men; buried without friend; without decent rites; her tomb the evil report her enemy raised above her; her grave the sands of that dreary shore" (*Falkner*, 1: 276). Gerard theatricalizes the event, calling Osborne (Falkner's hireling) a "participator in, a frightful tragedy" (*Falkner*, 1: 278). This latest information confirms Gerard's suspicions and strengthens his resolve to discover his mother's murderer, just as Hamlet determines to expose Claudius's guilt.

Gerard's likening himself to Hamlet prompts Elizabeth to reread Shakespeare's tragedy:

> She was soon buried, not only in the interest of the drama itself, but in the various emotions it excited by the association it now bore to one she loved more even than she knew. It was nothing strange that Neville, essentially a dreamer and a poet, should have identified himself with the Prince of Denmark; while the very idea that he took to himself, and acted on sentiments thus high-souled and pure, adorned him yet more in her eyes, endowing him in ample measure with that ideality which the young and noble love to bestow on the objects of their attachment. (*Falkner*, 1: 186).

Although she is caught up as a spectator of drama, Elizabeth refrains from playing roles. She draws parallels between real life and fictional/dramatic people; however, she does not equate them or expect events to play out as a Shakespearean tragedy. She has a firm grasp on the realities of life and an optimistic rather than idealistic outlook. The narrator describes her maturing into a young adult: "Vague forebodings are awakened; a sense of the opening drama of life, unaccompanied with any longing to enter on it — that feeling is reserved for the years that follow; but at fourteen and fifteen we only feel that we are emerging from childhood, and we rejoice, having yet a sense that as yet it is not fitting that we should make one of the real actors on the world's stage. . . . We look upon the menaced evils of life as a fiction" (*Falkner,* 1: 113). This passage implies that an adolescent does not yet see herself as a principal actor in life's drama. Yet it also suggests that Elizabeth, like Ethel Lodore, is more concerned with with real life than with theatrical metaphors. She possesses neither an obsessive dramatic sensibility nor a debilitating Romantic subjectivity. When Falkner reads about historic heroes, his reaction to literature and the imagination is much like that of Victor Frankenstein's; in contrast, Elizabeth's is like that of Henry Clerval's and Elizabeth Lavenza's: "When they read of the heroes of old, or the creations of the poets, she dwelt on the moral to be deduced, the theories of life and earth, religion and virtue, therein displayed; while he compared them to his own experience, criticised their truth, and gave pictures of real human nature, either contrasting with, or resembling, those presented on the written page" (*Falkner,* 1: 161-162). Elizabeth may allude to the dramatic metaphor, but she always recognizes it as an analogy. On the other hand, Falkner confuses the boundaries between life and art. Like the dark Romantic figures in Gothic novels, he can only see the weak or malevolent side of humanity. Guiltless, Elizabeth recognizes the duality of human nature and accepts it.

In the tradition of the sentimental novel, Mary Shelley offers a typically happy ending to the trials endured by these characters: Elizabeth is received by the Rabys; she and Gerard marry with full approval of their families; and Falkner takes up residence near them. However, the warning message is not diffused by the end result. The dangers of inventing or reconstructing of life as we wish it to be or as we wish it had been too often leads to dramatic role-playing at the expense of all that we hold dear. As the narrator remarks, "there are moments when the future, with all its contingencies and possibilities, becomes glaringly distinct to our foreseeing eye; and we act as if that was, which we believe must be" (*Falkner,* 1: 288). Not an explicit moralist, Mary Shelley nonetheless makes clear the debilitating and often tragic results of Romantic idealism and obsessive individualism; Cornelia Lodore and Falkner are merely more fortunate than Mathilda or Victor Frankenstein. She has also emphasized the importance of fidelity. Recall her comment to Maria Gisborne that the novel stresses "fidelity as the first of human virtues." The action in this work, as in her others, reinforces Shelley's remark — fidelity to others and to one's self is indeed an all-encompassing virtue.

Chapter 9 Notes

1. Shelley was upset with Ollier on two counts: she believed that *Lodore*'s sales had probably exceeded 600 copies and that Bentley owed her the extra £50 promised; she felt that Ollier had reneged on a £100 payment to Edward Trelawny for a second edition of his *Adventures of a Younger Son*. Shelley, who had arranged the contract terms for Trelawny, was also angry with herself for trusting an oral agreement with Ollier and not carefully examining the written contract, which did not specify an extra payment for a second edition (*Letters*, 2: 252, 255).
2. Critics for *The Athenæum, Literary Gazette*, and *Monthly Repository* were others who recommended the novel. See Lyles 181-83.
3. Mary Shelley, *Falkner*, 2 Volumes (New York: Saunders and Otley, 1837), 2: 1; hereafter cited in text as *Falkner*.
4. William Godwin, *Mandeville*, ed. Pamela Clemit, Volume 6 of *Collected Novels and Memoirs of William Godwin* (London: William Pickering, 1992), 44.
5. Eliza Fenwick, *Secresy: or, the Ruin of the Rock* (London: Pandora, 1989).

CHAPTER TEN

Conclusion

The curtain rises on the scene,
With someone chanting to be free;
The play unfolds before my eyes,
There stands the actor,
Who is me.
— The Moody Blues, "The Actor"

The numerous dramatic conventions in Mary Shelley's novels demonstrate the disabling effects of a Romantic sensibility whose inward gaze and theatrical imagination construct an egocentric illusion of the world as a stage. In varying degrees, each work refigures the *theatrum mundi* motif to represent Shelley's theme: Victor's storytelling as a performance; Mathilda's perception of her life as a tragedy; Lionel's autobiography as a dramatic construct; Castruccio, Beatrice, Richard, Cornelia Lodore, and Falkner's self-conscious role-playing; Frion and Monina's masks and disguises. For all these characters, the theatrical metaphor is a reality, and the confusion of this boundary between life and stage causes further confusion of self/other and public/private.

Throughout her works, Mary Shelley uses plays as metaphors for her characters' actions and perspectives, and Shakespeare's dramas in particular provide her with a plethora of analogies: *As You Like It* (*Mathilda*), *Macbeth* (*The Last Man*), *Troilus and Cressida* (*Valperga* and *Lodore*), *The Tempest* (*Lodore*), and *Hamlet* (*Falkner*). Shakespeare's dramas enjoyed a revival during the Romantic period, and Shelley could expect that her audience was quite familiar with these major plays from attending the theater or through publication. As "objective correlatives," these references certainly highlight the novels' themes and intensify her characters' theatricality and their tendency to view life as a drama. Mathilda mentally re-enacts Rosalind's search for her father; Lionel Verney translates the power struggles and despair of *Macbeth*'s Scottish court to his world; and Gerard adopts Hamlet's mission as his own. Such parallels are subtle reminders to the novels' readers that they are witnessing a dramatic performance. They also add another layer of artificiality that addresses the question of what is real and what is illusion in the minds of the characters.

Like the stage settings for Romantic dramas, the landscapes in Shelley's novels become mere backdrops to foreground the characters' theatrics, and carefully staged *tableaux* intensify their perception that life is art. The dramatic metaphor is also enhanced by the melodramatic language that the characters employ to describe their actions and emotions, a language that clearly is theirs, not Mary Shelley's. When comparing Shelley's crisp, and often economical, prose in her criticism and in her biographies, one recognizes her skill in presenting her characters' point-of-view in their own voices.

Nevertheless, Mary Shelley's personal writing frequently exhibits a disabling sensibility like that of her characters and reflects the same apprehension toward it. Shelley knew well the dangers of indulging the emotional self. Although she eschewed the spotlight herself, she understood that human nature possesses an ego that yearns for recognition and a subjective sensibility that focuses on the self. The journals she kept throughout most of her life helped her delineate the boundary not only between a desired imaginary world and the actual one, but also between the public and private spheres. Empowered by imagination and stimulated by disappointment and tragedy, Shelley was able not only to see life as drama and to create an illusory world, but also to recognize how one can mask or disguise oneself through roles to conceal or subordinate the private, inner soul. Consider this 19 October 1822 journal entry: "How painful all change becomes to one who entirely & despotically engrossed by their own feelings, leads — as it were — an *internal* life quite different from the outward & apparent one. While my life continues its monot[on]ous course within sterile banks, an under current disturbs the smooth face of the waters, distorts all objects reflected in it — and the mind is no longer a mirror in which outward events may reflect themselves, but becomes itself the painter & creator" (*Journals*, 2: 438). Mary Shelley's fourth journal book, in which the above entry was written, marks a departure from the previous journals that primarily record social, literary, and domestic activities; it reveals deeply personal emotions that Shelley kept from all but her closest friends.

The fourth journal begins on 2 October 1822, nearly three months after Percy Shelley and Edward Williams were drowned in the Gulf of Spezia. After her husband's death, Mary Shelley used it as a private outlet for her depression and loneliness.[1] Entries such as the following in 1823 reveal that Shelley could relate to the fears of characters such as Mathilda and Falkner with regard to the frightening depths that despair and self-pity can take one: "This is madness — my brain whirls — I must not write, or scream — I must hush — hush the dreadful feelings that work within me — silence oh silence!" (*Journals*, 2: 459). She also identified with the isolation that Frankenstein, Walton, and Perkin/Richard feel. On 21 October 1822, she writes the following: "No one seems to understand or to sympathize with me. They all seem to look on me as one without affections — without any sensibility — my sufferings are thought a cypher–& I feel myself degraded before them; knowing that in their hearts they degrade me from the rank which I deserve to possess. —I feel dejected & cowed before them, feeling as if I might be the senseless person they appear to consider me. But I am not" (*Journals,* 2: 440-441). Although Shelley made her own circle of friends and acquaintances when she returned to England in 1823, she did not feel an integral part of a sympathetic and nurturing environment as she had before Percy Shelley's death — despite the difficulties with Claire Clairmont, money troubles, and marital tension resulting from the loss of her children, Clara and William.[2]

Subjective emotion demonstrated in the above journal passages parallel that expressed by Victor Frankenstein, Mathilda, Lionel, Beatrice, and Falkner. However, unlike her characters, Shelley could shake the debilitating sensibility and re-direct her gaze outward: "to bear [solitude] I must indeed string my mind — I must awaken conscious worth" (*Journals,* 2: 487). "I close my book," she wrote, "Tomorrow I must begin this new life of mine" (*Journals,* 2: 438). Neither was she one to put herself forward into the public spotlight. Although she depicts characters who enjoy playing the "starring" role in their illusory dramas, Shelley did not in hers. Rather she acts as "a permanent chorus," demonstrating an ability to step out of herself and into other personages, as she indicates in her introduction to the 1831 edition of *Frankenstein:* "I did not make myself the heroine of my tales. Life appeared to me too common-place an affair as regarded myself. I could not figure to myself that romantic woes or wonderful events would ever be my lot; but I was not confined to my own identity, and I could people the hours with creations far more interesting to me at that age, than my own sensations" (*Mary Shelley Reader,* 168).

Like Euthanasia and Katherine, Mary Shelley was an intensely private person, despite her fame as a novelist and her "notoriety" as Wollstonecraft's and Godwin's daughter and as Percy Shelley's wife. Perhaps, as Marilyn May suggests, Shelley was acutely aware of how misrepresented the private can be, as she witnessed the troubles that Godwin experienced as her mother's biographer.[3] Although her novels clearly invite biographical analogies, Shelley did not use them as confessional vehicles. Her journals and letters to close friends provided that release. As she wrote in a 2 October 1822 entry, "White paper — wilt thou be my confident? I will trust thee fully, for none shall see what I write" (*Journals,* 2: 429). Later, she records, "And thus ends this year? —It has struck me what a very imperfect picture (only *no one* will ever see it) these querulous pages afford of *me* — This arises from their being the record of my feelings & not of my imagination" (*Journals,* 2: 542).

While acknowledging the various literary traditions which permeate Mary Shelley's works, especially the influence of Mary Wollstonecraft, William Godwin, and Percy Bysshe Shelley, this study has primarily focused on her artistry based on its own merits. Too often Shelley is examined in the shadow of her mother, father, or husband rather than as an artist in her own right, and too often her works are read for biographical revelations rather than for their own intrinsic worth. That she herself felt an obligation to be talented as the daughter of Wollstonecraft and Godwin and as the wife of Percy Shelley is undisputed, as she indicated in an 1838 journal entry: "To be something great and good was the precept given me by my father: Shelley reiterated it" (*Journals*, 2:554). That she drew on her own experience and life as a basis for her fiction is also uncontested; like most of the Romantic writers, her writings reflect an expressive approach to her art. However, Shelley's works demonstrate that she created her own shadow of influence and that she possessed an original imagination and skilled craftsmanship that many writers could only hope for. If Shakespeare's Jaques is right in his view of the world as a stage and men and women merely players on it, then Mary Shelley — as a public author and a private woman — played her part with admirable distinction.

Chapter 10 Notes

1. See Mary Jean Corbett's essay "Reading Mary Shelley's *Journals*: Romantic Subjectivity and Feminist Criticism," which closely examines how the journal represents a "tentative effort to adopt an individualist idiom as a means of self-expression" (74).

2. Claire was ever an annoyance to Mary Shelley; living with the Shelleys for most of their time together, she seldom afforded them any privacy. The financial problems stemmed from many areas, including Percy Shelley's generous subsistence of others, including Godwin and Leigh Hunt. Clara, a year old, died from dysentery 24 September 1818, as Mary Shelley was travelling to Venice to help resolve tension between Claire Clairmont and Lord Byron regarding their daughter, Allegra. Three-year old William died in Rome, 17 June 1819, probably from cholera or typhoid. In 1815, Shelley had also lost her first daughter, a few weeks after the child's premature birth.

3. Godwin revealed Wollstonecraft's affair with Gilbert Imlay and her attempted suicide in his memoir of her, revelations that the general public long held against Wollstonecraft, already suspect for her feminism and political radicalism.

Bibliography

Abbott, Anthony. *The Vital Lie: Reality and Illusion in Modern Drama.* Tuscaloosa: University of Alabama Press, 1989.

Abel, Lionel. *Metatheatre: A New View of Dramatic Form.* New York: Hill and Wang, 1963.

Adams, M. Ray. *Studies in the Literary Backgrounds of English Radicalism.* Lane: Franklin and Marshall Press, 1947.

Alexander, Meena. *Women in Romanticism.* Totowa, NJ: Barnes and Noble, 1989.

Auerbach, Nina. "Victorian Players and Sages." In *The Performance of Power: Theatrical Discourse and Politics,* ed. Sue-Ellen Case and Janelle Reinelt. Iowa City: University of Iowa Press, 1991.

———. *Private Theatricals: The Lives of the Victorians.* Cambridge: Harvard University Press, 1990.

Austen, Jane. *Mansfield Park.* Vol. IV of the Oxford Illustrated Jane Austen. Oxford: Oxford University Press, n.d.

———. *Northanger Abbey and Persuasion.* Vol. IV of the Oxford Illustrated Jane Austen. Oxford: Oxford University Press, n.d.

Baillie, Joanna. *Orra.* In *The Dramatic and Poetical Works of Joanna Baillie.* 2nd ed. London: Longman, Brown, Green, and Longman, 1851.

———. *De Montfort.* In *Seven Gothic Dramas: 1789–1825,* ed. Jeffrey N. Cox, 231–314. Athens: Ohio University Press, 1992.

Baldick, Chris. In *"Frankenstein's" Shadow: Myth, Monstrosity, and Nineteenth-Century Writing.* Oxford: Clarendon Press, 1987.

Barbour, Judith. "'The meaning of the tree': The Tale of *Mirra* in Mary Shelley's *Mathilda*." In *Iconoclastic Departures: Mary Shelley After "Frankenstein,"* ed. Syndy M. Conger, Frederick S. Frank, and Gregory O'Dea, 98–114. Madison: Fairleigh Dickinson University Press, 1997.

Bate, Jonathan. *Shakespeare and the English Romantic Imagination.* Oxford: Clarendon Press, 1986.

Baum, Joan. "The Lessons of *Frankenstein*." *Rendezvous* 12 (1977): 5–8.

Bennett, Betty T. "Finding Mary Shelley in Her Letters." In *Romantic Revisions*, ed. Robert Brinkley and Keith Hanley, 291–306. Cambridge: Cambridge University Press, 1992.

———. "Mary Diana Dod's, Not Mary Shelley's, Poetic Lament: A Correction." *Keats-Shelley Review* 4 (1989): 27–30.

———. "The Political Philosophy of Mary Shelley's Historical Novels: *Valperga* and *Perkin Warbeck*." In *The Evidence of the Imagination: Studies of Interactions Between Life and Art in English Romantic Literature*, ed. Donald H. Reiman et al, 354–371. New York: New York University Press, 1978.

———. Introduction to *The Fortunes of Perkin Warbeck*, by Mary Shelley. 3 Vols. Reprint. Norwood Editions, 1976.

Bentley, Eric. *The Life of the Drama.* New York: Atheneum, 1975.

Birkhead, Edith. *The Tale of Terror.* 1921. Reprint. New York: Russell and Russell, 1963.

Bloom, Harold. "Frankenstein, or the New Prometheus." *Partisan Review* 32 (1965): 611–618.

Blumberg, Jane. *Mary Shelley's Early Novels.* Iowa City: University of Iowa Press, 1993.

Booth, Michael. *Victorian Spectacular Theatre 1850–1910.* Boston: Routledge and Kegan Paul, 1981.

———. *Prefaces to English Nineteenth-Century Theatre.* Manchester: Manchester University Press, 1980.

———. *English Melodrama.* London: Herbert Jenkins, 1965.

Boren, Lynda S. "The Performing Self: Psychodrama in Austen, James and Woolf." *Centennial Review* 30 (1986): 1–24.

Botting, Fred. "Frankenstein and the Language of Monstrosity." In *Reviewing Romanticism*, ed. Philip Martin and Robin Jarvis, 51–59. London: Macmillan, 1992.

Bowerbank, Sylvie. "The Social Order vs. the Wretch: Mary Shelley's Contradictory-Mindedness in *Frankenstein*." *ELH* 46 (1979): 418–431.

Bowers, Fredson Thayer. *Elizabethan Revenge Tragedy: 1587–1642.* Gloucester: Peter Smith, 1959.

Brontë, Charlotte. *Villette.* London: J. M. Dent & Sons LTD, 1969.

Brooks, Peter. *The Melodramatic Imagination.* New Haven: Yale University Press, 1976.

Brown, Charles Brockden. *Arthur Mervyn.* New York: Holt, Rinehart and Winston, 1962.

———. *Wieland, or The Transformation.* New York: Harcourt, Brace & World, 1926.

Burney, Frances. *Evelina.* London: Oxford University Press, 1970.

Burroughs, Catherine. *Closet Stages: Joanna Baillie and the Theater Theory of British Romantic Women Writers.* Philadelphia: University of Pennsylvania Press, 1997.

Butler, Judith. *Bodies That Matter: On the Discursive Limits of "Sex."* New York: Routledge, 1993.

———. *Gender Trouble: Feminism and the Subversion of Identity.* New York: Routledge, 1990.

Butler, Marilyn. "The First *Frankenstein* and Radical Science." *TLS* 9 April 1993: 12–14.

Byron, George Gordon, Lord. *George Gordon, Lord Byron: Selected Works,* ed. Edward E. Bostetter. NewYork: Holt, Rinehart and Winston, Inc., 1972.

———. *Don Juan,* ed. Leslie A. Marchand. Boston: Houghton Mifflin Company, 1958.

———. *The Poems and Dramas of Lord Byron.* Chicago: Belford, Clarke & Co., 1885.

Calderòn de la Barca, Pedro. *Life is a Dream,* ed. William E. Colford. Great Neck: Barron's Educational Series, Inc., 1958.

Cantor, Paul. *Creature and Creator: Myth-making and English Romanticism.* Cambridge: Cambridge University Press, 1984.

Carlisle, Janice. "The Face in the Mirror: *Villette* and the Conventions of Autobiography," in *Critical Essays on Charlotte Brontë,* ed. Barbara Timm Gates, 262–289. Boston: G. K. Hall, 1990.

Carson, James P. "'A Sigh of Many Hearts': History, Humanity, and Popular Culture in *Valperga.*" In *Iconoclastic Departures: Mary Shelley After "Frankenstein,"* ed. Syndy M. Conger, Frederick S. Frank, and Gregory O'Dea, 167–192. Madison: Fairleigh Dickinson University Press, 1997.

Chatterjee, Ranita. "*Mathilda*: Mary Shelley, William Godwin, and the Ideologies of Incest." In *Iconoclastic Departures: Mary Shelley After "Frankenstein,"* ed. Syndy M. Conger, Frederick S. Frank, and Gregory O'Dea, 130–149. Madison: Fairleigh Dickinson University Press, 1997.

Clemit, Pamela. *The Godwinian Novel: The Rational Fictions of Godwin, Brockden Brown, Mary Shelley.* Oxford: Clarendon Press, 1993.

Coleridge, Samuel Taylor. *Osorio: A Tragedy: as originally written in 1797 by Samuel Taylor Coleridge.* London: John Pearson, 1873.

Conger, Syndy McMillan. Introduction to *Sensibility in Transformation*, ed. Syndy McMillan Conger. Rutherford: Fairleigh Dickinson University Press, 1990.

Corbett, Mary Jean. "Reading Mary Shelley's Journals: Romantic Subjectivity and Feminist Criticism." In *The Other Mary Shelley: Beyond "Frankenstein,"* ed. Audrey A. Fisch, Anne K. Mellor, and Esther H. Schor, 73–88. New York: Oxford University Press, 1993.

Cox, Jeffrey N. *In the Shadows of Romance: Romantic Tragic Drama in Germany, England, and France.* Athens: Ohio University Press, 1987.

———, ed. *Seven Gothic Dramas: 1789–1825.* Athens: Ohio University Press, 1992.

Cude, Wilfred. "Mary Shelley's Modern Prometheus: A Study in the Ethics of Scientific Creativity." *Dalhousie Review* 52 (1972): 212–225.

Dacre, Charlotte. *Confessions of the Nun of St. Omer; a Tale.* New York: Arno Press, 1972.

Dante [Dante Alighieri]. *The Portable Dante.* Translated by Laurence Binyon. New York: Viking Press, 1969.

Dawson, Anthony B. *Indirections: Shakespeare and the Art of Illusion.* Toronto: University of Toronto Press, 1978.

Defoe, Daniel. *Journal of the Plague Year.* Oxford: Oxford University Press, 1990.

———. *Moll Flanders*, ed. Edward Kelly. Norton Critical Edition. New York: W. W. Norton & Company, 1973.

———. *Roxana.* New York: The New American Library, Inc., 1979.

DeLamotte, Eugenia. *Perils of the Night: A Feminist Study of Nineteenth-Century Gothic.* New York: Oxford University Press, 1990.

Dobzhansky, Theodosius. "Evolutionism and Man's Hope." *Sewanee Review* 68 (1960): 274–288.

Donahue, Joseph. *Theatre in the Age of Kean.* Totowa, NJ Rowman and Littlefield, 1975.

Drabble, Margaret, ed. *Oxford Companion to English Literature.* 5th edition. Oxford: Oxford University Press, 1985.

Drake, Nathan. *Literary Hours; or, Sketches Critical and Narrative.* New York: Garland Press, 1970.

Dunn, Jane. *Moon in Eclipse: A Life of Mary Shelley.* New York: St. Martin's Press, 1978.

Dunn, Richard. "Narrative Distance in *Frankenstein*." *Studies in the Novel* 6 (1974): 408–417.

Dussinger, John. "Kinship and Guilt in Mary Shelley's *Frankenstein*." *Studies in the Novel* 8 (1976): 38–55.

Ellis, Kate Ferguson. *The Contested Castle: Gothic Novels and the Subversion of Domestic Ideology.* Urbana: University of Illinois Press, 1989.

Evans, Bertrand. *Gothic Drama from Walpole to Shelley.* Berkeley: University of California Press, 1947.

Fenwick, Eliza. *Secresy: or, the Ruin of the Rock.* London: Pandora, 1989.

Fielding, Henry. *Amelia.* Harmondsworth, England: Penguin, 1987.

———. *The History of the Adventures of Joseph Andrews.* New York: The New American Library, 1960.

———. *The History of Tom Jones, A Foundling.* New York: The New American Library, 1963.

Fisch, Audrey A. "Plaguing Politics: AIDS, Deconstruction, and *The Last Man*." In *The Other Mary Shelley: Beyond "Frankenstein,"* ed. Audrey A. Fisch, Anne K. Mellor, and Esther H. Schor, 267–286. New York: Oxford University Press, 1993.

Ford, John. "Perkin Warbeck," in *John Ford*, edited by Havelock Ellis. New York: Hill and Wang, 1957.

Forry, Steven Earl. *Hideous Progenies: Dramatizations of "Frankenstein" from Mary Shelley to the Present.* Philadelphia: University of Pennsylvania Press, 1990.

Review of *Frankenstein*, by Mary Shelley. *The British Critic* 9 (April 1818): 432–458.

———. *The Gentleman's Magazine* 8 (April 1818):334–335.

———. *The Monthly Review* 85 (April 1818): 439.

Gardner, Joseph. "Mary Shelley's Divine Tragedy." *Essays in Literature* 4 (1977): 182–197.

Gates, Eleanor M. "Leigh Hunt, Lord Byron, and Mary Shelley: The Long Goodbye." *Keats-Shelley Journal* 35 (1986): 149–167.

Gaull, Marilyn. *English Romanticism: The Human Context.* New York: W. W. Norton, 1988.

Gilbert, Sandra. "Horror's Twin: Mary Shelley's Monstrous Eve." In *The Madwoman in the Attic,* ed. Sandra Gilbert and Susan Gubar, 213–247. New Haven: Yale University Press, 1979.

Gisborne, Maria and Edward E. Williams. *Maria Gisborne and Edward E. Williams, Shelley's Friends: Their Journals and Letters,* edited by Frederick L. Jones. Norman: University of Oklahoma Press, 1951.

Glut, Donald. *The Frankenstein Legend: A Tribute to Mary Shelley and Boris Karloff.* Metuchen: Scarecrow Press, 1973.

Godwin, William. *Caleb Williams,* ed. David McCracken. New York: W. W. Norton, 1977.

———. *Fleetwood, or The New Man of Feeling.* London: R. Bentley, 1832.

———. *Mandeville,* ed. Pamela Clemit. Vol. 6. *Collected Novels and Memoirs of William Godwin.* London: William Pickering, 1992.

———. *St. Leon,* ed. Pamela Clemit. Oxford: Oxford University Press, 1994.

Goethe, Johann Wolfgang von. *The Sufferings of Young Werther.* Translated by Bayard Quincy Morgan. New York: Frederick Ungar Publishing Co., 1973.

Goldberg, M. A. "Moral and Myth in Mrs. Shelley's *Frankenstein.*" *Keats-Shelley Journal* 8 (1959): 27–38.

Goodwin, Sarah Webster. "Domesticity and Uncanny Kitsch in 'The Rime of the Ancient Mariner' and *Frankenstein.*" *Tulsa Studies in Women's Literature* 10 (1991): 93–108.

Gottleib, Erika. *Lost Angels of a Ruined Paradise: Themes of Cosmic Strife in Romantic Tragedy.* Victoria, British Columbia: Sono Nis Press, 1981.

Gray, Thomas. "Elegy Written in a Country Churchyard." In *Major English Writers of the Eighteenth Century,* ed. Harold E. Pagliaro, 844–47. New York: The Free Press, 1969.

Hallett, Charles A. and Elaine S. Hallett. *The Revenger's Madness: A Study of Revenge Tragedy Motifs.* Lincoln: University of Nebraska Press, 1980.

Harpold, Terence. "'Did you get Mathilda from Papa?': Seduction Fantasy and the Circulation of Mary Shelley's *Mathilda.*" *Studies in Romanticism* 28 (1989): 49–67.

Hays, Mary. *The Memoirs of Emma Courtney.* London: Pandora, 1987.

Haywood, Eliza. *The History of Miss Betsy Thoughtless.* London: Pandora, 1986.

Hazlitt, William. *A View of the English Stage, or, A Series of Dramatic Criticisms*. London: G. Bell, 1906.

Heilman, Robert. *Tragedy and Melodrama: Versions of Experience.* Seattle: University of Washington Press, 1968.

Heller, Janet Ruth. *Coleridge, Lamb, Hazlitt, and the Reader of Drama.* Columbia: University of Missouri Press, 1990.

Heywood, Thomas. *An Apology for Actors.* New York: Scholars' Facsimiles and Reprints, 1941.

Hill, J. M. "*Frankenstein* and the Physiognomy of Desire." *American Imago* 32 (1975): 335–358.

Hill-Miller, Katherine. *"My Hideous Progeny": Mary Shelley, William Godwin, and the Father-Daughter Relationship.* Newark: University of Delaware Press, 1995.

Himes, Audra Dibert. "'Knew shame and knew desire': Ambivalence as Structure in Mary Shelley's *Mathilda.*" *Iconoclastic Departures: Mary Shelley After "Frankenstein,"* ed. Syndy M. Conger, Frederick S. Frank, and Gregory O'Dea, 115–129. Madison: Fairleigh Dickinson University Press, 1997.

Hirsch, Gordon D. "The Monster Was a Lady: On the Psychology of Mary Shelley's *Frankenstein.*" *Hartford Studies in Literature* 7 (1978): 116–153.

Hornby, Richard. *Drama, Metadrama, and Perception.* Lewisburg: Bucknell, University Press, 1986.

———. *Script into Performance: A Structuralist View of Play Production.* Austin: University of Texas Press, 1977.

Houtchens, Lawrence Huston, and Carolyn Washburn Houtchens, ed. *Leigh Hunt's Dramatic Criticism, 1808–1831.* 1949. New York: Octagon Books, 1977.

Howells, Coral Ann. *Love, Mystery, and Misery: Feeling in Gothic Fiction.* London: Athlone, 1978.

Hume, Robert D. "Exuberant Gloom, Existential Agony, and Heroic Despair: Three Varieties of Negative Romanticism." In *The Gothic Imagination: Essays in Dark Romanticism,* ed. G. R. Thompson, 109–127. Pullman: Washington State University Press, 1974.

———. "Gothic versus Romantic: A Revaluation of the Gothic Novel." *PMLA* 84 (1969): 282–290.

Hunt, Leigh. Review of *Lodore,* by Mary Shelley. *London Journal* 58 (6 May 1835): 138–139.

Inchbald, Elizabeth. *A Simple Story.* London: Pandora, 1987.

James, Henry. *The Ambassadors,* ed. S. P. Rosenbaum. Norton Critical Edition. New York: W. W. Norton, 1964.

———. *The Turn of the Screw and Other Short Novels.* New York: New American Library, 1962.

Johnson, Barbara. "My Monster/My Self." *Diacritics* 12 (1982): 2–10.

———. "The Last Man." In *The Other Mary Shelley: Beyond "Frankenstein,"* ed. Audrey A. Fisch, Anne K. Mellor, and Esther H. Schor, 258–266. New York: Oxford University Press, 1993.

Jonson, Ben. *The New Inn,* edited by Michael Hattaway. The Revels Plays series. Manchester: Manchester University Press, 1989.

Joseph, Gerhard. "Frankenstein's Dream:The Child as Father of the Monster." *Hartford Studies in Literature* 7 (1975): 97–115.

Jung, Carl Gustav. *The Basic Writings of C. G. Jung.* Princeton: Princeton University Press, 1990.

Keats, John. *John Keats,* ed. Elizabeth Cook. Oxford: Oxford University Press, 1990.

Kelly, Gary. *English Fiction of the Romantic Period: 1789–1830.* London: Longman, 1989.

———. *The English Jacobin Novel: 1780–1805.* Oxford: Clarendon Press, 1976.

Kerr, James. *Fiction Against History: Scott as Storyteller.* Cambridge: Cambridge University Press, 1989.

Kiely, Robert. *The Romantic Novel in England.* Cambridge: Harvard University Press, 1972.

Knoepflmacher, U. C. "Thoughts of the Aggression of Daughters." In *The Endurance of "Frankenstein,"* ed. George Levine and U. C. Knoepflmacher, 88–119. Berkeley: University of California Press, 1979.

Kyd, Thomas. "The Spanish Tragedy." In *Drama of the English Renaissance I: The Tudor Period,* ed. Russell A. Fraser and Norman Rabkin, 169–203. New York: Macmillan Publishing Co., 1976.

Laden, Marie-Paule. *Self-Imitation in the Eighteenth-Century Novel.* Princeton: Princeton University Press, 1987.

Review of *The Last Man,* by Mary Shelley. *The Literary Gazette* No. 473 (18 February 1826): 102–103.

———. *The Monthly Review* 1 (March 1826): 333–335.

Lennox, Charlotte. *The Female Quixote,* ed. Margaret Dalziel. London: Oxford University Press, 1970.

Levine, George. "The Ambiguous Heritage of *Frankenstein*." In *The Endurance of "Frankenstein,"* ed. George Levine and U. C. Knoepflmacher, 3–30. Berkeley: University of California Press, 1979.

Lew, Joseph. "God's Sister: History and Ideology in *Valperga*." In *The Other Mary Shelley: Beyond "Frankenstein,"* ed. Audrey A. Fisch, Anne K. Mellor, and Esther H. Schor, 159–181. New York: Oxford University Press, 1993.

Lewis, Matthew Gregory. *The Monk*. New York: Grove Press, Inc., 1952.

———. "The Castle Spectre." In *Seven Gothic Dramas: 1789–1825*, ed. Jeffrey N. Cox, 149–224. Athens: Ohio University Press, 1992.

Litvak, Joseph. *Caught in the Act: Theatricality in the Nineteenth-Century Novel*. Berkeley: University of California Press, 1992.

Lok, Henry. "This stately stage where we players stande." In *Microcosmos: The Shape of the Elizabethan Play*, by Thomas B. Stroup, 18. Lexington: University of Kentucky Press, 1965.

Lovell, Ernest A. Jr. "Byron and the Byronic Hero in the Novels of Mary Shelley." *Studies in English* 30 (1951): 158–183.

Lowe-Evans, Mary. *Frankenstein: Mrs. Shelley's Wedding Guest*. New York: Twayne Publishers, 1993.

Lyles, W. H. *Mary Shelley: An Annotated Bibliography*. New York: Garland Publishing, 1975.

MacAndrew, Elizabeth. *The Gothic Tradition in Fiction*. New York: Columbia University Press, 1979.

MacCarthy, B. G. *The Female Pen: Women Writers and Novelists, 1621 – 1818*. New York: Cork University Press, 1994.

Mackenzie, Henry. *The Man of Feeling*. London: Oxford University Press, 1967.

Markley, Robert. "Sentimentality as Performance: Shaftesbury, Sterne, and the Theatrics of Virtue." In *The New Eighteenth Century*, ed. Felicity Nussbaum and Laura Brown. New York: Methuen, 1987.

Marshall, David. *The Figure of Theater: Shaftesbury, DeFoe, Adam Smith, and George Eliot*. New York: Columbia University Press, 1986.

———. *The Surprising Effects of Sympathy: Marivaux, Diderot, Rousseau, and Mary Shelley*. Chicago: University of Chicago Press, 1988.

Maturin, Charles Robert. *Melmoth the Wanderer*. Lincoln: University of Nebraska Press, 1961.

May, Marilyn. "Publish and Perish: William Godwin, Mary Shelley, and the Public Appetite for Scandal." *Papers on Language and Literature* 21 (1990): 489–512.

Mays, Milton A. "*Frankenstein*, Mary Shelley's Black Theodicy." *Southern Humanities Review* 3 (1969): 146–153.

McCalmon, George and Christian Moe. *Creating Historical Drama.* Carbondale: Southern Illinois University Press, 1965.

McIntyre, Clara F. "Later Career of the Elizabethan Villain-Hero." *PMLA* 40 (1925): 874–880.

———. "Were The 'Gothic Novels' Gothic?" *PMLA* 36 (1921): 645–667.

Mellor, Anne K. *Mary Shelley: Her Life, Her Fiction, Her Monsters.* 1988. New York: Routledge, 1989.

———. "Why Women Didn't Like Romanticism." In *The Romantics and Us: Essays on Literature and Culture,* ed. Gene W. Ruoff, 274–287. New Brunswick: Rutgers University Press, 1990.

Middleton, Thomas. *A Game at Chess,* ed. T. H. Howard Hill. The Revels Plays series. Manchester: Manchester University Press, 1993.

Milton, John. *John Milton: Complete Poems and Major Prose.* Edited by Merritt Y. Hughes. Indianapolis: The Odyssey Press, 1957.

Moers, Ellen. "The Female Gothic." In *Literary Women,* by Ellen Moers, 77–87. London: Women's Press Limited, 1978.

The Moody Blues. "The Actor." *In Search of the Lost Chord.* London: Decca Record Company Limited, 1968.

Morgan, Charlotte E. *The Rise of the Novel of Manners.* 1911. Reprint. New York: Russell and Russell, Inc. 1963.

Mrozek, Slawomir. "Theatre versus Reality." *New Theatre Quarterly* 12 (1992): 299–304.

Napier, Elizabeth. *The Failure of the Gothic: Problems of Disjunction in an Eighteenth-century Literary Form.* Oxford: Clarendon Press, 1987.

Newmann, Bonnie Rayford. *The Lonely Muse: A Critical Biography of Mary Wollstonecraft Shelley.* Salzburg: Institut fur Anglistik und Amerikanistik, 1979.

Nitchie, Elizabeth. *Mary Shelley: Author of Frankenstein.* Westport: Greenwood Press, 1953.

O'Rourke, James. "'Nothing More Unnatural': Mary Shelley's Revision of Rousseau." *English Literary History* 56 (1989): 543–569.

O'Sullivan, Barbara Jane. "Beatrice in *Valperga*: A New Cassandra. In *The Other Mary Shelley: Beyond "Frankenstein,"* ed. Audrey A. Fisch, Anne K. Mellor, and Esther H. Schor, 140–158. New York: Oxford University Press, 1993.

Ozolins, Aija. "Dreams and Doctrines: Dual Strands in *Frankenstein*." *Science Fiction Studies* 2 (1975): 103–111.

Palacio, Jean de. *Mary Shelley dans son œuvre*. Paris: Editions Klincksieck, 1969.

Paley, Morton D. "Mary Shelley's *The Last Man*: Apocalypse Without Millennium." *Keats-Shelley Review* 4 (1989): 1–25.

Palmer, D. J. and R. E. Douse. "*Frankenstein*: A Moral Fable." *Listener* 68 (1962): 281–284.

Pavis, Patrice. "From Text to Performance." *In Performing Texts*, ed. Michael Issacharoff and Robin F. Jones, 86–100. Philadelphia: University of Pennsylvania Press, 1988.

Peake, Richard Brinsley. "Presumption; or, The Fate of Frankenstein." *Hideous Progenies: Dramatizations of "Frankenstein" from Mary Shelley to the Present*. Philadelphia: University of Pennsylvania Press, 1990.

Review of *Perkin Warbeck*, by Mary Shelley. *The Athenæum*. No. 135 (29 May 1830): 323–25.

———. *The Edinburgh Literary Journal*. No. 84 (19 June 1830): 350–52.

Phy, Allene Stuart. *Mary Shelley*. San Bernadino: Borgo Press, 1988.

Pollin, Burton R. "Philosophical and Literary Sources of *Frankenstein*." *Comparative Literature* 17 (1965): 97–108.

Poovey, Mary. *The Proper Lady and the Woman Writer – Idealogy as Style in the Works of Mary Wollstonecraft, Mary Shelley, and Jane Austen*. Chicago: University of Chicago Press, 1984.

Pope, Alexander. "Essay on Man." In *The Poetry and Prose of Alexander Pope*, edited by Aubrey Williams, 120–157. Boston: Houghton Mifflin, 1969.

Powers, Katharine Richardson. *The Influence of William Godwin on the Novels of Mary Shelley*. New York: Arno Press, 1980.

Praz, Mario. *The Romantic Agony*. 2nd edition. London: Oxford University Press, 1951.

Punter, David. *The Literature of Terror*. London: Longman, 1980.

Quarles, Francis. *The Complete Works in Prose and Verse of Francis Quarles* ed. Alexander B. Grosart. 3 Volumes. New York: AMS Press, 1967.

Radcliffe, Ann. *The Italian*, ed. Frederick Garber. London: Oxford University Press, 1968.

———. *The Mysteries of Udolpho*, ed. Bonamy Dobrée. London: Oxford University Press, 1970.

——. *Gaston de Blondeville*. Philadelphia: H. C. Carey and I. Lee, 1826.

——. *The Romance of the Forest,* ed. Chloe Chard. Oxford: Oxford University Press, 1986.

——. *The Sicilian Romance*, ed. Alison Millbank. Oxford: Oxford University Press, 1993.

——. "On the Supernatural in Poetry." *New Monthly Magazine* 7 (1826): 145–150.

Rahill, Frank. *The World of Melodrama.* University Park: Penn State University Press, 1967.

Railo, Ernest. *The Haunted Castle: A Study of the Elements of English Romanticism.* New York: E. P. Dutton and Co., 1927.

Ranger, Paul. `Terror and Pity reign in every Breast': Gothic Drama in the London Patent Theatres, 1750–1820.* London: The Society for Theatre Research, 1991.

Reiman, Donald. "Gender and Documentary Editing: A Diachronic Perspective." *Text* 4 (1988): 351–360.

Richardson, Samuel. *Clarissa, or the History of a Young Lady.* Edited by John Angus Burrell. New York: The Modern Library, 1950.

——. *Pamela, or Virtue Rewarded.* New York: W. W. Norton & Co., 1958.

Richetti, John. "Richardson's Dramatic Art in *Clarissa.*" In *British Theatre and the Other Arts, 1660–1800,* ed. Shirley Strum Kenny, 288–308. Washington: Folger Shakespeare Library, 1983.

Richter, David. "Reception of the Gothic Novel in the 1790s." In *The Idea of the Novel in the Eighteenth Century*, ed. Robert W. Uphaus, 117–137. East Lansing: Colleagues Press, 1988.

Roberts, Marie. "Mary Shelley: Immortality, Gender and the Rosy Cross." In *Reviewing Romanticism*, ed. Philip Martin and Robin Jarvis, 60–68. London: MacMillan, 1992.

Robinson, Charles E. "Mary Shelley and the Roger Dodsworth Hoax." *Keats-Shelley Journal* 24 (1975): 20–28.

Rogers, Katharine. "The Contribution of Mary Hays." *Prose Studies.* 10 (1987): 131–142.

——. *Feminism in Eighteenth-Century England.* Urbana: University of Illinois Press, 1982.

Rousseau, Jean Jacques. *The Confessions*, trans. and ed. J. M. Cohen. New York: Penguin Press, 1953.

——. *Emile.* New York: Dutton, 1974.

————. *La nouvelle Héloise. Julie; or, the New Heloise,* trans. and ed. Judith H. McDowell. University Park: Pennsylvania State University Press, 1968.

Rubenstein, Marc A. "'My Accursed Origin': The Search for the Mother in *Frankenstein.*" *Studies in Romanticism* 15 (1976): 165–194.

Rudowski, Victor Anthony. *The Prince: A Historical Critique.* New York: Twayne Publishers, 1992.

Ruffo-Fiore, Silvia. *Niccolo Machiavelli.* Boston: Twayne Publishers, 1982.

Sanford, Wendy Coppedge. *Theater as Metaphor in Hamlet.* Cambridge: Harvard University Press, 1967.

Schechner, Richard. *Performance Theory.* New York: Routledge, 1988.

Scott, Sir Walter. *The Bride of Lammermoor,* ed. Fiona Robertson. Oxford: Oxford University Press, 1991.

————. "Remarks on *Frankenstein; or, the Modern Prometheus*: A Novel." *Blackwood's Edinburgh Magazine* 2 (March 1818): 613–620.

————. *Rob Roy,* ed. Edgar Johnson. Boston: Houghton Mifflin Co., 1956.

Shaftesbury, 3rd Earl of [Anthony Ashley Cooper]. *Characteristics of Men, Manners, Opinions, Times,* ed. John M. Robertson. Indianapolis: Bobbs-Merrill, 1967.

Shakespeare, William. *As You Like It.* In *The Riverside Shakespeare,* 365–402. Boston: Houghton Mifflin, 1974.

————. *Hamlet.* In *The Riverside Shakespeare,* 1135–1197. Boston: Houghton Mifflin, 1974.

————. *Henry V.* In *The Riverside Shakespeare,* 930–975. Boston: Houghton Mifflin, 1974.

————. *Macbeth.* In *The Riverside Shakespeare,* 1306–1342. Boston: Houghton Mifflin, 1974.

————. *Merchant of Venice.* In *The Riverside Shakespeare,* 250–285. Boston: Houghton Mifflin, 1974.

Shelley, Mary Wollstonecraft. *Falkner.* 2 vols. New York: Saunders and Otley, 1837.

————. *The Fortunes of Perkin Warbeck,* with an introduction by Betty T. Bennett. 3 Volumes. Norwood Editions, 1976.

————. *Frankenstein,* ed. James Kinsely and M. K. Joseph. 1831 edition. Oxford: Oxford University Press, 1969.

————. *Frankenstein.* [1818 edition]. In *The Mary Shelley Reader,* ed. Betty T. Bennett and Charles E. Robinson, 11–171. New York: Oxford University Press, 1990.

————. *The Journals of Mary Shelley 1814–1844*, ed. Paula R. Feldman and Diana Scott-Kilvert. 2 vols. Oxford: Clarendon Press, 1987.

————. *The Last Man*, ed. Hugh J. Luke, Jr. Lincoln: University of Nebraska Press, 1965.

————. *The Letters of Mary Wollstonecraft Shelley*, ed. Betty T. Bennett. 3 vols. Baltimore: The Johns Hopkins University Press, 1980–1983.

————, and others. *Lives of the Most Eminent French Writers*. 2 vols. Philadelphia: Lea and Blanchard, 1840.

————. *Lodore*, ed. Lisa Vargo. Ontario: Broadview Literary Press, 1997.

————. *Lodore*. New York: Wallis & Wallis, 1835.

————. *Mary Shelley: Collected Tales and Stories* ed. Charles E. Robinson. Baltimore: Johns Hopkins University Press, 1976.

————. *The Mary Shelley Reader*, ed. Betty T. Bennett and Charles E. Robinson. New York: Oxford University Press, 1990.

————. "Mathilda." In *The Mary Shelley Reader*, ed. Betty T. Bennett and Charles E. Robinson, 173–246. New York: Oxford University Press, 1990.

————. *Mathilda*, ed. Elizabeth Nitchie. Chapel Hill: University of North Carolina Press, 1959.

————. *Mythological Dramas: Prosperine and Midas*, ed. Charles E. Robinson. New York: Garland, 1992.

————. "A Review of William Godwin's *Cloudesley*." In *The Mary Shelley Reader*, ed. Betty T. Bennett and Charles E. Robinson, 372–376. New York: Oxford University Press, 1990.

————. *Valperga: or, the Life and Adventures of Castruccio, Prince of Lucca*. 3 Volumes. London: G. and W. B. Whittaker, 1823.

————. *Valperga: or, the Life and Adventures of Castruccio, Prince of Lucca*, ed. Stuart Curran. New York: Oxford University Press, 1997.

Shelley, Percy Bysshe. *Shelley's Poetry and Prose*, ed. Donald H. Reiman and Sharon B. Powers. Norton Critical Edition. New York: W. W. Norton, 1977.

————. *Zastrozzi and St. Irvyne*. Oxford: Oxford University Press, 1986.

Sheridan, Richard Brinsley. "The Rivals." In *British Dramatists from Dryden to Sheridan*, ed. George H. Nettleton and Arthur E. Case, 789–830. Revised by George Winchester Stone, Jr. Carbondale: Southern Illinois University Press, 1969.

Small, Christopher. *Ariel Like a Harpy: Shelley, Mary and "Frankenstein."* London: Gollancz, 1972.

Smith, Charlotte. *Emmeline*, ed. Anne Henry Ehrenpreis. London: Oxford University Press, 1971.

———. *The Old Manor House*, ed. Anne Henry Ehrenpreis. London: Oxford University Press, 1969.

Smith, Susan Harris. "*Frankenstein*: Mary Shelley's Psychic Divisiveness." *Women and Literature* 5 (1977): 42–53.

Spark, Muriel. *Mary Shelley*. Revised from *Child of Light: A Reassessment of Mary Shelley*. 1951. New York: E. P. Dutton, 1987.

———. "Mary Shelley: A Prophetic Novelist." *The Listener* 45 (1951): 305–306.

Spatt, Hartley S. "Mary Shelley's Last Men: The Truth of Dreams." *Studies in the Novel* 7 (1975): 526–537.

Spencer, Jane. *The Rise of the Woman Novelist: From Aphra Behn to Jane Austen*. Oxford: Basil Blackwell, 1986.

Spender, Dale. *Mothers of the Novel*. London: Pandora Press, 1986.

St. Clair, William. *The Godwins and the Shelleys*. Baltimore: Johns Hopkins University Press, 1989.

de Staël, Madame. *Corinne, or Italy*. New Brunswick: Rutgers University Press, 1987.

Steiner, George. *Death of Tragedy*. New York: Knopf, 1961.

Sterne, Laurence. *A Sentimental Journey*, ed. Graham Petrie. Harmondsworth, England: Penguin Books Ltd, 1967.

Stroup, Thomas B. *Microcosmos: The Shape of the Elizabethan Play*. Lexington: University of Kentucky Press, 1965.

Summers, Montague. *The Gothic Quest*. 1938. Reprint. New York: Russell and Russell, 1964.

Sunstein, Emily. *Mary Shelley: Romance and Reality*. Boston: Little, Brown, 1989.

Swingle, L. J. "Reading Mary Shelley, Well—." *Review* 12 (1990): 119–133.

Tannenbaum, Leslie. "From Filthy Type to Truth: Miltonic Myth in *Frankenstein*." *Keats-Shelley Journal* 26 (1977): 101–113.

Thompson, G. R. "Introduction: Romanticism and the Gothic Tradition." In *The Gothic Imagination: Essays in Dark Romanticism*, ed. G. R. Thompson, 1–10. Pullman: Washington State University Press, 1974.

Thornburg, Mary K. Patterson. *The Monster in the Mirror*. Ann Arbor: UMI Research Press, 1987.

Thorslev, Peter. *The Byronic Hero*. Minneapolis: University of Minnesota Press, 1962.

Todd, Janet. "Frankenstein's Daughter: Mary Shelley and Mary Wollstonecraft." *Women and Literature* 4 (1976): 18–27.

———. *Sensibility*. London: Methuen, 1986.

———. *The Sign of Angellica: Women, Writing and Fiction, 1660–1800*. London: Virago, 1989.

Tropp, Martin. *Mary Shelley's Monster: The Story of Frankenstein*. Boston: Houghton Mifflin, 1976.

Tysdahl, B. J. *William Godwin as Novelist*. London: Athlone, 1981.

Review of *Valperga; or, the Life and Adventures of Castruccio, Prince of Lucca*, by Mary Shelley. Blackwood's Edinburgh Magazine. 13 (March 1823): 283–293. *Romantic Circles* [online] www.rc.umd.edu/reference/mschronology/reviews/valpbn.html.

———. *The Examiner* No. 788 (2 March 1823): 154.

———. *La Belle Assemblée, or Court and Fashionable Magazine*. 28 (August 1823): 82–84.

———. *London Literary Gazette*. No. 319 (1 March 1823): 132–33.

Varma, Devendra P. *The Gothic Flame*. 1957. Reprint. New York: Russell and Russell, 1966.

Vasbinder, Samuel Holmes. *Scientific Attitudes in Mary Shelley's Fiction*. Ann Arbor, MI: UMI Research Press, 1984.

Veeder, William. *Mary Shelley and Frankenstein: The Fate of Androgyny*. Chicago: University of Chicago Press, 1986.

Wade, Philip. "Shelley and the Miltonic Element in Mary Shelley's *Frankenstein*." *Milton and the Romantics* 2 (1976): 23–35.

Wake, Ann M. Frank. "Women in the Active Voice: Recovering Female History in Mary Shelley's *Valperga* and *Perkin Warbeck*.," In *Iconoclastic Departures: Mary Shelley After Frankenstein*, ed. Syndy M. Conger, Frederick S. Frank, and Gregory O'Dea, 235–259. Madison: Fairleigh Dickinson University Press, 1997.

Walling, William. *Mary Shelley*. Twayne English Author Series. New York: Twayne, 1972.

Walpole, Horace. "The Castle of Otranto." In *The Castle of Otranto, The Mysteries of Udolpho, and Northanger Abbey*, ed. Andrew Wright, 3–116. New York: Holt, Rinehart and Winston, 1963.

———. *The Mysterious Mother, A Tragedy*. Dublin: J. Archer, W. Jones, and R. White, 1791.

Watkins, Daniel. *A Materialist Critique of English Romantic Drama.* Gainsville: University Press of Florida, 1993.

Webb, Timothy. "The Romantic Poet and the Stage: A Short, Sad History." In *The Romantic Theatre,* ed. Richard Allen Cave, 9–86. Totowa: Barnes and Noble, 1986.

Wells, Lynn. "The Triumph of Death: Reading and Narrative in Mary Shelley's *The Last Man.*" In *Iconoclastic Departures: Mary Shelley After Frankenstein,* ed. Syndy M. Conger, Frederick S. Frank, and Gregory O'Dea, 212–234. Madison: Fairleigh Dickinson University Press, 1997.

Wilshire, Bruce. *Role Playing and Identity; The Limits of Theatre* as Metaphor. Bloomington: Indiana University Press, 1982.

Wollstonecraft, Mary. *Letters Written During a Short Residence in Sweden, Norway, and Denmark,* ed. Carol H. Poston. Lincoln: University of Nebraska Press, 1976.

———. *Maria, or the Wrongs of Woman.* New York: W. W. Norton, 1975.

———. *A Vindication of the Rights of Woman,* ed. Charles W. Hagelman, Jr. New York: W. W. Norton, Inc., 1967.

Wolstenholme, Susan. *Gothic (Re)visions: Writing Women as Readers.* Albany: State University of New York Press, 1993.

Wordsworth, William. *The Borderers,* edited by Robert Osborn. Ithaca: Cornell University Press, 1982.

Young, Arlene. "The Monster Within: The Alien Self in *Jane Eyre* and *Frankenstein.*" *Studies in the Novel* 23 (1991): 325–338.

Youngquist, Paul. "*Frankenstein*: The Mother, the Daughter, and the Monster." *Philological Quarterly* 70 (1991): 339–359.

Zdanys, Jonas. "Raskolnikov and Frankenstein: The Deadly Search for a Rational Paradise." *Cithara* 16 (1976): 57–67.

Zonana, Joyce. "'They Will Prove the Truth of My Tale'" Safie's Letters as the Feminist Core of Mary Shelley's *Frankenstein.*" *Journal of Narrative Technique* 21 (1991): 170–184.

Index